Dear Howard —

I do hope you
will enjoy these stories
as much as I have —
Being in my backyard has
helped — and knowing
Backcountry
a couple of them has
helped ~~too~~!

Mary

This anthology of contemporary West Virginia writing had its beginnings as a course project in the Department of English at West Virginia University. The West Virginia University Press thanks Professor James Harms and his students in English 271 for all of their preliminary work on Backcountry.

The students of English 271 were Nathan Bennett, Jason Bryant, Frankie Michelle Dennison, Erik Evanto, Jason Freeman, Patrick Granelli, Jessie Harriman, Jeffrey Harvey, Nathan Hayes, Colin Helb, Rachel Krause, James Marinelli, Alex Matzureff, Alvis Minor, Lori Placek, Meryl Ratzman, Natalie Sypolt, Chris Wheeler, and Keith Woofter.

Vandalia Press publishes fiction and non-fiction of interest to the general reader concerning Appalachia and, more specifically, West Virginia.
See our website at vandaliapress.com to learn of forthcoming titles.

Dear Howard & Louise,

Hope you enjoy this book as much as I have —

Fondly
Mary Tormuly

Backcountry

Contemporary Writing in West Virginia

Edited by Irene McKinney

Vandalia Press

Morgantown 2002

Vandalia Press, Morgantown 26506

© 2002 by West Virginia University Press
All rights reserved
First edition 2002

Printed in the United States of America

10 09 08 07 06 05 04 03 02   10 9 8 7 6 5 4 3 2 1

ISBN 0-937058-72-6

Library of Congress Cataloging-in-Publication Data

  Backcountry: Contemporary Writing in West Virginia / [edited] by Irene McKinney.
     p. cm.
  1. Literature—American—West Virginia. 2. Poetry—American—West Virginia. 3.
  Fiction—American—West Virginia. 3. Autobiography—American—West Virginia.
  4. Literature—American—Appalachian. I. Title. II. McKinney, Irene.

Library of Congress Control Number: 2002108962

Vandalia Press is an imprint of West Virginia University Press

Book design by Alcorn Publication Design
Cover photo courtesy Jim Clark
Printed in USA

This volume is dedicated to the memory of

Tom Andrews
Davis Grubb
Louise McNeill
Breece Pancake

Contents

Acknowledgements

Anderson, Maggie: "Spitting in the Leaves," "Independence Day, Terra Alta, West Virginia, 1935," "Among Elms and Maples, Morgantown, West Virginia, August 1935," and "Mining Camp Residents, West Virginia, July 1935" from *Cold Comfort*, by MaggieAnderson, © 1986. Reprinted by permission of the University of Pittsburgh Press. "Marginal," "Long Story," and "Ontological" from *Windfall*, by Maggie Anderson, © 2000. Reprinted by permission of the University of Pittsburgh Press.

Andrews, Tom: "Evening Song" and "Hymning the Kanawha" from *Hemophiliac's Motorcycle*, by Tom Andrews, © 1994. Reprinted by permission of the University of Iowa Press.

Benedict, Pinckney: "The Sutton Pie Safe" from *Town Smokes* by Pinckney Benedict, © 1987. Reprinted by permission of Ontario Review Press. "Odom" from *The Wrecking Yard* by Pinckney Benedict ©1992. Reprinted by the kind permission of the author.

Currey, Richard: "The Wars of Heaven" from *The Wars of Heaven* by Richard Currey, ©1990. Reprinted by the kind permission of the author.

DeFoe, Mark: "Driving the Gauley River, Listening to the Radio," and "Late Winter Snow: South of Morgantown, WV" from *Aviary* by Mark DeFoe ©2002. Reprinted by permission of Pringle Tree Press. "Air," "Leaving the Hills," and "The former Miner Returns from his First Day as a Service Worker" from *Air* by Mark DeFoe, ©1998. Reprinted by permission of Green Tower Press.

Depta, Victor: "When Your Ego Bloats," "The Mad Whore of Peachtree," "It Didn't Come from Hallmark," and "Charlene's Ex" from *A Doorkeeper in the House* by Victor Depta, ©1993. Reprinted by kind permission of the author.

Gates, Henry Louis, Jr: "Sin Boldly" from *Colored People: A Memoir* by Henry Louis Gates, Jr., ©1994 by Henry Louis Gates, Jr. Used by permission of Alfred Knopf, a division of Random House, Inc.

Giardina, Denise. "Rondal Lloyd" from *Storming Heaven* by Denise Giardina, ©1987 by Denise Giardina. Reprinted by permission of W.W. Norton and Co.

Grubb, Davis. "The Burlap Bag" from *The Siege of 318: Thirteen Mystical Stories* by Davis Grubb, ©1978. Reprinted by kind permission of the Estate of Louis Delaplaine Grubb.

Koger, Lisa: "Extended Learning" from *Farlanburg Stories* by Lisa Koger, ©1990. Reprinted by kind permission of the author.

Maynard, Lee: "Chapter 1 and 6" from *Crum* by Lee Maynard. ©2002 by West Virginia University Press. Reprinted by permission of WVU Press.

McKernan, John: "On the Edge of Highway 10." Printed by kind permission of the author.

McKernan, Llewellyn: "The Only Old Timer in the Neighborhood," "The Peaceful Kingdom," and "In Spring" from *Many Waters: Poems from West Virginia* by Llewellyn McKernan, ©1993. Reprinted by permission of Mellen Poetry Press: Lewiston, NY. "Aunt Anna" from *Short and Simple Annals* by Llewellyn McKernan, ©1983. Reprinted by kind permission of the author.

McKinney, Irene: "Twilight in West Virginia: Six O'Clock Mine Report," "Visiting My Gravesite: Talbott Churchyard, West Virginia," and "Deep Mining" from *Six O'Clock Mine Report*, by Irene McKinney, ©1989. Reprinted by permission of the University of Pittsburgh Press. "For Women Who Have Been Patient All Their Lives" from *Quick Fire and Slow Fire* by Irene McKinney, ©1989. Reprinted by kind permission of the author. "Fodder" from *Artful Dodge*, 1999. by Irene McKinney ©1999. Reprinted by permission of the author. "Viridian Days" from *American Voice*, No. 49, 1999 by Irene McKinney ©1999.

McNeill, Louise: "The Long Traveler" from *Fermi Buffalo*, by Louise McNeill, ©1994. Reprinted by the permission of the University of Pittsburgh Press. "A Patch of Earth," and "Night at the Commodore" from *The Milkweed Ladies*, by Louise McNeill, ©1988. Reprinted by permission of the University of Pittsburgh Press. "Granny Saunders," and "The River" from *Hill Daughter: New and Selected Poems*, by Louise McNeill, ©1991. Reprinted by permission of the University of Pittsburgh Press. "The Road" from *Gauley Mountain* by Louise McNeill, ©1939. Reprinted by permission of Pocahontas Communications Cooperative. "Memoria" and "The Roads" by Louise McNeill, © 1972 by West Virginia University Foundation. Reprinted by permission of West Virginia University Foundation.

Pancake, Ann: "Jolo" from *Given Ground* ©2001 by Ann Pancake, reprinted by permission of University Press of New England.

Pancake, Breece D'J: "Trilobites" and "Fox Hunters" from *The Stories of Breece D'j Pancake* by Breece D'J Pancake, ©1983 by Helen Pancake. Reprinted by Permission of Little Brown and Co.

Phillips, Jayne Anne: "Bess" from *Fast Lanes* © 1987 by Jayne Anne Phillips, reprinted by kind permission of the author. "Cheers" from *Black Tickets* © 1979 by Jayne Anne Phillips, reprinted by kind permission of the author.

Russell, Timothy: "In Consieratione Praemissorum," "In Aegri Somnia," "In Actu," and "In Dubio" from *Adversaria* ©1993 by Timothy Russell, reprinted by permission of Northwestern University Press.

Settle, Mary Lee: Excerpt from *Addie* by Mary Lee Settle ©1998. Reprinted by permission of the University of South Carolina Press.

Stringer, A.E.: "Ruins in Reverse," "Listen," and "My Friend Told Me" by A.E. Stringer, reprinted by kind permission of the author.

Willis, Meredith Sue: "Family Knots" from *The Mountains of America* ©1994 by Meredith Sue Willis. Published by Mercury House, San Francisco, CA, and reprinted by permission. <http://www.mercuryhouse.org.>

Introduction
Backcountry: Contemporary Writing in West Virginia

*T*his collection of stories, poems, and memoirs attests to the fact that there are still places in America that are unknown or poorly-known. These are places of shelter and secrecy in the heart of the Appalachian mountains, or hills, as their inhabitants call them, harking back to the naming practices of the home countries of Ireland and Scotland, as Merrill Gilfillan reminds us in his travel notes. In Ireland, one might refer to the Hills of Antrim, as here we say the hills of West Virginia. And when we are asked where we're from, we are more likely to mention McDowell County or Greenbrier County than to name a town, as in Ireland one would say County Mayo or County Clare. The countryside and forest has precedence over the towns, since most of our towns are small and blend quickly into the country, and there are no real cities of any size. The state is only thirty-nine per cent urban, and even the larger towns like Charleston or Huntington are still close enough to the countryside so that one can be on some little winding mud road in a matter of minutes. West Virginia is the only state that lies entirely within the Appalachian range of mountains, and most of the region is back in the hills, back of the beyond.

This is the backcountry. Gary Snyder wrote about the West that there was the country, and then beyond it and behind it, the backcountry. A traveler need only drive slowly into the interior of the state to feel what this means. In his book *Burnt House to Paw Paw*, Gilfillan describes this sense of intimate revelation:

> Five miles in, I pull over at a high spot to let pushy traffic pass and look off to the East, off and over at the great secrecy and fertile closure of the mountains and their hollows and runs, the soft hill upon hill, ridge after ridge, all buffered and screened by the beneficent canopy of the broadleafed deciduous forest. It is always a surprise and an uplift, the first intimation of the magnitude, of the vast continuity of the Appalachians…(14)

The writing that has recently emerged from West Virginia rises up out of these dense forests, coal mines, small towns, wet roads, mountain music, and the High Lonesome voice of it, the deep privacy of the layered and textured forests, vegetation, and surrounding animal life.

West Virginia and its arts and literature have not been known, partly because of the tendency of urban publishing centers to lump together all rural regions. In his review of Eudora Welty's *The Optimist's Daughter* in *The New York Times*, Howard Moss expressed some surprise and warned readers that Welty wrote of "a South where real distinctions are made between Texas and Mississippi, and Mississippi and West Virginia." (1972) Reviewers, critics, and the general reading public have not learned to see the difference between Appalachia and any other rural region. Nor have they discerned the differences between the regions in Appalachia itself. Ruel Foster, who was a professor for many years at West Virginia University, often extended a plea for responsible criticism of the writing from the region, and felt that a critical limbo existed because of the lack.

West Virginia is not the beautifully-groomed Parkway through the Blue Ridge Mountains of Virginia, (despite John Denver's inaccurate "Take Me Home, Country Roads") nor Tidewater Virginia with its lowland centers of commerce and activity, nor is it the Bluegrass of Kentucky. It is not even the mountains of Kentucky, a region with a history, an accent, a musical and literary tradition and flavor all its own, although there are some commonalities. West Virginia is not the Deep South, and despite the fact that our writers have learned much from the writers of the South, the two regions are very different in preoccupations and development. The Southern Literary Renaissance was well-established before we even began to occupy a place on the literary map, and because of our differing histories and geographies, West Virginia writers have not been so obsessed with the subject matter of the Civil War and its legacy, since there were no plantations or widespread slavery to defend, no genteel tradition, very few aristocratic aspirations. There were battles and skirmishes, and the armies marched back and forth throughout the region, but the mountain terrain did not admit easy access. Historian John Williams tells us that supply wagons sometimes fell off the sides of the mountains and landed on the tops of trees below, and he quotes a western Virginia soldier who wrote in a letter from a Union camp on Cheat Mountain: "There is nobody lives here and it is very lonesome." "I have not saw but one woman since we came here and she is about sixty years old..." (63) In the interior of the region, there were just the isolated hill farms, the little communities, the small county courthouses with their piddling local graft, and the groundhogs, blacksnakes, deer, foxes, and bears. But as a result of the struggle, West Virginia became a separate state in 1863, a fact that many of our fellow citizens across the country have still not heard about. Our writers have been characteristically concerned with more recent history, like the West Virginia Mine Wars, the battle of Blair Mountain, the War on Poverty, the human and ecological disasters at Hawk's Nest and Buffalo

Creek, and the devastation caused by man mountaintop removal mining in the southern part of the state.

The chorus of native voices we hear in this collection is comparatively recent. Of the writers represented here, Louise McNeill, Mary Lee Settle, and Davis Grubb stand at the head of the hollow, with the rest of the writers occupying a position that is roughly contemporaneous. McNeill is the first poet of note from the state. Her poetic history *Gauley Mountain: A History in Verse* was published in 1939 to substantial critical acclaim, and has often been compared favorably to Edgar Lee Masters' *Spoon River Anthology*. She continued to write and publish until near the end of her life in 1993. Mary Lee Settle began publishing novels in the 1950s, with *The Love Eaters* (1954), and *The Kiss of Kin* (1955). Davis Grubb published his first and subsequently best-known novel *The Night of the Hunter* in 1953. Breece Pancake published his first story in *The Atlantic* in 1977, although his book was not published until after his premature death. He died shortly before his twenty-seventh birthday in 1979, and his collected stories appeared in 1983. My own first book, *The Girl With the Stone in Her Lap*, (1976) was produced in the same period. Local color writing and genre writing had dominated the limited scene throughout most of the century, and with the exception of Rebecca Harding Davis' 1861 novel *Life in the Iron Mills*, there was no serious fiction from the state previous to our own time.

This is as closely-knit an anthology as you are ever likely to see. It is though a large, extended family were drawing on the same store of family stories, jokes, symbols, landscapes, animals, trees, language, and vernacular. How many snakes are in this book? How many foxes, possums? Fossils? And how very many coal mines. But it is not merely local references that unites these writers. There is a larger vision that ties these works together.

The connection is not so much in mutual influence, though there is some of that, but in each writer's total immersion in place. Even those writers who no longer live in the state remember the feel, the physical texture, the overwhelming and enfolding vegetal surround of the place. In her novel *MotherKind*, Jayne Anne Phillips remembers the road home this way:

> Kate drives. The old road home is a two-lane winding past clustered houses and abandoned coal tipples. Closed roadside gas stations still wear the weathered, upright jewelry of their empty pumps. No trucks rumbling through, no travelers stopping to buy sandwiches and soda pop. Here the same battered green metal signs are peppered with BB holes, lettered with the names of settlements and the legend "Unincorporated." Across the hilly yards of the houses Kate sees chickens strutting, a kid with a wagon. The air, the sky, the leaning buildings; all seem less dusty, the land more green, the storefronts preserved and oddly alone, as though they will vanish beyond this deserted grace into a future that already exists...(51)

Richard Currey's country musician Sapper Reeves in the novel *Lost Highway* drives home after years on the road:

> Inside the coming distance I will turn from Lexington and cross the river into West Virginia and a world built on memory collapsing into the present, abandoned farmhouses cocked oddly under hillsides, once palatial ice-whites gone to shades of charcoal, attics given over to nesting dens for swallows and thrushes, verandas and ground floors patrolled by the local insane. Out in the emerald fields vagrant horses stand beside splintered barns, gutted back roads anchoring the meridians of a harbored universe, all returned to me under what will by then be an opening sunrise. (1-2)

These entries and reentries are defining moments in this literature. The place may be remembered as suffocating or comforting, depending on the temperament of the writer, but it is always remembered. As Eudora Welty wisely tells us, place has a more enduring identity than we do and we are therefore drawn to our place of origin. ("On Writing" 119) It is here that we learn the original language of feeling and the names, names that are forever evocative of a primal reality, names which roll off the tongue: The Gandy and the Sinks of Gandy, Dolly Sods, the Kanawha, Glady Fork, Cheat Mountain, and the Canyon of the Gauley. Not incidentally, Welty's mother was from West Virginia, and Welty credits her own childhood summers spent at the mountain-top homeplace in Clay County as the source of her independent spirit. She writes: "I think when my mother came to Jackson she brought West Virginia with her. Of course, I brought some of it with me too." (*One Writer's Beginnings* 55) Even after spending most of her life in Mississippi, Welty was drawn back to those origins, and gives them expression in *The Optimist's Daughter* and *Losing Battles*. In her essays on regional writing, she advances the opinion that all powerful writing is local: it draws on the locale, speaks out of it, and gives it a habitation and name. "Location is the ground conductor of all the currents of emotion and belief and moral conviction that charge out from the story in its course." ("On Writing" 128) The late Jim Wayne Miller said that writers were always engaged in making local life conscious of itself. It can reasonably be argued that this is just as true of urban locales as it is of rural. And isn't Thoreau's *Walden* regional? And *Huckleberry Finn*?

These writers are also naturally connected because of their awareness of the living presence of history in daily human life. Louise McNeill was a professor of history as well as literature, and her poems and prose display a detailed knowledge of where we've come from and where we are now. And Mary Lee Settle has produced what is arguably the most sustained and ambitious work of historical fiction of our time, *The Beulah Quintet*, a work which begins in Cromwell's England and traces the evolution of democracy up to the present in Appalachia. Denise Giardina also exercises an historical imagination and a political vision in her Appalachian novels as well as the ones set in King Henry's England or Dietrich Bonhoeffer's Germany. These writers have not succumbed to mainstream America's cultivated loss of memory. In Louise McNeill's memory, nine generations of family and political history were alive.

So when I speak of the livingness of history, I am not referring only to the history of social and political events. First, many of these writers are intimately bound up in family history: Jayne Anne Phillips' luminous story "Bess" is partially a search for the source of current family patterns, an imaginative recreation of the deep isolation and self-sufficiency of mountain culture in the lives of grandparents and parents, based on legends, half-remembered fragments and family stories. Maggie Anderson is also concerned with family history and the effacement of her relatives into some broad social vision of Appalachian small town and rural life as depicted in the photographs of Walker Evans. Many of Llewellyn McKernan's poems are concerned with family members, as many of my own poems are. Victor Depta's *A Doorkeeper in the House* is a group portrait of an eccentric and brilliant southern mountain family, and his book *The Helen Poems* is a series of biographical poems about his daughter. Pinckney Benedict's stories in this collection present father-son relationships and their inner tensions and illuminations. Meredith Sue Willis and Lisa Koger explore the dynamics of small-town family life. Henry Louis Gates' affectionate memoir of his family and its interactions in a small community, Mary Lee Settle's portrait of a powerful precursor, her grandmother Addie, Tom Andrews' brilliantly painful evocation of his brother's illness and death: these writers are the self-chosen ones to carry the burden of the tale. This emphasis on family of course is hardly unique in contemporary literature: grandmothers and fathers abound in current poetry. Burt we might claim uniqueness in our particular meld of family history, social and political history, and ecological history.

A further source of connection among these writers, and perhaps most unusual in contemporary writing, is an awareness of non-human history, the history of the earth itself. Around our own small lives, there are constant reminders of geologic time which we can physically see in the folds and uplifts, the rolling quality of the hills like a slowed-down ocean, even in the telling layers of the road-cuts. The Kentucky writer Elizabeth Madox Roberts, in her novel, *The Time of Man*, (1926) follows the development of an uneducated little girl, Ellen Chesser, who first becomes aware of pre-human and ancient history by paying attention to the fossils she finds in rocks as she and her father till the field. She is moved by a sense of awe as she speculates about other races and peoples who have walked where she walks now. That awareness is also present in Kentucky writer James Still's character Brother Sim Mobberly (*River of Earth* 1940):

> My eyes were sot upon the hills from the beginning. Till I come on the Word in the good Book I used to think a mountain was the standingest object in the sight o' God. Hit says here that they go skipping and hopping like sheep, a-rising and a-falling. These hills are jist dirt waves, washing through eternity. My brethren, they hain't a valley so low but what hit'll rise again. They hain't a hill standing so proud but hit'll sink to the low ground of sorrow. Oh, my children, where air we going on this mighty river of earth, a-borning, begetting, and a-dying— the living earth and the dead riding the waters? Where air it sweeping us? (*River of Earth* 76)

To the young male protagonists in Breece Pancake's stories, this awareness is often the source of despair. In his signature story "Trilobites," Colly stands looking at the hills, thinking of how it took over a million years for them to be formed. Beside that knowledge, his own life appears as a tiny dot in an eternal continuum. He knows that the vital connection with the land is breaking down in his generation, the out-migration to Ohio and elsewhere continuing steadily, leaving him feeling left behind in an abandoned landscape. He goes searching for trilobite fossils, hoping for a way to connect with that deep past. He sees the planet's past everywhere he looks, and thinks of the ancient river Teays, flowing where he now stands, and the bison grazing in the river valley, and the formation of the ancient fossil gases now being sucked out of the ground for fuel. To Louise McNeill, there is a consolation in these evidences of pre-human life. In her mind, she connects her own family's graves with the fossil remains and chunks of coral scattered on the farm. There is also a natural evolution of humility and a sense of proportion when we see such clear evidence of our brief and tiny presence in space and time. For McNeill, such insight constitutes basic human knowledge. It leads us to understand that "the earth holds us and not the other way," and the human control of the non-human is an illusion.

The natural world of plants, animals, insects, rivers, and streams surrounds us with this basic knowledge. In Breece Pancake's stories, he depicts the struggles in an animal's life with the same attention that he pays to human life: he notes the mother possum's distress at the human presence which disturbs her search for a winter home, and he follows the movement of the fox, its evasions and escapes, in "Fox Hunters." The hunting tradition is shown in both its honorable and debased forms. He notes the interactions of owl, rabbit, fox, and human. McNeill reconnects us with the pungent world of plant life and its vital connection to human life, to the old peasant calendar of the seasons. And Ann Pancake's sensual evocation of the girl Connie's sexuality in the context of the fecund life of river and meadow pulls us back to the mysterious, common source of all life. We become aware that we occupy a liminal zone between the human and non-human. As Maggie Anderson puts it in "Marginal," we exist "at the line where the forest intersects the field," on the margins. As I sit here writing in my small house at the edge of the woods, on any given day I might look out the window and see dozens of varieties of trees, shrubs, plants, along with the accompanying red and grey squirrels, red foxes, groundhogs, chipmunks, rabbits, deer, and from the other side of my vision, our cattle moving leisurely over the rolling meadow. In this landscape, it is nearly impossible for human beings to believe themselves to be the only actors in the web of life. These surroundings soak into our view of the world as we pass back and forth over the margins.

But at the heart of this writing and this culture, there is a profound conflict. We also occupy another kind of margin, the periphery between mainstream American culture and mountain culture. We are aware that the core culture views the periphery with a mixture of envy and contempt. In this view, the central culture is civilized and all marginal cultures are uncivilized. Little wonder then that young people often feel the need to repudiate their origins and the upwardly-mobile or affluent natives of the region deny any connection with the mountain culture, and indeed insist that there is no culture here except for the one that they import. They are anxious to be identified with mainstream America, and have already relegated their less-enlightened fellows to the stagnant backwaters of history. But to exiles from the region, this tension often manifests itself as an intense, lifelong homesickness, a longing for the place of origin, against all reason or worldly self-interest. In Mary Lee Settle's novel *Charley Bland*, (1989) a talented and sophisticated young woman who has traveled far and has now returned home to southern West Virginia describes this pull with a kind of bitter helplessness.

> I am a Southerner, and there is bred in us, as carefully as if we were
> prized hounds, a sense of betrayal in leaving our roots. We sit in cafes
> in Paris and pubs in London, everywhere we have landed, and tell
> stories that sustain us about funny uncles and people up hollows or in
> small towns with chinaberry trees. (31-32)

A less self-consciously sophisticated narrator in Denise Giardina's novel *The Unquiet Earth* is a little girl named Jackie, who lives in a coal camp and is troubled by the disconnection between the core culture she has been educated to value, and her daily experience. She has been listening to her Uncle Brigham tell her a tall tale, and even though she has been fascinated by it, she feels compelled to dismiss it, because it has "no handsome prince to rescue anybody. It's not a real story like you would hear someplace else."

> When I got back from his house I'd get a notebook and figure I would write a real story with a happy ending. But never worked. I'm not a real writer. Real writers live in New York apartments or sit at sidewalk cafes in Paris. (124)

Jackie feels defeated by her identification with the stereotype, and concludes that "there is not a thing to write about, only hillbillies, and nobody cares about hillbillies. I go inside and watch TV." (125) When this destructive self-view is internalized, the young person may feel that she cannot be happy or free unless she leaves. In "Trilobites," Colly's girl-friend Ginny has fled the region, and in Mark Defoe's "Leaving the Hills," the woman is "shedding self like a snake skin" as she drives away. Currey's Sapper Reeves, in his old age, remembers his youthful rejection of his roots:

> There was a time when I wanted to disavow my home, deny it, claim I was from a gentleman's Virginia, perhaps. West Virginia was on nobody's map of the present, in nobody's casual vocabulary, a derelict set of coordinates misplaced during the Civil War and never brought to mind again. (2)

For some expatriates, return is almost economically impossible. In Timothy Russell's steel mill poems, the men sit around during break and exchange stories of down home, "down happy," reminiscing about hunting and the loved landscape, but then their break is over.

Curiously, this pull toward home in West Virginia extends to those who have not been born or grown up in the state, but whose parents or grandparents have. Eudora Welty's mother creates the connection in her daughter's psyche and imagination, and in John O' Brien's *At Home in the Heart of Appalachia*, he remembers trips from Philadelphia back to his father's hometown of Piedmont, and the joyous yell of "West, by God, Virginia!" as they cross over the state line. Later, O'Brien leaves his home in Philadelphia and attends university in West Virginia. Later still, he moves with his wife and children to West Virginia, and as they drive in, the sense of sanctuary increases: "Every time I have come back to Appalachia, I reach this point, the moment of reentry." (48) In our secular age, there is a hesitancy about the speaking of the sacred space. Merrill Gilfillan, an Ohio native, grew up on the edge of the mountains, and feels in their heights "the sanctuary resonant with pre-social thought pools and the spirit-spoor of how many centuries, pure and lost and glady enough to connect with Thracian and Dravidian woods dancers." (27)

For many writers and non-writers alike, this struggle with place is a lifelong one, a constant vacillation between wanting to leave and search for the approval of the mainstream culture, and wanting to return to one's roots. Settle's novel is a poignant depiction of that struggle, which she compares to the Biblical story of Jacob wrestling with the angel:

> There was, I know now, another reason, as deep as a taproot. For better or worse, this was my country, and I could not let it go until it blessed me. What form that blessing would take I did not know yet. I only knew that when it came I would recognize it through its disguises. It is this that keeps poets in their countries through namelessness, doors closing, hungers, and there are many kinds, until they are forced to abandon home, which can, in itself, become a *felix culpa*, a blessing. (160)

This implies that home is not static, nor is it limited to the physical. Instead, it raises the question of how we wrestle with our longing, and how we may define and re-define what home is. The energy of much of the writing from the region twists and turns around this question. But ultimately, what matters to us is the talent and accomplishment of the writing. And I believe that the writers assembled here are strong and entertaining and authentic. I'm confident that readers will agree.

There are additional writers whose work I would like to have included but could not, for various reasons, such as the difficulty of excerpting from a longer work and publishers' constraints. Among them are John O'Brien, Chuck Kinder, and Sara Vogan,

I would like to thank the following people for their valuable help with the book:
Patrick Conner for his leadership and direction; James Harms for the original idea; his graduate class for their preliminary editorial work; Maggie Anderson for her sustained interest in this writing; John Saunders and Devon McNamara for listening; Mike Mazzolini and his Backcountry writers for use of the term; and Stephanie Grove for her able assistance.

Works Cited

Merill Gilfillan. *Burnt House to Paw Paw.* (Hard Press, Inc. 1997).

Howard Moss. "Eudora Welty's New Novel About Death and Class." *The New York Times.* May 21, 1972.

John Alexander Williams. *West Virginia: A History.* (West Virginia University Press, 2001).

Jayne Anne Phillips. *MotherKind.* (Alfred A. Knopf 2000).

Eudora Welty. *The Eye of the Story.* "On Writing." (Vintage Books 1979).

Eudora Welty. *One Writer's Beginnings.* (Harvard University Press 1984).

James Still. *River of Earth.* (The University Press of Kentucky 1940).

Mary Lee Settle. *Charley Bland.* (Carol & Graf Publishers 1989).

Denise Giardina. *The Unquiet Earth.* (W. W. Norton & Co. 1992).

Richard Currey. *Lost Highway.* (Houghton Mifflin Co. 1997).

John O'Brien. *At Home in the Heart of Appalachia.* (Alfred A. Kropf 2001).

Backcountry

Marginal

Maggie Anderson

This is where I live,
at the edge of this ploughed field
where sunlight catches meadow grasses
and turns them silver-yellow
like the tines of the birches
at the rim of the forest, where
lumps of earth are scabbed over
with rust colored pine needles
and one noisy crow has been
traversing them all morning.
Deep in these woods
his feathers have fallen so often
in some places they have started
to pile up like black snow.

I prefer it here, at the line
where the forest intersects
the field, where deer and groundhog
move back and forth to feed
and hide. On these juts and outcroppings
I can look both ways, moving
as that crow does, all gracelessness
and sway across the heaved-up fields,
then tricky flight between
the overhanging branches he somehow
manages never to scrape against.
This life is not easy,
but wings mix up with leaves here,
like the moment when surf turns into
undertow or breaker, and I can
poise myself and hold
for a long time, profoundly
neither one place nor another.

Independence Day
Terra Alta, West Virginia, 1935

Maggie Anderson

Maple trees rise around the picnic tables
as if an extension of the crowd. The young man
in the white linen suit and cap imagines himself
more dapper, and the girls selling kisses
under the striped canopy bend their heads.
Another girl, in a middy blouse with a party hat
tilted on her head, snarls at Walker Evans.
She doesn't want her picture made beside her mother
who is wearing a cloth coat with a fur collar
in early July, with the heat washing the fairgrounds
and everyone she knows standing around. She knows
what Evans doesn't: the talk behind the chance booth,
the way every gesture falls on her in a long shadow
of judgment and kin, her small mother in her stupid
cloth coat, clutching her purse to her bosom.

Among Elms And Maples
Morgantown, West Virginia, August, 1935

Maggie Anderson

Houses are wedged between the tall stacks
of Seneca Glass beside the Monongahela
and waffle up steep hills. Here, the terrain
allows photographers to appear acrobatic.
Walker Evans liked standing on a hill, focusing
down so it seemed he was poised on a branch.
He liked the single telephone pole against
the flat sky, crossed off-center like a crucifix.
Beneath it, among elms and maples, is the house
my mother lived in with her sister and their mother
nearly fifty years ago. In this shot, Evans
only wanted the rough surfaces of clapboard
houses, their meshed roofs and slanted gables.
He didn't want my mother peeling the thin skin
from tomatoes with a sharp knife, my clumsy
Aunt Grace chasing the ones she'd dropped
around the linoleum floor. That would be another
picture, not this one. I look back from the future,
past the undulating, unremitting line of hills
Evans framed my family in, through the shaggy fronds
of summer ferns he used as foreground and as border.

Mining Camp Residents
West Virginia, July, 1935

Maggie Anderson

> They had to seize something in the face of the camera.
> The woman's hand touches her throat as if feeling
> for a necklace that isn't there. The man buries one hand
> in his overall pocket, loops the other through a strap,
> and the child twirls a strand of her hair as she hunkers
> in the dirt at their feet. Maybe Evans asked them to stand
> in the little group in the doorway, a perfect triangle
> of people in the morning sun. Perhaps he asked them
> to hold their arms that way, or bend their heads. It was
> his composition after all. And they did what he said.

Spitting In The Leaves

Maggie Anderson

In Spanishburg there are boys in tight jeans,
mud on their cowboy boots and they wear huge hats
with feathers, skunk feathers they tell me.
They do not want to be in school, but are.
Some teacher cared enough to hold them. Unlike
their thin disheveled cousins, the boys on Matoaka's
Main Street in October who loll against parking meters
and spit into the leaves. Because of them, someone
will think we need a war, will think the best solution
would be for them to take their hats and feathers,
their good country manners and drag them off somewhere,
to Vietnam, to El Salvador. And they'll go.
They'll go from West Virginia, from hills and back roads
that twist like politics through trees, and they'll fight,
not because they know what for but because what they know
is how to fight. What they know is feathers,
their strong skinny arms, their spitting
in the leaves.

Long Story

Maggie Anderson

> To speak in a flat voice
> Is all that I can do.
>
> —James Wright

I need to tell you that I live in a small town
in West Virginia you would not know about.
It is one of the places I think of as home.
When I go for a walk, I take my basset hound
whose sad eyes and ungainliness always draw
a crowd of children. She tolerates anything
that seems to be affection, so she lets the kids
put scarves and ski caps on her head
until she starts to resemble the women who have to dress
from rummage sales in poverty's mismatched polyester.

The dog and I trail the creek bank with the kids,
past clapboard row houses with Christmas seals
pasted to the windows as a decoration.
Inside, television glows around the vinyl chairs
and curled linoleum, and we watch someone old
perambulating to the kitchen on a shiny walker.
Up the hill in town, two stores have been
boarded up beside the youth center, and miners
with amputated limbs are loitering outside
the Heart and Hand. They wear Cat diesel caps
and spit into the street. The wind
carries on, whining through the alleys,
rustling down the sidewalks, agitating
leaves, and circling the courthouse steps
past the toothless Field sisters who lean
against the flagpole holding paper bags
of chestnuts they bring to town to sell.

History is one long story of what happened to us,
and its rhythms are local dialect and anecdote.
In West Virginia a good story takes awhile,
and if it has people in it, you have to swear
that it is true. I tell the kids the one about
my Uncle Craig who saw the mountain move
so quickly and so certainly it made the sun
stand in a different aspect to his little town
until it rearranged itself and settled down again.
This was his favorite story. When he got old,
he mixed it up with baseball games, his shift boss
pushing scabs through a picket line, the Masons
in white aprons at a funeral, but he remembered
everything that ever happened, and he knew how far
he lived from anywhere you would have heard of.

Anything that happens here has a lot of versions,
how to get from here to Logan twenty different ways.
The kids tell me convoluted country stories
full of snuff and bracken, about how long
they sat quiet in the deer blind with their fathers
waiting for the ten-point buck that got away.
They like to talk about the weather,
how the wind we're walking in means rain,
how the flood pushed cattle fifteen miles downriver.

These kids know mines like they know hound dogs
and how the sirens blow when something's wrong.
They know the blast, and the stories, how
the grown-ups drop whatever they are doing
to get out there. Story is shaped
by sound, and it structures what we know.
They told me this, and three of them
swore it was true, so I'll tell you
even though I know you do not know
this place, or how tight and dark the hills
pull in around the river and the railroad.

I'll say it as the children spoke it,
in the flat voice of my people:
down in Boone County, they sealed up

forty miners in a fire. The men who had come
to help tried and tried to get down to them,
but it was a big fire and there was danger,
so they had to turn around
and shovel them back in. All night long
they stood outside with useless picks and axes
in their hands, just staring at the drift mouth.
Here's the thing: what the sound must have been,
all those fire trucks and ambulances, the sirens,
and the women crying and screaming out
the names of their buried ones, who must have
called back up to them from deep inside
the burning mountain, right up to the end.

Ontological

Maggie Anderson

This is going to cost you.
If you really want to hear a
country fiddle, you have to listen
hard, high up in its twang and needle.
You can't be running off like this,
all knotted up with yearning,
following some train whistle,
can't hang onto anything that way.
When you're looking for what's lost
everything's a sign,
but you have to stay right up next to
the drawl and pull of the thing
you thought you wanted, had to
have it, could not live without it.
Honey, you will lose your beauty
and your handsome sweetie, this whine,
this agitation, the one you sent for
with your leather boots and your guitar.
The lonesome snag of barbed wire you have
wrapped around your heart is cash money,
honey, you will have to pay.

from Addie: A Memoir

Mary Lee Settle

*I*n 1927, when the Florida boom burst, we went home in a Model T Ford with what was left packed in orange crates tied to the running boards. We went to Cedar Grove, Kanawha County, West Virginia, the only place my mother ever called home in her life.

So that was why, on an early summer afternoon when I was eight years old, I was lying in the same hammock where my mother had lain in her Peter Thompson suit with her high-buttoned shoes in 1908, smiling at a camera. The hammock had a design of flowers and leaves, vaguely oriental. Fringe hung down, even though it was pretty ratty by 1927. It had always been suspended catty-cornered at the foot of the back stairs, between the old, thin wooden columns of the back porch, shaded by a huge trumpet vine that made a mat which kept the sun away.

I was half asleep, weighed down with heat that stuck my dress to my stomach. There was only the creak of the hammock, and then silence, and then again the creak of the hammock when I put a foot down to move it. I remember especially the silence that seemed blessed since it was such a rare thing in that house where there were so many people.

There was always talk at Cedar Grove, oceans of it, afternoons of it, evenings of it. But I never in all the time I was growing up saw one of the aunts, uncles, or in-laws touch another, ever, in love or sympathy or anger, except when Addie, my grandmother, smoothed my hair as she passed by, or broke a switch off her favorite tree, swished it to test it, and said, "If you won't listen, you'll have to feel."

From the corner where I lay I could see the place where she had had the breezeway between the dining room and the kitchen filled in with brick. In that magic time Before the War, it had been open, and slaves had brought the food through the open air from the kitchen. My mother said that it was wrong to change things like that in a lovely old historic place. Not house. Place. She had said that ever since I could remember, as if she were seeing the house that once was, or could be, but never as it was at the time.

My grandmother, Addie, hadn't changed the back porch, though. She said that suited her. So it remained what it had been since the house was built in 1844. The well was under the roof at the long side of an ell. It was table height so you could hike yourself up on the stone ledge, lean over when there were no grown ups around, look down a long way and see yourself, a little scared face in the black water. Beside the well, the smoke house and the milk house were built into the brick ell behind the main house, both of them dark and cool even in the hottest days of summer. The breeze-way between them and the kitchen which had matched the one between the kitchen and the dining room had been left open. Addie said she had a use for that, an easy way to get to the corncrib and the hog pen to slop the huge sow with her evil eyes and her squealing piglets. My nastiest cousin said that if I fell into the pigpen, the old sow would eat me. There would be nothing left. The pen and the corncrib were in a row away on the east side of the backyard with the chicken house which had once been my mother's playhouse.

I didn't hear her walk onto the porch. Like many heavy women, Addie had silent feet. I did not know she was close to me until she spoke. "The Catholic Church is the Whore of Babylon in the Book of Revelation," she said to wake me up. She wanted to talk. She said she thought I ought to know that about the Catholics, in case.

I was still half asleep, and I saw The Whore of Babylon on the Great Beast, riding astraddle, as Miss Addie put it, across the hot white summer sky beyond the back porch, and I heard again the creak of the hammock.

If she had found any of the other ten grandchildren, she would have routed them out for a chore, made up on the spur of the moment to get them moving. Then we would hear her voice of thunder, "Shame on you! A great big thing like you asettin down," or, if she caught them smoking, "You put out them coffin-nails! You'll stunt your growth," or, worst of all, "Quit that, you little HESSIAN!"

But I was privileged. Because she had lifted me up and taken me to Serena's breast when I was, she said, just lying there waiting to die at a month old, she still thought when I was eight that my mother wouldn't raise me. She would say, "You rest, honey. You never can tell when the knell will sound."

I heard the creak of Miss Addie's rocker when she settled herself to talk. I opened my eyes. She was wearing the blue and white checked poke bonnet that made wings down both of her cheeks and partly hid her face, red from working in the summer heat. It had a frill at the back to protect her neck from the sun when she bent over. She made the bonnets for herself, and she wore them when she went into the garden, no matter how much it embarrassed the girls. She didn't refer to her daughters any other way. "My girls," she would say, glancing over her shoulder at them whenever they were gathered at the center of the house, the huge kitchen table, discussing their troubles, "have not got one iota of gumption." Then she would add, "except for your mother." It was the only nice thing, at least I suppose it was nice, that she ever said about my mother. "Not one iota" was a favorite size with her. She could use that diminishment like a club.

She sat there on the back porch foursquare upon her hams, with her legs apart, leaning on a hoe. I recognized that stance later when I saw statues of Athena that seemed to grow out of the ground. I never thought of Miss Addie as fat, but she had a thick body like the trunk of an old tree.

There she is, as alive for me as she was that afternoon, an old woman in summer, looking in memory like the goddess of justice, timeless and chthonic, in the shade of the porch, in her straight-backed rocker nobody else dared sit in, keeping a rocking rhythm on the stone floor. The shadows of afternoon filtered through the trumpet vines and swayed over the stone sides of the well, the flagstones of the floor, fluttered across the wall of bricks behind her that had been made by slaves, and time had changed to soft pink.

The places where she sat became, when she was there, the center of the house, and when she left them, and walked away, always alone, into the garden, or up the hollow to the tenant houses that had once been slave cabins, the ever-present voices of the "girls," her daughters, my mother and aunts, rose in volume as if they had been released and flew as they called to each other from floor to floor and room to room, from the upstairs back veranda rail, from the wide front lawn or the spreading front porch.

Addie's voice, that day, drifted in and out of dreams and summer until I was awake and watching her, which was what she had waited for. Then, out of some thought deep within herself that she made into words, she decided for the first time to tell me her version of the always whispered about but never admitted family scandal.

"Let me tell you something," she began, as she often did, to draw us to her whenever she caught us drifting. She talked mostly to her grandchildren. Her daughters had stopped listening. "I been thinking about this in the garden. My Lord, it's hot out there." The acre of formal garden that had been laid out when the house was built Before the War in patterns of herbs and peonies and roses and tiny English boxwood had long since been turned by her into a vegetable garden. Little wisps of its neglected and ignored past still showed forlornly in the spring. She said nobody but a fool would have too many flowers and too few vegetables, with things the way they were. "Things the way they are" was another one of her choruses.

"Well, this is how it was. I was no more than fifteen years old when I married that devil Chris Morris. By the time I was eighteen years old I already had three daughters. Chris Morris was mean to me." She settled back into her story, still grasping the hoe like a spear. A bandanna rose slowly and she wiped her forehead under the poke bonnet and began, as she did whenever she rested, to talk about Jesus. "You can't tell Him a thing," she complained. "You just have to set there and listen." She was completely familiar with Jesus, and her conversations with him were on as equal terms as she could manage.

Once, being smart aleck, I asked her what Jesus sounded like, and, instead of punishing me for taking the Lord's name in vain, she thought for a long time, and then she said, "Near as I can explain, real quiet, a little bit like your grandfather."

Her language was a mixture of Bible, fairy tale, ghost story, coal operator, and hillbilly. At any time, out of the house of her own recall and contemplation, one of the days or nights of life would come forth for me, from some kind of darkness that she lit with words. So much of it was legend, legend that now she believed and stated as facts.

"One Saturday night I heared Christopher Morris a'comin home from the saloon and I knowed he was drunk. He was always drunk on a Saturday night. He was a'comin up that road hell-bent for election, mutterin to hisself, and I knowed what that meant. I clumb a tree to get away from him. And there I was a'settin in that tree, no more than eighteen years old, and already married three years to that devil, and I looked down through the branches and there was Chris Morris mean drunk and lurchin around down there a'lookin for me."

Her voice changed, quieted. "Right there up that tree I heard the voice of Jesus." She began to sway and use her witness-bearing voice. "Jesus said unto me, Addie, you are nuthin but a damn fool. Ain't you ever heard of divorce?"

That was the way she remembered her Christian holy past, a victim up a tree, with Jesus to give her courage to act, a battered woman among so many battered women.

Nobody had ever said directly what had happened; we gathered around it later, picking up fragments, some malicious, some true, I suppose, but when I found the court records, I found the pathos and violence she had replaced with Jesus.

All the time I had known her I thought of her as Miss Addie. I would not have dared to do otherwise. But when I began to glimpse the woman she had been, she became, for me, Addie, more familiar and more mysterious than she was in life, Addie young, Addie hurt and proud, Addie beautiful, and finally, again, an old woman, sitting that day on the back porch, looking as she did when she entered my own childhood memory and stayed there and still does, as strongly as if she has just left the room I am in now, having shaken the curtains because somebody had been smoking coffin nails.

She had not been eighteen, she had been twenty-six when she filed for divorce, and she had already met my grandfather. It had been one of the first divorces in West Virginia, but the facts are misty, the legends crossed, and I saw more truth if not more fact in the way Addie told it that day.

The records of the divorce, the births, the marriage to my grandfather had remained ever since in the County Courthouse. When I finally saw them, they were less believable than the story of the voice of Jesus. The courage that she had shown was almost unbearable.

Christopher Morris said he wanted to get rid of her anyway. He didn't like being married and his mamma couldn't stand her. He had already left her three times in the course of their eleven-year marriage. She had made her living and fed her children by being a seamstress. They had lived in one of those board and batten houses, with inch-thick walls, three or four rooms, and a front stoop. Later, when the coal companies built housing for their miners, such dwellings were called "Jenny Lind houses" after the cheap method of building used at the Jenny Lind mine in Colo-rado. But they had long been built that way in West Virginia. The farmers used board and batten to cover the logs of they cabins as a sign that they were moving up in the world. The next stage toward gentility was broad clapboard, overlapping and painted white.

Addie had been a beautiful woman, the most beautiful, they said, in the valley. There are no pictures of her then, only people's memories, and in memory, beauty grows. She was of her time – the chestnut hair she could sit on, the tiny waist, even after three daughters born in the single bedroom of that poor house on the south bank of the river. If she screamed it was to a local midwife, and when the third daughter came the other two watched from the doorway. "There wasn't nobody to make them scat," she said. "Chris Morris was off drunk somewheres." Her birth stories were not calculated. She would have scorned calculations. They were simply facts of life, often too strong for the blood of her daughters and granddaughters.

She sued for divorce on the grounds of cruelty and desertion. She was represented by the leading law firm in the city of Charleston, twenty miles downriver, where, because of the new coal business, lawyers had gathered like a plague of locusts. My grandfather had hired the law firm that had been there years longer that the "new people," and whom she never would have heard of or been able to pay for.

It was obvious from the court records that they were prepared to do a favor for the old friend who had "kicked the end out of the same cradle" and who they sat with on the porch of the Ruffner Hotel, looking at the river, drinking juleps, and talking politics.

In the legal layer presented of past events, her husband had "deserted" her three times. The last time, in 1889, he did not return. She said she saw him sometimes across the road in the town at the foot of the hollow in a wide place in the valley, where a ferry plied across the Kanawha River.

The Kanawha runs west to the Ohio. Its direction has dictated industry, economics, marriages, and mores ever since the valley was settled in 1775. Its direction had formed the longings and lies of so many of its people—dreams of gentility east of the Alleghenies in Virginia, dreams of fortunes west along the Ohio at Cincinnati. It has flowed past coal companies with their shack towns, narrow bottomland, and knife-cut hollows between steep hills on its south side. It passed large old farms with several small towns grown up around on the north side until, a few miles east of Charleston, beyond the lush beautiful farmland and virgin forests on the hills, the land had once been blackened and denuded of trees when the salt business had been the first of the exploitive industries in the valley. Upriver, the cultural banks were farther apart than the mere fact of a hundred or so feet of deep water.

According to Addie's testimony, the river had held for her a terrible way out. She had tried twice to drown herself in it. The first time, she said, had been in the first two years of the marriage, the second within the year of her statement. She had tried to kill herself by taking a bottle of laudanum when she was eight months pregnant. She had bought it at the Company Store. She said she had tried to go to the station to catch the train to see her mother, and Chris Morris had followed her and forced her home by pulling a knife on her. She said her mother had died without Addie being able to visit her.

Her first witness was her housekeeper, who had looked after the children while Addie earned her living after the desertion. In her testimony she said that she had seen Addie jump into the river, had seen Addie's husband beat her. She added that he was a mean drunk and that the children weren't safe with him. Addie's oldest daughter, Minnie, was put on the stand to testify that her father beat her mother. She was eleven years old.

It had been Chris Morris, though, who came back to the house after threatening Addie with the knife and found her insensible on the bed, with the empty bottle of laudanum beside her. He called the family doctor. The doctor testified that he nearly lost her that time.

Jesus and the legal evidence were only the first two layers of the event. The third consisted of rumor, memory, facts let slip, a patchwork of events that had to be put together like a quilt, the kind that Addie and her friends stretched across two big trestles and quilted all through the winter. Some of the gossip came from daughters-in-law who didn't like her, some from my mother when her memories of "home" slipped into reality without her being aware that she had spoken. My mother tended literally to speak her mind, let out in words the secret scenes that she was seeing.

All the memories are real. Of course they are, like dreams are real, like old wounds that insist until they heal and leave a twinge of memory in the scars.

Chris Morris did pull a knife on Addie, not because she wanted to visit her mother, but because he knew she was pregnant with another man's child. She did try to go to the station, where the trains then ran several times a day and made the whole valley into one railroad town, a forty-mile corridor down the south side of the river. But she was not going to meet her mother who had been dead for years, but her lover, my grandfather.

By the time of the trial she was buried in scandal, unable to breathe. The doctor told the truth until he said he knew nothing against her reputation. He must have pitied her, he, nearly eighty, too old for judgment, she still young, still lovely.

She had seen a way out, a way that was taboo. She took it and then, for too long, had the door slammed in her face. Her dreams while she worked at her sewing machine, over the washtub, calling the children, patching, darning, quilting, cooking, became nightmares. The laudanum was real. The bottle was empty.

She was surrounded by catcalls and rumors, that Chris Morris was paid off, that my grandfather had bought her from him for a sack of corn. Chris Morris and his buddies played sandlot baseball on a Saturday afternoon, got drunk at the saloon on Saturday night, and threw five sticks of dynamite from the mine on the front porch of her stepfather's house, where she had gone to wait for the divorce to be final. Addie ran out, stamped on the long fuse, picked up the bound sticks and threw them into the woods. She saved her children's and her stepfather's lives, and her own, which by then wasn't worth a plugged nickel. No wonder that, in those days, when she heard the voice of Jesus, he must have sounded like Mr. Tompkins, my grandfather.

⟶⇥◎⇤⟵

What Addie called her home in heaven was as sensuous as a Moslem's. One morning she caught me sulking on the front porch with my legs hanging over the porch floor. I was kicking rambler roses. To cheer me up she told me, "Oh, honey, last night I had the most wonderful dream. I dreamed that I passed over at last and I went to heaven, and when them great gold gates parted, there in front of me was a big table laden with golden dishes and every dish was full of beautiful food, and there was flowers and silks and satins and purple for the kings and blue for the saints, and there was all my relatives that had gone before all waiting to welcome me at the great table, and all their relatives and friends that had gone before, a great host at the banquet . . ."

She stopped; she had heard me make a small sound, a humph, and she said, "What's the matter with you?"

I said that didn't sound much like heaven to me, that I lived with too many people already who didn't understand me and I certainly didn't want to get stuck with them forever in heaven when I got there.

"All right," she said. "Go on to hell where you don't know nobody."

All her life she loved Jesus, ghosts, my grandfather, and food. Her dinner table was always laden with food, and she looked at it as if it might disappear.

Much of Virginia beyond the mountains had been Confederate in sentiment during the occupation of Federal troops in western Virginia, which became West Virginia in 1863. The army took the people's mules and their livestock. Secretly the southern sympathizers called the new state the bastard of political rape.

In 1865 men from both armies were straggling home. Some had given up and lit out for the territories. Some were simply never heard of again—dead or missing. Addie said her real father had been a Confederate spy and had been hanged when he was caught. She was ashamed of that. My grandfather told her that it was braver to be a spy than a soldier, but she never quite believed it.

She had been taken up by a family called either Ross or Elswick. None of her children knew whether her father had been called Ross and her stepfather Elswick, or the other way round. No mention had ever been made of her mother, who had not survived the starving time. All that was known was her mother's last name—Martin.

Sometimes Addie said she was descended from Pocahontas. Pocahontas's only child has been accused of having a million descendants in Virginia. But sometimes Addie just told us that her great-great-grand-mother was a squaw. In the early days of the Virginia colony, women were rounded up and sent over from England to be wives. Up to the early eighteenth century the saying in the colony was "Better a clean squaw than a London whore." By the mid-eighteenth century, of course, many of the settlers were younger sons of peers, according to their descendants, but Addie scorned what she called that piece of foolishness. The shape of Addie's face and her eyes hinted at the truth of the squaw.

During the Civil War (the greatest of all historic oxymorons) there were only the old people and the children to work the steep fields of the small farms. They gathered wild greens in the woods when the spring came to cure the cabin fever and the scurvy that came from eating only jerky, the dried meat that had been put up for winter, after the dried beans and yarbs and corn and the vegetables in the root cellar had long since run out. They lived as people on the frontier had always lived, long after the frontier had passed them by.

Gradually the young men straggled back and the fields were plowed again. A mule was a luxury few could afford. Addie remembered how the women steered while the men were hitched to the ancient plows their grandparents had brought over the mountains. She followed with corn seed, and stinking fish, three seeds for the hole – one for the critters, one to rot, and one to grow. She laid a piece of rotten fish in the hole for fertilizer. She still planted corn that way when she was an old woman, but she said the three seeds were the Father, the Son, and the Holy Ghost.

When Addie was nine years old, her world changed more profoundly than we can fathom. The coming of the railroads and the opening of the coal mines in the Kanawha Valley were as violent a change to the farmers of Addie's childhood as the great industrial revolutions were to earlier Americans. We are seeing something like it in our own lives, and are now once again in a frightening economic upheaval, this time requiring intelligence, a new language, more delicate skills, instead of the once-proud working man's muscular strength.

John Henry has been replaced by a fourteen-year-old computer genius in a garage. The newly honored intelligence that was once derided when muscle was needed at the coal face is leaving bitterness, as the men Addie grew up with became embittered when their mules were "commandeered" by war and their farm skills were no longer needed. Some retired deeper into the hollows, like animals after a flood has passed, then, as now, leaving dangerous residues that turned into hatred of what had passed them by.

In 1873 the Chesapeake and Ohio railroad was completed on the south side of the river, and later the Kanawha and Michigan railroad on the north. Coal barges plied the river below Cedar Grove in the months when the river was navigable, following the way of the salt barges, on their way to Cincinnati in the salt boom of the early 1800s.

The new boom was coal. Cash money poured into the valley with the opening of the great coal seams. A farmer who had had sense enough not to sell his mineral rights could (and did) become a millionaire overnight. Coal had names as overblown as the hopes that came with it – black diamonds, black gold, King Coal. Later F. Scott Fitzgerald, who was at Princeton with coal baron heirs, was to call a coal fortune "The Diamond as Big as the Ritz." Most of the money went to stockholders who didn't know or care about how people were living in West Virginia. The saying on "the street" was "dividends don't make demands."

In the next five years of Addie's growing up, the soil darkened with coal dust. Spurs of the railroad snaked up the hollows. Rich men came in their private railroad cars. The train engines belched long lines of smoke. If you traveled on the train you could smell coal dust, clean linen, furniture polish, good whiskey, and fat cigars. It was the smell of new money. My father told me that the first time he ever saw a grapefruit was through the window of a diner on the C&O.

The hillbillies watched the trains go by and made up songs. "Here she comes, look at her roll, there she goes eatin' that coal." Billy Richardson of Hinton became immortal when a song told about how he was beheaded by a projecting signal on the water tower but brought the train to a halt in the station anyway. John Henry challenged a mechanical pile driver in the digging on No. 9 tunnel under Gauley Mountain on the C&O. Casey Jones died at the throttle when he lost his average on a three-mile grade. At the railroad town of Thurmond on the New River, new kinds of men gathered, glamorous men—coal operators, railroad men, speculators. A poker game in the Dunglen Hotel went on for thirty-four years.

Life, for a while, was good. Local men had work that paid cash or the scrip that meant they could buy, but only at the Company Store. There were things at the Company Store that they would have had to go all the way to Charleston for in the past, if they had the cash, which they usually didn't. It stocked gingham and shoes and clothes, and overalls that the women didn't have to make.

There were barrels of dill pickles, huge wheels of store-bought cheese, white bread, drugs and whiskey, and mangles for the washtub. At Christmastime there were oranges from Florida and Skookam apples all the way from the West Coast. There was sheet music from New York. They could order pianos, upright and player and even baby grand. There were cans of fruit and vegetables the women didn't have to put up, the essence of luxury. When my grandfather asked a miner who had ten children how he was managing to feed them, he answered, "Well, Mr. Tompkins, we don't eat no canned peaches."

They came down out of the hills, from the farms, off the immigrant boats from Europe. An Italian consulate opened at Montgomery, a few miles upriver from Addie's home. It was a new "volunteer" fashion for ladies from Charleston to go upriver to teach the Italian women to speak

English, to cook (when they had been cooking Italian food all their lives), and to be "American."

Then, as it has ever since, in a kind of systalic, diastalic progression, the bottom dropped out of the coal business. For the first of many times, people who had come to work in the mines were thrown out of the shacks the companies had built. The United Mine Workers began to grow on the rocky soil, now poisoned by acid from the slag.

Addie had married at fifteen into the Morris family, who were victims of a change that had been going on since 1812, when the salt wells were dug north of the river at Burning Springs, a few miles east of Charleston. Christopher Morris, her husband, like most of the men, had gone into the new mines. He was a drunkard, but then so many of them were. He did beat her, but in that world of coal mining, day long, night long, where petrified tree trunks called kettles could loosen and kill, where the white bones of ancient fish in the coal caught the light from the miners' head lamps, and the crystal skeletons of plants were known as flowers of darkness, where accidents waited for millennia when the earth was disturbed, the men were all edged with fear, like people in a perpetual war who go about their business as best they can.

There were too many shootings on Saturday nights. From the new language of machinery and the railroad they took the phrase "letting off steam." In winter, when he had work, Chris Morris left home before dawn with his carbide lamp lit on his miner's hard hat to show him the way; he made the daily trip by mule-drawn tram into the mine, sometimes as far as two or three miles. When he returned, long after dark, with his lamp lit to show him the way home, Addie heated water on the kitchen range and tried to scrub off the black gold while he sat in the washtub.

You could tell a coal miner by his eyes, and it was still so when I was a child there. They were darkened around the rims with coal dust that never came off – Nefertiti eyes. Yes, he beat her. Yes, he drank. Men then lived hard, died early, carried guns, gambled, and, being so on the tether of some decision made someplace else by men who didn't know their names, they swaggered even more. Those with brains fought their way downriver, to college, but carried the scars of the coal business, and still do. The feudalism. The exploiting of earth and men. Owner and worker, each far from the other, were threatened by the same diseases of danger and indifference, recognized each other as brothers who don't claim kin.

We are all marked, who have lived and been blooded by the coal fields. We never get away because it is deep in us, whether our fathers have worked the coal face, or bought our clothes and our college educations with money that was as black as the rims of coal miners' eyes. We have all been formed long before human ancestry or our culture or kindness or hatred or lack of money has affected us. These are all personal. And they can twist and stunt, or lie fallow in us, or help us grow strong.

But the coal mines, the darkness, like the mark of Cain, are as deep within us as the eons that formed us both, slowly and inexorably, millions of years ago, where patient time has crushed and dried ancient seas, swamps, forests, animals into something mysterious that seduced the world we lived in, made us rich, made us poor, broke the health of some of us, made some of us refugees. Like people who have been deserted by a lover, we may hate it, but we never forget it.

We who have the stigma recognize each other. Sometimes the recognition goes unrealized for years. At least ten years after I grew close to a fine singer, Bobby Short, I found out that his father had been mashed in a mine in Kentucky. Ann Beattie, who is a writer of Mozartean prose, told me after I had known her for twenty years that her mother was brought up in a coal town. An Englishman I nearly married and whom I knew only as an RAF pilot turned out to be the heir to a coal fortune. What is it that is between us, deeper than country, race, or sex? Is it a residue of genetic fear, the fear of the exploited depths?

Even if we have lived far from it, maybe we inherit a residue, too, daily and unnoticed, the awareness of darkness, listening and not listening for accidents, for boom or bust, for failure, for wild success, all from the earth-stabbing we are born into. Mining, the boring for oil, gas, minerals, unlike farming or the making of things, is the taking of something that only more eons can give back. It informs politics, too. The ones who do the dangerous work produce paper profit for people without names or responsibility or care.

Almost directly across the river from where Addie was born was the house my great-grandfather had built with money from salt. It was one of the three largest farms in the valley, a place that must have seemed a mirage to her in the starving time. On early mornings as a child in linsey-woolsey, she would have seen the horses and the cattle, and a few black people who had stayed and were getting wages of a sort and enough to eat, all like shadows, moving too far away for her ever to reach.

Then, when Addie was twenty-three or -four, there was a moment so short, so far-reaching, that it still haunts my dreams and my habits as it did my mother's. It fashioned our bones. My mother was brittle with imitations of some faraway gentility, always thin, always upright, always watchful, and yet, within, she carried the voice of Addie, mocking her as she mocked herself. The moment was the meeting of my grandparents.

There has always been a mystery to how Addie and my grandfather met and what they could have had in common. Maybe they shared the immediacy of memory of a better, richer earth before the black change came in their lifetime. Was the meeting on the ferry that plied between her town and his?

Or was it on a country road? I like to think so. Make it a hot morning and sandy bottom at the mouth of one of the hollows. The althea is in bloom, and scraggly roses crawl over a stump in the sandy front yard—a hot morning that smells of grass and sand and the wet wash that flaps on the line.

I see Addie standing by the fence, as if she is resting for a minute from too much work. The sweat, the glow, as Mr. Tompkins would have called it, stands out on her lovely forehead. She is small and lithe and beautiful. One of her daughters clings to her skirt. The two older girls are playing in the yard, but quietly, watching her from time to time as if they don't know which way the cat will jump. Behind her is the small white-washed house with a stoop. Two rocking chairs stand still beside a corrugated tin washtub with a hand wringer clamped to it. On the other corner of the stoop, where it can catch the sun, is an incongruously elegant wire stand that holds a huge blooming lily.

She had whitewashed the house herself. She never in her life, she told me when she was an old woman, could get a man to do a damned thing. I think that just at the moment he passed by, she leaned forward on the fence and sighed and he could see the sun glistening on the hair at the nape of her neck.

He was driving downriver. Maybe. Addie made her legends come true by lodging them with us. There were our own legends and hers, elusive and ponderous, and there behind them all, deep within the heavy old woman, was Addie when she was young, slim, beautiful, on a sand road by the river in the summertime, the valley lush around her, as it is still, so lush that it hides its scars and its sins every summer until the leaves fall on the slag heaps and the forgotten shacks and the car graveyards and the piles of old tires.

She told me that the first time she saw him, he wore a flaring red tie, a poet's tie, she called it when she told the story, and he drove the fastest four-in-hand, the lord of the valley, she said, when he got his hands on those reins. She said he cut a dash. He had been the valley's eligible bachelor as long as anybody could remember and still was what they called a great catch.

The tools Miss Addie had to change the only life she could have chosen as the wife of a coal miner, were, first, her imperious eyes. She had, too, hidden maybe even from herself, a will, a passion as strong and as inevitable as the river's current.

But on that morning her life was confined by the huddled coal town, the Company Store, her stepparents' house, the little church, Church of

God Holy Roller, the washtub that sat on a bench on the stoop. The sun behind her made a halo around her head of glossy hair. That was what I think he saw at that moment, at that place or at another place, a glance and then a look, and the lives of so many would spin out from it, including her children's, my cousins,' my brother's, and my own.

After they met, did she dream at the washtub, in the privy, in the tumbled bed where she had to do her marital duty, calling the children, wandering down to the riverbank and watching the river flow toward where he might be? A whole new life opened up, a dream come true and turning terrible. All she knew was passion. It was all that her life had taught her, that and work, passion and work, and for herself, all her life afterwards, an imagination the people around her never had, except for my mother, the only child out of all of them who inherited it, and was teased, it being the time when women were derided for such things. It terrified her. She threw the talent away. I picked it up—a hidden gauntlet, grandmother to mother to child—as carelessly as if I had found it in an alley and wondered what it was. I was punished for years for picking up something that might be dirty.

I guess that the year they met was 1887. I think the passion caught fire so that perhaps neither of them, certainly not Addie, could ever have withstood it. He, in his mid-forties, may have been more calculating in his watching as he passed, judging as he would have judged a dog, a horse, another man. He was the favorite son. Whatever he wanted, he got, or took with all the charm that was so famous. He wanted her. At last he had found somebody who could give him a family, which was the only thing in human relations he hadn't tasted, one way or another.

And Addie, who had never been in a house that had an upstairs? She watched across the river that had nearly taken her life and saw far-away, wide green fields and slow-moving horses feeding, and in the distance, almost out of sight, nestled in the hills beyond the river, a tiny red brick house. Its many windows caught the sun, and she knew that it was not tiny, but huge, bigger than any house she had ever seen. But the river was between her and my grandfather, impossible. She must have stood there, as she had when she was a child, long before she met my grandfather, and gazed across to the north side, the far, far side of the river.

"Across the river," the house where Addie's lover lived, was as far from the coal dust she knew as the moon. It rose above the river mist as unattainable as Paradise, and as near as the ferry that ran between East Bank and Cedar Grove. But what she saw in the distance was more a mirage than just green hills, rolling fields, and calm. She saw feudal divisions of money, property, and power in what had been, such a short time ago, a frontier valley.

Late Winter Snow:
South Of Morgantown, WV

Mark DeFoe

The scene is too beautiful, a Rockwell
straight from *Country Home*. Such moments we take
without judgment, and we join the traffic,
moving with a Sunday's benediction.

The ruddy sun, cooling beyond the sweep
of shaggy horizon, stretches fingers
into these old hills, humped like the backs
of great drowsing, long gone buffalo.

In this watercolor, snow has sketched log
and trunk and ridgeline, glyphs in black and gray.
Each meadow is a page where deer browse amid
the brush strokes of our musings.
      Taillights string
ruby beads across the hills. We follow,
linking up our little glow. Dark holds off
until our driveway. It seems we have been
gone for years. But one look up at the gables,
the pitch of roof, and we know things—though
a bit worse for wear—are as we left them.
        We open the car doors
and the air's kindness surprises.
Around us, spring whispers—soon, soon.

Leaving The Hills

Mark DeFoe

She's shedding self like a snake skin,
sculpting her makeup for new nights,
bound for where habits run shallow,
where dreams don't hang limp in her closet.

She's flying the hollow, larking
for a land too wide for whispers,
where no kin is kin. Where the terms
"roof fall ," "knocked up," or "covered dish"

are discouraging words. This land
wants to drape her in wren song, catch
her ankles in chicory, cloud her
with cool fog. Autumn might dazzle

with homey gold. Summer might drug
with cricket song. Oh, No. She loads
her red Camaro with quilts to pawn.
She chooses gritty March, early,

when light spares nothing, when her fear
of leaving is a copperhead fear,
but not as deadly as the bile
that comes when she thinks of staying.

As she flashes by the high school,
she shoots her memories the bird
and then feels ashamed. She recalls
the night in Kevin Holt's backseat.

Who was that panting child who gave
her flesh away to wear his jacket?
She squares her shoulders—like Mom said—
slips on her new Oakley's, pumps up

the volume, and serpentines the curves.
She laughs into her sun, rising
like a neon promise, scarlet
and gaudy over the interstate.

Driving The Gauley River, Listening To The Radio West Virginia

Mark DeFoe

I see King Coal has sprinkled his favors—
new jeeps, wives on riding mowers, fresh paint.

But this is a tale of hard times. Set it
in these hills. Say she walked home
in November rain—caught cold, of course.
It ran to pneumonia. Drowning, Doc said,
lungs filling with the dank
that settles in these hollows.
The preacher, the gathered kin, sang
of sweet solemn hope, crossing over
to tarry on that brighter shore.

Her blue eyes clouded; she squeezed their hands,
saying give Sis my best dress,
Cletus my fourth grade speller,
said it like she had it by rote,
like it came to her from a country song.
And those anvil faces, that circle of skulls, sang,
rising toward a light above their shrouded hills.
And each year they ran her picture
in the county paper—a small girl
with receding chin, limp hair and bad teeth.

And the tale became a song. It's maudlin,
but I sing along with my radio,
caught on the brambles of that twang,
hooked on the briars of her blue, blue eyes.
I drive beside the green river, pulled
curve by curve into the trees—
my own voice rising in terrible joy,
held in the circle of her thin arms,
certain she is asleep in Jesus.

The Former Miner Returns From His First Day As A Service Worker (at McDonald's—somewhere in Appalachia)

Mark DeFoe

All day he crushed the spongy buns, pawed at
The lids of burger boxes and kiddie packs
As if they were Chinese puzzles.

All day his hands ticked, ready to latch on
Or heave or curl around a tool
Heavier than a spatula.

All day he rubbed his eyes in the crisp light.
All day the blue tile, the polished chrome, said
Be nimble, be jolly, be quick.

All day he grinned while the public, with bland
Or befuddled faces, scowled over his head
And mumbled, whispered, snarled and snapped.

All day his co-workers, pink and scrubbed,
Prattled and glided and skipped while he,
All bulk and balk, rumbled and banged.

Near shift's end he daydreamed—of the clang
Of rock on steel, the skreel
Of a conveyor belt, the rattling whine
Of the man trip, the miner's growl of gears
As it gnarled, toothing at the seam.

He makes his slow way home, shadow among
Roadside shadows, groping back in himself
For that deep sheltering dark.
He has never been so tired.
His hands have never been so clean.

Air

Mark DeFoe

Listen. Sweet the air with tiny bells, souls
of those who might as well have never been.
Leaves rustle with their almost moans. They cry—
"Once I strode the street with a red bandana,
with burnished earrings that dazzled sun."

The air eddies, swirls rife with souls, the air
luminous, gauzy with prayers.

                        And we turn
from tossing the salad, mowing the lawn,
shake our heads, as if we heard whispers low,
like the scrape of a moth's wing on the dark.

We turn to our work, cocking heads to what
pings among the dust motes.   to what pleads
beneath any human ear—fluttering
husk and chaff of lives, some white noise—
I was. I was. I was. I was.

The Sutton Pie Safe

Pinckney Benedict

$\mathcal{A}$ blacksnake lay stretched out on the cracked slab of concrete near the diesel tank. It kept still in a spot of sun. It had drawn clear membranes across its eyes, had puffed its glistening scales a little, soaking up the heat of the day. It must have been three feet long.

"There's one, dad," I said, pointing at it. My father was staring at the old pole barn, listening to the birds in the loft as they chattered and swooped from one sagging rafter to another. The pole barn was leaning hard to one side, the west wall buckling under. The next big summer storm would probably knock it down. The winter had been hard, the snows heavy, and the weight had snapped the ridgepole. I wondered where we would put that summer's hay.

"Where is he?" my dad asked. He held the cut-down .410 in one hand, the short barrel cradled in the crook of his elbow, stock tight against this bare ribs. We were looking for copperheads to kill, but I thought maybe I could coax my dad into shooting the sleeping blacksnake. I loved the crack of the gun, the smell of sulphur from the opened breech. Again I pointed to the snake.

"Whew," he said, "that's a big one there. What do you figure, two, two and a half feet?" "Three," I said. "Three at least." He grunted.

"You gonna kill it?" I asked.

"Boys want to kill everything, don't they?" he said to me, grinning. Then, more seriously, "Not too good an idea to kill a blacksnake. They keep the mice down, the rats. Better than a cat, really, a good-sized blacksnake."

He stood, considering the unmoving snake, his lips pursed. He tapped the stock of the gun against his forearm. Behind us, past the line of willow trees near the house, I heard the crunch of gravel in the driveway. Somebody was driving up. We both turned to watch as the car stopped next to the smokehouse. It was a big car, Buick Riviera, and I could see that the metallic flake finish had taken a beating on the way up our lane.

My father started forward, then stopped. A woman got out of the car, a tall woman in a blue sun dress. She looked over the car at us, half waved. She had honey-colored hair that hung to her shoulders, and beautiful, well-muscled arms. Her wave was uncertain. When I looked at my dad, he seemed embarrassed to have been caught without a shirt. He raised the gun in a salute, decided that wasn't right, lowered the gun and waved his other hand instead.

It was too far to talk without shouting, so we didn't say anything, and neither did the woman. We all stood there a minute longer. Then I started over toward her.

"Boy," my dad said. I stopped. "Don't you want to get that snake?" he said.

"Thought it wasn't good to kill blacksnakes," I said. I gestured toward the house. "Who is she?" I asked.

"Friend of your mother's," he said. His eyes were on her. She had turned from us, was at the screen porch. I could see her talking through the mesh to my mother, nodding her head. She had a purse in her hand, waved it to emphasize something she was saying. "Your mom'll take care of her," my dad said. The woman opened the porch door, entered. The blue sun dress was pretty much backless, and I watched her go. Once she was on the porch, she was no more than a silhouette.

"Sure is pretty," I said to my father. "Yeah," he said. He snapped the .410's safety off, stepped over to the diesel pump. The snake sensed his coming, turned hooded eyes on him. The sensitive tongue flicked from the curved mouth, testing the air, the warm concrete. For just a second, I saw the pink inner lining of the mouth, saw the rows of tiny, backward curving fangs. "When I was ten, just about your age," my dad said, levelling the gun at the snake, "my daddy killed a big old blacksnake out in our back yard."

The snake, with reluctance, started to crawl from the spot of sun. My dad steadied the gun on it with both hands. It was a short weapon, the barrel and stock both cut down. It couldn't have measured more than twenty inches overall. Easy to carry, quick to use: perfect for snake. "He killed that blacksnake, pegged the skin out, and gave it to me for a belt," my dad said. He closed one eye, squeezed the trigger.

The shot tore the head off the snake. At the sound, a couple of barn swallows flew from the haymow, streaked around the barn, swept back into the dark loft. I watched the body of the snake vibrate and twitch, watched it crawl rapidly away from the place where it had died. It moved more quickly than I'd seen it move that afternoon. The blood was dark, darker than beets or raspberry juice. My dad snapped the bolt of the gun open, and the spent cartridge bounced on the concrete. When the snake's body twisted toward me, I stepped away from it.

My dad picked the snake up from the mess of its head. The dead snake, long and heavy, threw a couple of coils over his wrist. He shook them off, shook the body of the snake out straight, let it hang down from his hand. It was longer than one of his legs. "Wore that belt for a lot of years," he said, and I noticed that my ears were ringing. It took me a second to understand what he was talking about. "Wore it 'till it fell apart." He offered the snake to me, but I didn't want to touch it. He laughed.

"Let's go show your mother," he said, walking past me toward the house. I thought of the woman in the sun dress, wondered what she would think of the blacksnake. I followed my dad, watching the snake. Its movements were slowing now, lapsing into a rhythmic twitching along the whole length of its body.

As we passed the smokehouse and the parked Riviera, I asked him, "What's her name?" He looked at the car, back to me. I could hear my mother's voice, and the voice of the other woman, couldn't hear what they were saying.

"Hanson," he said. "Mrs. Hanson. Judge Hanson's wife." Judge Hanson was a circuit court judge in the county seat; he'd talked at my school once, a big man wearing a three-piece suit, even though the day had been hot. It seemed to me that his wife must be a good deal younger than he was.

The snake in my father's hand was motionless now, hung straight down toward the earth. His fingers were smeared with gore, and a line of blood streaked his chest.

"Why'd you kill the blacksnake?" I asked him. "After what you said, about rats and all?" I was still surprised he'd done it. He looked at me, and for a moment I didn't think he was going to answer me.

He reached for the doorknob with his free hand, twisted it. "Thought you'd know," he said. "My daddy made a belt for me. I'm gonna make one for you."

The woman in the sun dress, Mrs. Hanson, was talking to my mother when we entered the porch. "I was talking to Karen Spangler the other day," she said. My mother, sitting at the other end of the screen porch, nodded. Mrs. Spangler was one of our regular egg customers, came out about once every two weeks, just for a minute. Mrs. Hanson continued. "She says that you all have just the best eggs, and the Judge and I wondered if you might possibly . . ." She let the sentence trail off, turned to my father.

"Why, hello, Mr. Albright," she said. She saw the snake, but she had poise: she didn't react. My father nodded at her. "Mrs. Hanson," he said. He held the snake up for my mother to see. "Look here, Sara," he said. "Found this one sunning himself out near the diesel pump."

My mother stood. "You don't want to bring that thing on the porch, Jack," she said. She was a small woman, my mother, with quick movements, deft reactions. There was anger in her eyes.

"Thought I'd make a belt out of it for the boy," my dad said, ignoring her. He waved the snake, and a drop of blood fell from his hand to the floor. "You remember that old snakeskin belt I had?"

Mrs. Hanson came over to me, and I could smell her perfume. Her skin was tan, lightly freckled. "I don't think we've met," she said to me, like I was a man, and not just a boy. I tried to look her straight in the eye, found I couldn't. "No'm," I said. "Don't think we have."

"His name's Cates," my mother said. "He's ten." I didn't like it that she answered for me. Mrs. Hanson nodded, held out her hand. "Pleased to meet you, Cates," she said. I took her hand, shook it, realized I probably wasn't supposed to shake a lady's hand. I pulled back, noticed the grime under my fingernails, the dust on the backs of my hands. "Pleased," I said, and Mrs. Hanson gave out a laugh that was like nothing I'd ever heard from a woman before, loud and happy.

"You've a fine boy there," she said to my dad. I bent my head. To my father, my mother said, "Why don't you take that snake out of here, Jack. And get a shirt on. We've got company."

He darted a look at her. Then he waved the snake in the air, to point out to everybody what a fine, big blacksnake it was. He opened the screen door, leaned out, and dropped the snake in a coiled heap next to the steps. It looked almost alive lying there, the sheen of the sun still on the dark scales. "Mrs. Hanson," he said, and went on into the house. He let the door slam behind him, and I could hear him as he climbed the stairs inside.

Once he was gone, Mrs. Hanson seemed to settle back, to become more businesslike. "The Judge and I certainly would appreciate the opportunity to buy some of your eggs." She sat down in one of the cane bottom chairs we kept on the porch in summer, set her purse down beside her. "But Sara—may I call you Sara?" she asked, and my mother nodded. "Something else has brought me here as well." My mother sat forward in her chair, interested to hear. I leaned forward too, and Mrs. Hanson shot a glance my way. I could tell she wasn't sure she wanted me there.

"Sara," she said, "you have a Sutton pie safe." She pointed across the porch, and at first I thought she meant the upright freezer that stood there. Then I saw she was pointing at the old breadbox.

My mother looked at it. "Well, it's a pie safe," she said. "Sutton, I don't know—"

"Oh, yes, it's a Sutton," Mrs. Hanson said. "Mrs. Spangler told me so, and I can tell she was right." Mrs. Spangler, so far as I knew, had never said anything to us about a pie safe. Mrs. Hanson rose, knelt in front of the thing, touched first one part of it and then another.

"Here, you see," she said, pointing to the lower right corner of one of the pie safe's doors. We'd always called it a breadbox, kept all kinds of things in it: canned goods, my dad's ammunition and his reloading kit, things that needed to be kept cool in winter. The pie safe was made of cherry wood—you could tell even through the paint—with a pair of doors on the front. The doors had tin panels, and there were designs punched in the tin, swirls and circles and I don't know what all. I looked at the place where she was pointing. "SS" I saw, stamped into the wood. The letters were mostly filled with paint; I'd never noticed them before.

Mrs. Hanson patted the thing, picked a chip of paint off it. My mother and I watched her. "Of course," Mrs. Hanson said, "this paint will have to come off. Oh, a complete refinishing job, I imagine. How lovely!" She sounded thrilled. She ran her hands down the tin, feeling the holes where the metal-punch had gone through.

"Damn," she said, and I was surprised to here her curse. "What's the matter?" my mother asked. Mrs. Hanson looked closely at the tin on the front of the pie safe. "It's been reversed," she said. "The tin panels on the front, you see how the holes were punched in? It wasn't put together that way, you know. When they punched this design in the tin, they poked it through from the back to the front, so the points were outside the pie safe."

"Oh," my mother said, sounding deflated. It sounded ridiculous to me. I couldn't figure why anyone would care which way the tin was put on the thing.

"Sometimes country people do that, reverse the tin panels," Mrs. Hanson said in a low voice, as if she weren't talking to country people. My mother didn't disagree. "Still, though," Mrs. Hanson said, "it is a Sutton, and I must have it. What will you take for it?"

I guess I should have known that she was angling to buy the thing all along, but still it surprised me. It surprised my mother too. "Take for it?" she said.

"Yes," Mrs. Hanson said, "it's our anniversary next week—mine and the Judge's—and I just know he would be thrilled with a Sutton piece. Especially one of the pie safes. Of course, I don't think it'll be possible to have it refinished by then, but he'll see the possibilities."

"I don't know," my mother said, and I couldn't believe she was considering the idea. "Is it worth a lot?" It was an odd way to arrive at a price, and I laughed. Both women looked at me as if they had forgotten that I was on the porch with them. I wondered what my father would say when he came down from putting on a shirt.

Mrs. Hanson turned back to my mother. "Oh, yes," she said. "Samuel Sutton was quite a workman, very famous throughout the Valley. People are vying to buy his pieces. And here I've found one all for myself. And the Judge." Then, as if understanding that she wasn't being wise, she said, "Of course, the damage to it, the tin and all, that does lower the value a great deal. And the paint." My father had painted the breadbox, the pie safe, when it had been in the kitchen years ago, to match the walls. We'd since moved it out to the porch, when my mother picked up a free-standing cupboard she liked better.

"I don't know," my mother said. "After all, we don't use it much anymore, just let it sit out here. And if you really want it . . ." She sounded worried. She knew my father wasn't going to be pleased with the idea. "We should wait, ask my husband." Mrs. Hanson reached into her handbag, looking for her checkbook. I knew it wasn't going to be that easy.

"Didn't that belong to Granddad?" I asked my mother. She looked at me, didn't answer. "Dad's dad?" I said, pressing.

"It was in my husband's family," my mother said to Mrs. Hanson. "He might not like it."

"Could we say, then, three hundred dollars? Would that be possible?" Mrs. Hanson asked. She wasn't going to give up. Just then, my father opened the door and stepped out of the house onto the porch. He had washed his hands, put on a blue chambray shirt, one I'd given him for Christmas.

"Three hundred dollars?" my father said. "Three hundred dollars for what?" I saw my mother's face set into hard lines; she was determined to oppose him.

"She wants to buy the pie safe," my mother said. Her voice was soft, but not afraid.

My father walked over to the breadbox, struck the tin with two fingers. "This?" he said. "You're going to pay three hundred for this?" Both my mother and Mrs. Hanson nodded. "I think that's a fair price, Mr. Albright," Mrs. Hanson said. I noticed she didn't call him Jack.

"You could use it to get someone over to help you work on the barn," my mother said. My father didn't even look at her. I moved to his side.

"Didn't know the breadbox was for sale," he said. "Didn't know that it would be worth that much if it was for sale."

"My father owned that," he said. "Bought it for my mother, for this house, when they were first married." He turned to my mother. "You know that," he said.

"But what do we use it for, Jack?" she asked. "We use the barn. We need the barn. More than some pie safe."

My father put his hand on my shoulder. "You're not going to leave me anything, are you?" he said to my mother. She flushed, gestured at Mrs. Hanson. Mrs. Hanson managed to look unflustered.

My dad looked at Mrs. Hanson. Her calm seemed to infuriate him. "We aren't merchants," he said. "And this isn't a furniture shop." He turned to me. "Is it, boy?" I nodded, then shook my head no, not sure which was the correct response. "Mrs. Hanson," my mother began. You could tell she didn't like my father talking like that to Mrs. Hanson, who was a guest in her home.

"Don't apologize for me, Sara," my dad said. "Go ahead and sell the damn breadbox if you want, but just don't apologize for me." My mother opened her mouth, shut it again.

"Boy," he said to me, "you want a snakeskin belt like I was talking about? Like my daddy made?" He gestured out the porch door, to where the headless snake lay. A big fly, colored like blue glass, was crawling on the body.

"Yes, sir," I said, glad not to have to look at the high color rising in Mrs. Hanson's cheeks.

"You come out back with me, then, and I'll show you how to skin it, how to stretch the hide. How'd that be?" Neither my mother nor Mrs. Hanson said a word. My dad pushed me ahead of him, and I headed out the door.

As he came after me, he turned and spoke through the screen. "I'll tell you something, Mrs. Hanson," he said. "You ought not to try to buy what hasn't been put up for sale."

Outside, my father groped in his pocket for a second, came up with his old Barlow knife, flicked the blade out. "You hold the snake for me," he said. "We'll take that skin right off him." He held out the body to me. I hesitated, reached out and took it.

It was heavy and rope-like, cool and limp in my hands. The scales were dry as sand. "Set it down there," my dad said, " and hold it stretched out tight." I set the snake down.

"Belly up," my dad said. "We don't want to mess up the scales on his back. That's what makes a snakeskin belt so nice, so shiny, them back scales." I rolled the snake. The scales on the sausage-like belly were light-colored, looked soft, and I prodded them with a forefinger. The skin rasped against my fingernail.

"Here we go," my father said, and pressed the blade of the knife against the belly of the snake. He always kept the knife razor-sharp, had a whetstone at the house he kept specially for it. I looked away. The knife made a sound as it went in; I thought I could hear him slicing through muscle, thought I could hear small, cartilaginous ribs giving way under the blade.

Mrs. Hanson left the porch, and I could tell from the way she was walking that she must have gotten what she wanted. She moved with a bounce in her step. She looked over at us where we were kneeling, shook her hair back out of her face, smiled. My father paused in his cutting for a second when he heard the car door open. Mrs. Hanson backed the Buick around, headed back down the lane, toward the highway. A couple of low-hanging branches lashed the windshield as she went.

My mother stood on the porch, an outline behind the mesh of the screen, watching her go. When the car was out of sight, she turned and went back into the house.

My father gave a low laugh. When I looked at him, he was holding something gray between two fingers, dangled it back and forth in front of my face. "I'll be damned," he said. I looked down at the snake, the open stomach cavity, realized that he was holding a dead mouse by its tail. "No wonder that snake was so sleepy," my dad said. "He just ate." I stood, turned away from him.

"What's the matter?" he asked. I didn't answer. "You aren't gonna let that bother you," he said, and there was disdain in his voice. I put my arms over the top rail of the board fence around our yard, leaned my weight on it. I closed my eyes, saying nothing.

My father lowered his voice. "Thought you wanted that belt," he said. I wanted to turn to him, tell him that I did want the belt, just to give me a minute. I wasn't sure I could trust my voice not to break. "Guess not," he said.

Once again, I heard the sound of the knife, two quick cuts. I turned to look, saw that he had deftly sliced the body of the snake, had carved it into three nearly equal sections. It looked like pieces of bicycle tire lying there, bloody bicycle tire. My father rose, wiped his hands on his jeans.

"You think about that, boy," he said. "You think about that, next time you decide you want something." He walked past me, not toward the house, but toward the ruined barn.

Odom

Pinckney Benedict

Odom squats beside the fresh-cut stump of a hickory tree. The heavy gnarled trunk of the hickory lies in cubit sections, ready for splitting, at the edge of the small clearing. Odom clasps a slender length of slow-burning fuse in his left hand, marries it to the wooden kitchen match he holds in his right.

The fuse runs to two sticks of dynamite, unpacked now from their thick waxy skins, capped, and tamped into a hollow under the hickory stump. Odom peers at the flame, shields it with the bulk of his body from a light breeze that has sprung up. Still the flame dies.

Odom tosses the spent match away, and his son hands him a fresh one, which he strikes against the dry leather upper of his boot. The son kneels, breathless, presses his solid shoulder against his father's, cups his hands around the burning match. The fuse smolders, fires, and Odom drops it. He and his son scramble away crabwise, clamber over a windfallen oak, and drop prone in a drift of leaves, not daring to look past the defilade at the charge they've planted. A minute or so passes.

"It's gone out," the son says.

"I don't believe so," Odom says, head down among the stinking windrowed leaves. "I got it lit pretty good."

Before he finishes the sentence, the explosion detonates. Odom hears only a dull thud, winces at the painful pressure inside his ears and against his eyeballs. He feels suddenly heavy where he lies, thickened, and his belly presses into the cool ground. The leaves whip and rattle around his head. Dust patters down on him, powders his shoulders and hair, the back of his neck. He can taste it on his lips.

Beyond the windfall, the stump rises, turning, into the air. A slab of wood as thick as a man's arm whickers by overhead. At Odom's elbow, a distressed copperhead slides out from under its blanket of leaves and cobwebs and slips away, tongue flickering from between its delicate triangular jaws.

When Odom opens his eyes, he sees that his son is pointing over the windfall and laughing, but he can't hear the sound. A drifting pall of smoke gets into his eyes and his throat, makes him cough. "What," he says. "What is it?" His own voice makes a dull, distant sound in his ears, like a dog's barking somewhere. He looks where his son points, in front of them and above their heads.

At first there seems to be nothing extraordinary there, just the knobby greenless branches of a tall black locust tree and behind those the bright bland horizon-line of the next ridge over and the vanishing copper disk of the sun. Odom decides that he must be looking in the wrong place. Then he spots the hickory stump, blackened twisted roots to the sky, caught a dozen yards off the ground in the limbs of the locust.

"Too big a blast," Odom's son says, the words sounding flat and pinched as though they come to Odom through a piece of iron pipe.

"I thought I was deaf there a minute," Odom says. He is still crouched and tense, but his son is up and out of their place already. "Till I heard you talk," Odom says. The son is at the crater that the explosion made, tipping clods of dirt back into the ragged hole with the side of his foot, still looking up at the suspended stump. It is trapped in the crotch of two principal boughs. Odom waits another moment to see if it will fall.

When it doesn't, he rises to his feet, grimacing at the popping of his hinges and bones, and joins his son at the hole. The smells of cordite and nitroglycerine and singed wood are strong around them.

"Did you see it go?" he asks.

"No," the son says.

"Me neither," he says. "I was just staring into the ground."

"It must of went up like a mortar," the son says. He tucks the branch saw into his belt and levers himself onto the lowest limb of the locust tree, at the height of his chest. The limb is a sturdy one, doesn't sway at all with his weight. He grabs another branch, above his head, and begins to climb.

"Where you headed?" Odom asks.

"See if I can knock the stump loose out of there," his son says. He is a fast climber, already halfway up to where the stump hangs. Odom's ears continue their ringing, and he has to concentrate on the movement of his son's lips to know what he's saying. The tree's branches are skinny where the son is climbing now, and they bend dangerously under his weight.

"Just leave it," Odom says.

The son takes another branch, and another, before he answers. "I'm most the way there already," he says.

"What do we want it down here for?" Odom says.

The son shakes the branches around him, bounces on the springy limb. "Next big wind will just bring it loose," he says.

"Then let the wind do it," Odom says.

The son hesitates, then slips down the trunk of the tree. He drops the last seven or eight feet to the ground, lands on the balls of his feet, straightens up quickly. He grins at Odom. "I bet one stick's worth will do for stumps from here on out," he says.

"And a further place to go," Odom says. He is blinking rapidly. His eyes smart.

Odom's son looks at him strangely, then reaches out a hand as if to stroke the side of his head, which is raw and sensitive. Odom pulls away, grasps his son's wrist. He is surprised at the thickness of the wrist, and at the strength in the arm that shakes his grip off. "Let me," the son says, and he touches the tips of his fingers to Odom's ear. He draws his hand back, and there is blood on it.

"Your ear," the son says. He holds up his hand with its darkened fingerpads, revolves it before his eyes, then wipes it carefully on his pant leg. "You got blood coming out your ear," he says to his father, looking the man square in the face. He speaks the words slowly and carefully, as though he doesn't want his father to mistake the damage that has been done.

Odom puts a plate of bacon and beans on the table in front of his son, and another at his own place. A fine gray dust layers the skin and clothes of both men. Odom's eyes are traversed with broken blood vessels, feel hot and overlarge as he pads about the kitchen. He pulls the coffeepot off a glowing stove burner, pours two cups full.

The son is already well into his food, taking up grease with a piece of bread. There is a pile of slices on a saucer set next to his place. He holds his head low over his plate.

Odom draws a forkful of beans, chews them, swallows. He hasn't got much of an appetite. The beans are already cool though he pulled them off the stove only minutes before. He and his son live in a cold house. The floor is made of poorly finished pine boards. They are fitted loosely, and the chill of the soil under the place rises from between them.

"I've decided we'll take out that locust tree tomorrow," Odom says. He has packed his injured ear with a wad of cotton batting. The ruptured eardrum aches fiercely.

The son looks up. "You sure?" he says. "We don't strictly have to. It don't lie in the way of nothing."

"I'm sure," Odom says. "We'll knock it down first thing."

The son goes back to his plate of beans. Odom takes a slice of soft bread from the saucer, swabs at his food with it. He prefers a piece of coarse grainy cornbread hot out of the pan, with a dollop of salty butter, but he hasn't recently taken the time to make any. There is no butter in the place, and hasn't been for some while.

"Locust tree draws lightning," Odom says. "More than spruce or walnut or elm. More than any other tree in the forest."

"I heard that before," his son says.

"Not the kind of a thing to have near a house," Odom says.

His son stands up form the table, sets his empty plate and his coffee cup in the sink. He runs water on them. He wets his hands too, splashes water on his face, drags his fingers back through his hair. The fingers leave damp tracks. When he straightens up from the sink he says, "Believe I'll use the truck this evening."

"You got a place you need to go?" Odom asks.

"To the valley. Some folks I want to see there."

"Sure," Odom says. "You bet."

The son retrieves the truck keys from where they hang, on a coat hook near the door. He struggles into a denim jacket with a thick fleece collar. The jacket is a couple of sizes to small for him, and it is splitting down the seam between the shoulders.

"Listen," Odom says. He gestures at the thin unpainted walls around him. "I know this ain't much. It's nothing to come home to." He leans forward, braces his arms against the edge of the table. "But that new house. When we get that built," he says, and leaves the sentence unfinished.

"It'll be quite a day," his son says.

"It will be," Odom says. "We'd of been there already, but the crawler crapped out on us."

"I know that," the son says. "I know where we'd be." He is buttoning up the jacket. He has his index finger hooked through the key ring, and the truck keys jingle in his hand.

"Better to build it by hand anyway," Odom says. His son says nothing.

"Well," Odom says. "You have yourself a good time."

"I'll do her," the son says. He leaves the house. Odom can picture him crossing the meager dirt dooryard, unchocking the truck's front end, swinging himself into the cab as the truck starts to roll down the slope. He listens for the popping of the clutch and the rumble of the motor but hears only the new strange depthless rushing of his punctured eardrum. The truck's headlights sweep the kitchen walls, throwing slashed diagonals of light across the room in one direction as the truck backs, and then in the other as it heads off.

Odom's house is built at the edge of a steep bluff, overlooking the mountain road that leads away from his place. Odom watches from the window as the truck follows the road down, slaloming through the series of steep widening switchbacks: red taillights on one pass, dim canted head-lights on the next, growing smaller and more distant with each reversal. In a few minutes the truck executes the final tight S-curve and descends altogether out of the line of his sight.

Twice now Odom has made the long walk along the roads his son might have taken when he left several nights back. He goes as far down the mountain as he can get and reasonably hope to walk back: dirt roads and gravel cutoffs and blacktop one-lane highways streaked with slick red clay. He examines gullies and crumbling embankments and hop-scotches his way down wooded inclines, looking for the wrecked truck that he imag-ines, and the body of his son. His calves ache with the effort of descending and of climbing again.

In his searching he finds a desolate Volkswagen Beetle on its roof in a reeking sump and, further on, enmeshed in a rustling hedge of rhododen-dron, an elderly Nash convertible. The rhododendron has grown up through the floorboards of the car and out of the rotted cloth top. Caught in the Nash's shattered grillwork is the narrow rib cage of a deer.

Long after midnight, when he has been walking for hours, a black finned Lincoln with suicide doors rolls slowly past him, weaving down the road, left tires flirting with the cliffside edge of the pavement. It looks to Odom as though there are only little boys in the car, maybe half a dozen of them, the oldest no more than about eleven. They pass him at their sedate pace, and as they round the deep curve ahead, moving uphill, their faces gather at the wide rear window, pale as little moons behind the glass. They stare at him as though they think he might be a dangerous psychopath out wandering the roads alone.

Later, he follows the course of a dry stream that parallels the road. There he runs across a truck that is much like his own, and his breath catches in his throat. But this truck is a different color from his, has been stripped of its tires and wheels and engine long ago. The wooden stakes around the rusted truckbed sit loose in their sockets, and the wind rattles them as it rushes down the smooth-stoned channel.

The sheriff's deputy finds Odom in the partially cleared lot out behind the little shanty house on the bluff. Odom is perched in the saddle of the busted crawler, eating from a can of cling peaches that he has opened with the short blade of his pocketknife. His hands are dark with engine grease and there is a smear of the stuff on his forehead. He wipes his mouth with the back of his hand as the deputy approaches.

The deputy is a man in his middle years, dressed in loose comfortable khaki clothes and a short military-style jacket which is inadequate to keep him warm in the winter temperature. He has shaved carelessly, and there is a patch of light stubble under the shelf of his jaw. He makes a gesture of greeting at Odom. Odom fishes a yellow slice of peach from the can and holds it out to the deputy, pinned between the blade of the knife and his thumb. When the deputy shakes his head no, Odom slides the section into his mouth, drinks sweet juice from the can.

"You're Odom, ain't you?" the deputy asks. Odom says nothing, just looks at him. "Einer Odom," the deputy says.

Odom nods as if he has this moment recognized the name. "Yes," he says. "That's me."

"You got a boy," the deputy says. Odom has gone silent again. "A boy about seventeen." Coaxing, now.

"Yes," Odom says slowly, hesitant.

The deputy leans back, hooks his fingers in his wide gun-belt, hitches at the belt with its heavy revolver and cinch of brass cartridges. He takes a deep breath. "Look," he says, "I dealt with enough of you crazy backward ridge-running mountain rats in my lifetime." His words are measured and softly spoken, with no trace of anger in them. "I don't figure to freeze my ass out in the cold and listen to you hem and haw all day. Now why don't you tell me something about your boy."

"He went down into the valley, into town. He's been gone a few days," Odom says.

"Of course he has," the deputy says. "I got him in the county lockup. Drunk and disorderly. That your truck he's driving?"

Odom relaxes a little against the crawler's seat.

"I said, that your truck he's driving?"

Odom stirs, says, "Yes, it's my truck."

"Minus one fender," the deputy says. "He got into a scrape at a roadhouse in the levels. How much do you know about what he does when he's not here?"

Odom shrugs, wondering if that is response enough to satisfy this deputy. "Not much, I guess," he says.

"I guess," the deputy says. "He runs with a pretty rough crowd is what he does. Drinking and starting fights. We stopped him before he did anything real bad. Anyway, he's a minor, so I come up to tell you what he's been doing. You want my advice, I'd keep him closer to home now on."

"I will," Odom says. "Surely."

"The other evening he told me a thing that I found interesting," the deputy says. "I asked him what he does up here days, and he said you and him are clearing some land for your homestead. He said you were blasting stumps. I thought maybe that was what happened to your ear there." He points to the crude head bandage Odom has fashioned out of a neckerchief.

Odom's eyes narrow. He thinks of the crate of black-market dynamite sitting in the earthen root cellar under the house, filmed in a sweat of nitroglycerine. He thinks of the carton of blasting caps with its warnings printed in fading primary colors on the rotting cardboard, and the bale of brittle fuse.

"I see he's mistaken, though," the deputy says. His voice is still cool. "I see he was confused. You're snaking them trees out of here with that 'dozer, not fooling with any damn boot-leg dynamite."

Odom looks down at the crawler, which is clearly incapacitated. The offside tread is broken, has slid from the driving wheels and lies in a twisted loop behind the machine, its metal cleats clotted with mud. The blade is tilted against a granite outcropping, listing heavily to one side. The surface of the blade is carved and bent, and bright new metal shows through in half-a-dozen places where hard rock has scored the plate.

"Well," Odom says, setting the can of peaches on the bulldozer's running board and standing up, "we got a problem with the crawler at the moment."

"But you're fixing it," the deputy says, indicating the grease of Odom's hands. "It'll be all right here after a while and then you can start up again."

"Oh, sure," Odom says. His voice is small. He blew the crawler's engine trying to push the half-buried granite boulder aside, just as he broke the blade and snapped the tread. He has no chainfall to pull the engine, no new engine to replace it with, no way to get one. Too tired to trek the roads anymore, he's just been fooling with it for something to do.

"That's a good thing, then," the deputy says.

"My boy," Odom says. "He'll be coming home?"

"No doubt," the deputy says. "Anyway, we're releasing him."

Odom climbs down off the crawler, stands waiting for the deputy to leave. His legs are sore from all the walking, and he wants to sit again. The deputy glances around the clearing, and his gaze fastens on something behind Odom, high over his shoulder. The hickory stump, Odom realizes, still hung up in the black locust.

"The one occasion I recall fooling with dynamite," the deputy says, and he's looking at Odom now, and not at the stump, "was the time my uncle stole a few sticks from the limestone quarry where he was working. He got his hands on some underwater fuses, too, and he took me out fishing with him."

Odom shifts from foot to foot, and the deputy peers closely at him. "I ain't boring you with this, am I?" he asks. "I wouldn't want to keep you from something you got to do."

"Oh no," Odom says.

The deputy continues. "We went out on the lake in his little rowboat, no motor or nothing. He said he would take me if I did the rowing, so I pulled us all the way out into the middle of that lake. We sat out there in the mist on that black dark water and it was like we were a million miles from the shore. Then he snapped a fuse and chucked one of the sticks of dynamite over the side of the boat.

"I was leaning over the gunwale watching when it went off, and I like to got drownded in the geyser. The water come up and slapped me in the head and lifted the rowboat and us in it, and a minute later the fishes floated to the surface, all dead from the concussion. Bass, bluegill, pike, perch, some walleye. We just scooped them into the boat by the armload. You ever seen a fish that got wasted with dynamite?"

Odom shakes his head. "No," he says. "Never have."

"Well," the deputy says, "they look like they got the surprise of their life. Mouths agape, like this." He drops his jaw in imitation. "That first bunch filled the bottom of the boat, and then he popped another stick, and a third. We like to sank, we took in that many fish.

"We get them home in his little station wagon, which never did smell the same again, and we froze a mess of them and smoked a bunch more into fish jerky on wooden racks we built out behind the house. In the end we had so many left over we had to grind them up, bones and scales and all, and plow them into my mother's garden plot for fertilizer. It stank like hell in the heat, but you should have seen them squash and sunflowers grow."

"We're planning to put us in a garden," Odom says. "It'll go on the south side of the house. I figure we'll get most of the produce we need out of it if we're lucky, and won't have to make the haul down the mountain so much."

"Sure," the deputy says. "That's a fine idea." He stretches his arms out above his head, then slaps his hands against his thighs. "It is cold up here. I swear to God, it's twenty degrees colder on this ridge than it is anywhere in the county." He turns and heads off around the shanty. Odom follows him to where he has parked his cruiser. It is a blue Mercury with bubble lights on top and a riot gun fastened upright to the dashboard.

"Tell my boy when you see him to come on back up here," Odom says. "Tell him I need him to help me with the clearing."

"If I see him," the deputy says, climbing into the cruiser. "They'll probably of turned him loose by the time I get back." He starts the car, backs and fills, backs and fills in the little turnaround Odom has cut into the hillside, and finally gets his vehicle pointed in the direction from which he came, on the road that leads to the valley floor.

Odom takes his time dropping the black locust, figures all the angles, but in the end some unexpected thing—the weight of the hickory stump trapped in its branches, or an errant gust of wind fifty feet up, or an unseen inequity in the distribution of the flesh of the tree —causes it to fall wrong, and it catches against a slim dogwood that stands across the clearing, bends the smaller tree almost double. When the locust hits, the hickory stump slips from its branches and thumps to the ground.

With his smoking, chattering chainsaw, Odom sections the locust where it has wedged, excises it neatly and expertly from the dogwood, but the little tree is badly broken. It trails its sleek limbs on the ground. Though he wanted it for a sweet-blossoming decoration in his new front yard, Odom cuts the dogwood too, and lays its slight trunk next to the locust's dark burly one.

Odom examines the stump of the locust and finds that a groundhog has established its den, with two or three entrances, around and under the meaty roots of the tree. He won't have to sink a shaft under this stump as he did with the hickory tree. He grins, retrieves a stick of dynamite from the root cellar, with a blasting cap and a strip of fuse. He slits the damp casing of the dynamite with his knife, dumps the innards into his hand, forms the yielding mix of nitroglycerine and sawdust into a lump the size and approximate shape of a baseball.

He reaches into the hole nearest him. The ground is frosty to a depth of about six inches; below that the dirt is soft and unfrozen. Odom inserts his arm up to the elbow, then midway to the shoulder, finds what he takes to be an appendix to the tunnel. He tucks the ball of explosive into the pocket, withdraws his arm, and crimps the soft copper blasting cap around the fuse. When he slides his arm back into the hole to insert the cap into the dynamite, his hand follows a slightly different path, down a steeply slanting fork.

He gives a grunt of surprise when he doesn't find the dynamite where he expected it, thrusts his arm in up to the shoulder. His hand is in a large open space at the arm's full extension, cool air around it rather than warm dirt, and he is surprised by the apparent size of the tunnel complex. He pulls free of the groundhog hole, slides his arm in again, searches in vain for the dynamite. He extracts his arm, licks his lips, tries once more. This time he is lucky and locates the explosive right away. He sticks the blasting cap deep into it. Then he scoops loose earth from around the mouth of the hole back into the burrow and presses it against the dynamite.

He sits near the opening, brushing dirt from his hands and regarding the fuse. He has cut a piece about a yard long, which should give him three minutes or so to get clear. Plenty of time. He pats his pockets, searching for the box of matches. When he doesn't find them, he goes back to the shanty. The matches are on the kitchen table, where his son left them. They are Ohio Blue Tip matches, the kind with the Indian head on the cover. He takes them up, returns to the locust stump.

There he lights the fuse. As it burns its laggard way into the hole, he trots away form it. He moves toward the windfall oak, then cuts away from that shelter, crosses the clearing to the granite boulder and, on the other side of it, the crawler. He climbs over both of them, pleased with his agility and the fading soreness of his muscles. He settles with his back against the crawler, on the side where the tread is whole. He presses his hands lightly to his ears, facing the house.

When the dynamite goes off, the shanty's windows ripple like water in their frames. Putty crumbles from around one or two of the panes. Odom stands, checks himself all over, laughs to find that his hands are shaking. A plume of dust and smoke stand over the blast site, already ragged and dispersing in the breeze.

Odom trots back into the clearing, scanning the nearby trees for signs of the locust stump. It is nowhere to be seen, and he is puzzled, until he finds it still in its place. It lies on its side, many of its roots still sunk in the ground. A number of them have torn loose, enough for the stump to have toppled, and the wood there is blond and new. The groundhog's tunnels have vented off the force of the blast, and the stump has only been damaged, not torn loose and thrown clear as it should have been.

Odom puts his hands on the capsized stump, which is the size of a fifty-five-gallon drum, and shoves at it. It doesn't move. He shifts his grip, tucks his shoulder under a projecting root. He throws his weight against it, but the stump is immovable. His feet piston the ground, fight for purchase, slip on the dirt. Odom stands back from the stump for a moment and stares at it, breathing hard.

"You son of a gun," he says. He kicks the stump, and the pain of the impact jars a cry from him. He leans into it, claws at it, feels one of his fingernails peel away, feels bark slipping from the hard smooth wood underneath. He flings the loosened bark into the air around him, grinds it between his palms. "You don't think you're ever coming loose out of there, do you," he says. He begins to weep, and the sound echoes off the rocks and hollows that surround him.

After a time, he sits down on the stump, growing quiet. From where he sits, he can see into the groundhog's den. The locust stump has prized up the roof of the burrow in falling, and much of the dirt, sparkling with ice crystals, remains trapped in the wide tangle of its roots. The burrow itself consists of a maze of tunnels, laid in the earth like halved clay pipes. Many of them have collapsed from the force of the blast, but a number survived. Odom is astonished by the size of the warren.

He wonders how old the groundhog is that built it, and how long it took to dig the place. Though he cannot know, he suspects that there is a layer of tunnels set below this exposed level, and another below that, and another, down through the skin of the mountain to bedrock. He imagines that there is a groundhog down below him in its smooth-walled darkness, looking up with weak piggy eyes and snuffing the air for some clue as to what cataclysm has befallen the upper world.

He imagines that after the groundhog has paused briefly in wondering, it shambles down its close corridors in the direction it was already heading, and when it comes to the end of that tunnel, it sets it shoulder against the dense earth face, and its claws, and its teeth, and simply digs and digs and digs.

Odom sits on his haunches in the root cellar. The long coat he wears is rimed with frost. Sleet clatters against the cellar door, which is set into the ground at a slant, propped open now for light. The clay walls of the cellar are hung with thin sheets of crackling ice. Odom draws his shoulders in toward his neck. He is counting the sticks of dynamite that are left in the crate, toting them up in his head against the land he wants to clear. His lips move as he calculates, but he says nothing. When he counts a stick, he moves it delicately from one side of the crate to the other.

When he is finished with the dynamite, he moves on to the box of blasting caps. He takes up a handful of the pencil-width sticks, and another, stops when he is satisfied that he has enough. He measures off an arm's length of fuse, which is stiff from the cold, and cuts it with his pocketknife. His hands are grimy with ash, and they tremble. He stuffs the fuse into one of the long side pockets of his coat, drops in a couple of blasting caps after it.

He takes up a stick of dynamite, two. He stands a moment, considering. Then he takes up a third stick and quickly climbs the steep wooden stairs that lead up from the cellar. A rotten stair tread gives under his weight, and he stumbles, catching himself with one hand, clutching the dynamite to his breast with the other. He clucks his displeasure at himself, then rises.

Out in the slaty daylight, he swings the heavy door to and snaps shut the padlock that secures it. He straightens his coat around his legs, turns the collar up with his free hand, and heads off toward the clearing.

Odom's son switches off the truck, hops out, chocks the wheels before it can get away from him down the grade. The truck's crumpled right fender is fastened to the body with a twist of heavy-gauge baling wire. The son looks at the gray weathered shanty and the woods around but does not see his father. Then a sound comes to him from the clearing behind the house: an arrhythmic tolling, metal on metal; twice; three times; then it ceases.

"Hey," he calls. "I'm back." He leans into the truck cab, gathers a couple of grocery bags into his arms, pushes the door shut with his hip. The hammering sound starts up again. He pauses near the bed of the truck, where there are two battered canisters of LP gas, but decides to leave them where they are until later.

He enters the house, sets the bags down in the frigid kitchen. His breath mists when he exhales. He puts his hand on the propane heater in the corner and finds it cold. He shakes his head, goes to the window. When he looks out, he sees his father hunched against the granite outcropping, wielding a small claw hammer. He swings it clumsily, his grip high, just under the hammer's head. When the hammer comes down, metal chimes.

The son's eyes widen when he looks beyond Odom and the boulder to the clearing. The ground there is torn and pitted, as though an artillery barrage has walked through it. A large number of trees are gone. They have evidently been cut and sectioned, their branches sliced away and piled together for a coming bonfire, the stumps blown and removed. Those are the trees closest to the shanty.

Farther away, the trees are down, but they have not been cut. They have been blasted wholesale from the ground, and the seared trunks lie at startling removes from the tangles of their roots. The trees are tumbled pell-mell over one another, two and even three deep, in a welter of sap and pith and broken wood. Odom has cleared enough space for a mansion, for the home of a giant.

The son leaves the shanty and goes to Odom, who is still flailing at the rock. He grips a short stone drill in his left hand, strikes it with the hammer, turns the bit, strikes it again. As the son watches, the head of

Odom's hammer misses the drill, grazes his fingers, bounces off the boulder. A spray of broken rock flies up, and Odom turns his head aside to avoid it. He pulls the bit from the rock, drops it, sucks at his bruised fingers.

"Hey Poppy," the son says. His voice is quiet. "I come back." He has been gone for nine days. Odom has lost weight in his son's absence. His gabardines hang on him. There are dark crescents under his eyes, smears of sleeplessness like lampblack. The light hammer hangs at his side. When he bends to set it down, his son sees that the skin and hair on one side of his head have been crisped. The son catches briefly the scent of a burn.

"What happened to your head?" he asks.

Odom raises his right hand absently to the hurt place and touches it lightly, as though to familiarize himself with his changed profile. "Oh yeah," he says, and his voice is unnaturally loud in the stillness on the ridge. "Fire jumped right down the fuse a couple days back. Got a premature blast, and I didn't have time but to skip away a little."

The hand that scrapes at Odom's skull is wrapped in a stained bandanna. Because the hand is in continual motion, Odom's son cannot tell if there is a full complement of fingers inside the bandage. The nails of the fingers that he can make out are blackened and split. Odom turns away to look toward the clearing. "You see what I done?" he says.

"I seen," the son says. But Odom doesn't turn back to him or respond.

"I knocked them down." Odom says, gesturing at the cascade of flattened trees. "Now all we got to do is shift them trunks out of there, break up this rock, and we can lay the foundation. We'll be in by spring." He turns back to his son, stares at him. His bloodshot eyes are tearing, and he wipes at them with the back of his hand. "You see?" he says.

"I see," the son says. Odom nods enthusiastically.

"You should," he says. "You should see, when I light off a charge under a big pine tree. Sucker rides the blast up and up, just like a rocket, up into the sky. Branches flatten against the trunk. Then it turns and slides and falls back. Can't always tell where it's going to fall, though," he says, and his tone sounds as though it is born of regret, "so you got to keep a sharp eye out. Stay on your toes."

The son begins to reply, but Odom pushes past him, circles the boulder to where the crawler sits, returns with a four-pound sledgehammer and a long star drill cradled against his chest. He presses the hammer on his son, who holds the rough wooden haft of it, resting the rectangular head in the dirt at his feet.

"But now," Odom says, "you're back, and we can make some real progress."

"I brought some food up with me," the son says, but Odom has turned from him again. "I got canned goods."

"That was the simple part," Odom says. He swings his wounded hand out toward the trees, and the gesture is dismissive. He pats the side of the boulder, almost with affection. He fingers the hole he had begun in its side. "Now this," he says, "this here is the real bitch-kitty."

"I brought up some propane," the son says, and now his voice is almost pleading. He drops the handle of the hammer. Odom notices, stoops to pick it up, hands it once more to his son. "For the stove, and the heaters," the son says. He tries not to stare at his father's slightened figure. "Let's get you something to eat."

Odom inspects the cutting edge of the star drill, slips it into the hole in the granite. While he holds the long bit clumsily in both hands, he says to his son, "Go ahead on. I can't swing the hammer good, so I'll turn the bit."

The son raises the hammer, lowers it again. "I don't," he says. "I don't believe I can."

"Go to it," Odom says. "Faster you cut the hole, faster we can set the charge and blow this son of a gun."

The son cocks the hammer, makes a tentative pass with it at the end of the drill bit. The hammer's head clinks against it, skitters off, barely misses Odom. He doesn't flinch. "That's it," he says, and turns the bit in the hole. "Now get some fire into it."

"I'll mash your hands," the son says, but already he has the hammer in motion. It describes a brief arc through the air, strikes the bit, makes the metal clang and hum. The handle of the hammer vibrates, stings the palms of his hands. Rock dust puffs out of the hole.

"Go," Odom says, and he turns the bit again. The son brings the hammer over his shoulder, connects. Odom twists the drill. The son swings again.

"This is how they built the railroads," Odom says. He pauses to turn the drill, which is growing warm. It buzzes as though it might be alive with electricity. "They cut a hole in the rockbed by hand, then dropped the charge in." The son misses a stroke, stumbles forward. He moves back to his place, looks at his father, but Odom is concentrating on the quivering bit in his hands.

"They had a guy that sang to keep them in time," Odom says. The son strikes the drill bit solidly. "That way they never missed a beat," Odom says. Then he begins to sing.

The son stands and listens for a moment. He cannot recall ever having heard his father sing before. "Drill ye tarriers, drill," Odom sings. His voice is hard and tuneless. The son brings the hammer smartly down on the drill. He is surprised to see that the bit sinks appreciably with every blow.

"And blast, and fire," Odom sings. Soon the son finds the rhythm of the song, ignores the abrasions the hammer provokes on the skin of his palms. "And it's work all day for sugar in your tay," Odom bellows, "down behind the railway." The son finds that he is more accurate if he doesn't look at the wavering end of the bit but watches instead the blistered side of his father's head.

For his part, Odom keeps his eyes on the steadily deepening hole in the rock, singing at the top of his lungs, the vapor of his breath condensing and swirling around him in the cold. "Drill ye tarriers, drill," he sings, beginning again, and the son cannot tell whether it is the second time he has heard the verse, or the third, or the hundredth. He continues to heft the hammer. Each time its heavy head rings against the drill, Odom gives the bit a quarter turn. And joined together in that slow mechanical labor, the two men drive a narrow shaft toward the hidden bitter heart of the rock.

Hymning The Kanawha

Tom Andrews

1

> Day brings a steady
> hand, a sure breath every other day . . .

My brother again on the edge of his bed,
sitting up with his eyes closed,
his palms pressed, a brief prayer.

> *You see we're in trouble*

Spring, 1972. The last flare
of an April dusk. Sure breaths and relief
after a run on dialysis. He's telling
an old story, his slim translations
of Psalms, to whoever is listening.

> *Give us strength enough*

The passionate calm after a run—
his pulse grows as the fresh blood thins,
his drugged face opens like a fist.

*

Runnels of spring rain. Branches
like floating ribs from the camphor trees.

Someone is asking you to make a fist.
Someone is taking your pulse
and saying nothing, and starting to weep

over the jonquils and the yellow grass,
over the cold surge of the Kanawha River.

2

Slurs on the Psalms he calls these prayers.
And writes them out
in a notebook he keeps under his pillow,
and shows no one.

> *Death has fallen on me*
> *like a stone I can't budge*
>
> *Once death was my companion*
> *We walked together in your house*

It's an odd-numbered day,
the machine, like another child, bathed and asleep.

Before *he* sleeps tonight, my brother will forgive
his body anything—night sores, bad numbers,
pain like a word . . .

Before sleep, my brother will bless himself, and lie down.

❅

The blood in a black widow falls asleep.

Near an almond branch,
work ants gather their meals in the noon sun.

At the far edge of a field, a hospital
is erected and torn down
on the same day, the healers now

working double time, now obsolete,
your failed kidneys swelling from pinholes

to buttonholes, buttonholes to large red sacks.

3

What's in the doctor's pause and the heart's,
the needle placed like a root
in the red vein . . .

The machine drones through the afternoon.
My parents shuffle about him, keeping the lines clean,
smoothing the blood's slow run from the body.

> *But I am no one*
> *I am poured out like water*

Scissor-clamps, the pump, coils: the hours
are counted out. Like coins, like yesterday's
good news, they pile up
just out of reach.

> *Lord, be near*

✳

X rays of the hip joint, fat negatives,
milk-light your wronged bones.
For once you can hear yourself:

Syringe of sleep,
Syringe of another life,
close my eyes,
lift these white walls.

Your shadow ascends like a soul
from the stretcher but holds still.
In time, in good time, your own blood

mutters and wakes.

4

"Just to imagine
there is something larger than me, and purer."

Thus my brother, in a notebook, 1972.
A reason to rise in the long mornings.
Thus sun, moon, ghost-of-a-chance; what
the Psalms say.

> *How long will sorrow flow*
> *through my heart like bad blood*
> *How long will you be a stranger*
>
> *Like anyone*
> *I'm dying*

He writes at his desk, sure breath after
sure breath. Outside, the poplars; and I'm
spinning a ball through a netted hoop

over and over, getting better.

❋

Reedstem, cattail, eyelash, a leaf . . .
A fine rain peppers the Kanawha, a cold
wind hustles the yew bushes and hollyhocks
in Tuendiewei Park. The log cabin there

rests on your fingertip, twilit; inside,
your grandparents parade in your white gowns,
their eyes the color of your eyes, their wake
the dust prints you'll leave behind.

5

There's a photograph, a boy on a beach, 1961.
My father took it. My brother
didn't know it. He sat on the hot sands,
tracing his noon shadow with a Lego stick.

Heat came in with the waves. He was five.
Morning opened up
like a torn fingernail, and began to bleed.
Eleven years. He sits under himself now, the flush
and pull of dialysis; writing sentences.

       The river of God is full
       of water

The edge of his straw hat casts a shadow
like gray fingers, water reeds. Gulls
tattooed the beach. At five, my brother saw

his shadow as a circle. Widening, opening.

   ✳

The hallway goes out like a blown
candle, and you're back at your first house—

flies in the screen's light, white wings
fluttering through the grilled blackness.

You walk toward the coal cars by the riverbank:
damp smell of the cornfield at night;

over your head, the same stars
in their ordered slide . . .

Only this time it's wrong,
the face of the night nurse among the reeds

and birch branches, the whole landscape
caught like a moth in the renal room's dark.

6

Tonight, asleep, my brother walks
out into a mild rain on the driveway.
The pulse, he'll say, of drops collecting
into puddles is his pulse, the soft tick
against the windows his tick . . .

And tomorrow's an odd-numbered day,
nothing but sleep and a book.

> *a little sleep, a little folding*
> *of the hands*

My father goes out to bring him back
inside. He knows that he will keep this:
his son asleep in his pale flesh,

part of this rain and the black sky,
part of these black puddles filling the potholes
in the driveway.
                    (The hands ghostly, so steady . . .)

My brother is led to a dry bed, and lies down
whispering after a rain, the quiet
before a sleepwalker's footsteps . . .

    ✳

Your family, gathering themselves forever.

They play cards, or read, and wait for your step
and your suit of scars.
They stare past one another into

the river, and go on
waiting until your voice fills
the breezes again, until

the shine of the Kanawha
becomes their shine.

7

The machine drones like an old complaint.
My brother's shunt—a tubed sleeve, blood-vines
scaling the entire room, a red trellis
of veins. I'm eleven and looking on
for hours, as though over a roof's edge.

> *The peace of a good family*
> *like rare oil*
> *like your name*

We try to talk. Already, I know
the wrong words to say. I've rehearsed
the gestures of my hands, how fear
enters a child's voice. He's telling me
that it's all right, that if the mind
is lucid it can shine
like blown glass in a brilliant light . . .

His hands shake. His drugged face
blurs like a moon.

✳

You sit in a silence of rivers, the last
April driftings of the Kanawha, and watch
your own ashes being raised in wind

and scattered on the bank. Your family
looks on without a word. In a dry cove,
they've waited for your body to float by

like driftwood, for your one call
from the nettles, from the crickets' chirrs,
from the flash of fireflies low in the grass . . .

8

When God died my brother learned to sing.
When God died my brother slipped through the house
like wind, rustling his papers and spread sheets
before leaving under a door without a sound.

Lord, I look at the night sky
and see your fingerprints

What are we, almost you
There's sheep oxen birds
There's the sea there's the field

through which we see your vital hands

Scissor-clamps, the pump, coils. The hours
are counted out. But a sure breath fills
the planet, and another—what the Psalms say—

a sure breath, a steady hand, every other day.

❋

Along the east bank of the Kanawha River,
your shadow swells to its own poise

and walks into the chigger bush, burrs
clinging like tiny scabs to the silhouette.

It finds the warm grass in Tuendiewei Park
and lies down. It considers your guilt

and lies down. It turns back to the Kanawha
and rises, and slides into the black water,

your body drifting across the white
bedsheets, a slow erasure of your name . . .

Evening Song

Tom Andrews

The crickets go on with their shrill music.
The sun drops down.

What was it my brother said to me once
in Charleston, before he disappeared that spring
like the quick wake of a water mite?

This was 1980, evening, the porch lights burning.
He was reading from *The Cloud of Unknowing*.

Robins gossiped in the poplars,
moths spiraled across the uncut grass.
Moonlight wormed through the neighboring lawns.

> *We must therefore pray . . . not in many words,*
> *but in a little word of one syllable.*

Didn't he say forgiveness was his homely double?
Didn't he say what I wanted him to say? Maybe
I wasn't listening, chewing a branch of sassafras . . .

But I doubt it. As I doubt, now, that the life
of my lawn is a still life, the moon and shrill chants

opinions on despair. There are times
when the sound the world makes is a little word.
Something like *help, or yes* . . .

Extended Learning

Lisa Koger

*D*ella Sayer had promised to teach Vacation Bible School the first through the fifth of August, but when Frank phoned to say he and his family would be coming for a visit that same week, Della regretted her promise and decided to wiggle out of it. It wasn't that she didn't want to help her class make macaroni sculptures or pop-up Jesuses. Frank was her son, her only child, and he hadn't been home in two years. He was married to a dentist named Marjorie, a quiet, fragile-wristed woman with lovely teeth. Della looked forward to spending time with her son and his wife, but it was her grandson, eight-year-old T. Barry, she really wanted to see.

She knew God would understand her predicament. She wasn't sure about the pastor's wife, a tightly permed little woman named Mary Sue.

"Frank's living out west now, isn't he?" said Mary Sue when Della called the parsonage. Mary Sue was practicing church hymns on her old-fashioned organ, and she continued to play while she talked. Della could hear her chording.

"He's a professor at Oklahoma State," Della said. "He has tenure." She had never really understood what tenure meant, but it seemed impor-tant to Frank because he always mentioned it, so when someone struck up a conversation about her son and inquired as to the nature of his employ-ment, Della did what Frank did and casually tossed it in.

"A professor!" said Mary Sue. "Imagine! You just bring him right along with you. We'll find something for him to do."

"I can't ask him to do that," said Della. "It's his vacation."

There was a slight pause in the music as though the organ had hic-cupped or someone had turned a page. "Come alone then," said Mary Sue. "You'll be down here and back each morning before they even miss you."

Della considered it. "You're probably right, but I want to spend lots of time with my grandson. You know kids: 'Grandma, will you take me fishing? Grandma, will you take me berry picking?' I thought we'd all go over to Pritchett State park for a picnic one afternoon. It's a long way over there. We'll be gone most of the day."

"You'll have plenty of time," said Mary Sue. "You can leave right after you finish here and still get over there and back. You don't want to go too early anyway. It's cold up in those mountains until noon. Besides, if you cancel out on me, who's gonna teach your class? No one could do as good a job as you."

Mary Sue was in charge of the senior-high class. She requested them. "I'm a natural with teenagers," she often said. "It's amazing the influence the right teacher can have in just one week."

Della had the preschoolers. She taught them every year, though she doubted how much they got out of it. Ask them two weeks later what they remembered about Bible school, and nine times out of ten, they'd lick their lips and say, "Cookies." She often thought it might be just as effective and a whole lot cleaner to give them each a bag of Oreos and turn them loose outside where they could climb trees or roll in the grass and get on with the business of appreciating the world God had given them.

"I'm really sorry," said Della, "but you're going to have to find someone else. You've got plenty of time. You won't have any problem."

The music picked up a new sound, and Della guessed she was hearing a little touch of bass. "Let's be honest," said Mary Sue. "Can we? We've all got other things we'd rather do. There are fifty-two weeks in the year, and we're talking about one of them. Ten to fifteen hours total. Is that too much for the Lord?"

"I explained the whole thing to Him last night," said Della. "He didn't seem to think there was any problem."

The organ suddenly sounded as if someone had pulled out all the stops and floored the swell pedal. "Be that way," said Mary Sue.

Della threw herself into a fit of cleaning and preparation. "Don't go to any trouble," Frank said, and Della assured him she wouldn't. She papered rooms and painted porches, baked and froze rhubarb cake and gooseberry pie, carried woods dirt to revitalize her flowers, and conned a telephone repairman into helping her rig up a tire swing in the sycamore tree at the lower end of her yard.

"It's for my grandson," Della explained.

The repairman winked. "That's what they all say," he replied.

Della lived alone on a farm seven miles south of Farlanburg. It wasn't a farm in the working sense, but there were enough cows to keep the weeds down, and, at last count, a dozen chickens that occasionally scratched up enough energy to drop an egg in the grass. The nearest neighbors, the Peevys, lived more than a mile away, which meant Della could hoe her garden in her nightgown if she wanted, and when she felt the urge to get out her gasoline can and set fire to a pile of brush, there was no one whose permission she had to ask.

During the summer, she took her bath when evening first began to trickle into the hollow, then she would sit out on her back porch and revel in the beauty of her flowers and the smell of her own clean skin. She liked to watch the shadows creep up the hills, over rock and fence and thicket, climbing higher, covering ridge tops, until her world was submerged in darkness and the moon looked like the sun seen from the bottom of a clear blue lake. At the same time each night, if the dogs behaved themselves and didn't start their infernal yapping, a whippoorwill would slip out of the woods and sing on a hillside rock. Della would yawn and think her farm a dandy place to live and the best place in the world to visit, and she would climb the stairs to bed surprised she didn't have company more often.

Common sense told her the best part of her life was behind her and she ought to be depressed, but Royce had always said she was low on common sense, which explained, she supposed, why she woke most mornings feeling happy. Royce was her husband, dead now almost ten years. He was a big, florid-faced man who loved to eat, and when he wasn't eating, he worked at his sawmill. He was on his way to town one Saturday morning to get a haircut when the Volkswagen he was driving was hit head-on by a coal truck. The accident happened in the curve near the Pullman Creek Methodist church, and a woman named Oma Dalton was mowing the church cemetery at the time. She called Della. "They's a man dead over here, tore all to hell!" Oma shouted into the phone. "I don't know who he is, but a bunch of people standin' around down by the highway gave me your name and said I ought to call you."

Della was reluctant at the funeral to believe that the waxy, rouged thing in the casket had ever been Royce, but the weekly newspaper confirmed it: "Rescue Squad Uses 'Jaws of Life' to Extract Local Man from Car." The article featured pictures of the death car, or what was left of it, and though the pictures were in black and white, Della knew the real color of the dark spot that covered most of the front seat.

"In this life, you never count on nothing." Royce was fond of saying, and the suddenness of his departure seemed to bear that out. Even in death, he had a sly, knowing look on his face as if to say, "See. Told you I was right."

Frank and his family arrived on a Sunday night, exhausted from being on the road two days. They pulled their Volvo into Della's barn lot a little after ten o'clock and left a white trail of Styrofoam cups and empty food containers behind them as they lugged suitcases and pillows through the dewy, moonlit yard. Della met them on the porch, arms open wide. "Frank!" she said. "Son!"

"Hello, Mom," said Frank. He was a tall man with thinning hair and poor posture. He had a well-trimmed beard, a Ph.D. from Purdue University, and had been a forestry professor at OSU for the past eleven years. In photographs taken of him during professional meetings or departmental wingdings, he appeared bright-eyed and very distinguished, Della thought. But the Frank who came to her house always arrived bleary-eyed, with bugs on his windshield, and he acted as if some essential part of himself had been overlooked in the packing and left behind.

Della kissed her son and hugged him tightly, then turned and embraced Marjorie, who had lifted her foot and was frowning at something on the bottom of her left shoe.

"What is it?" asked Della, and Marjorie showed her.

"Ornery dogs," Della said. "Sorry about that."

While Frank headed back to the car for more suitcases, Marjorie stepped off the porch and wiped her sandal in the grass. She was thin and blonde, in her early forties, and the liveliest thing about her was her green pedal pushers and flowered blouse. When Frank first brought her home, Marjorie was still in dental school, and Della had been amazed that any person, especially one so young, could be so serene. She had kidded Frank on the phone and had written letters reminding him of the old saying: still water runs deep. But after fifteen years of observing her daughter-in-law, Della had amended the saying to create a new version which seemed more accurate: still water doesn't run at all.

Frank returned with more suitcases, and he handed Snapper, their new dog, to Marjorie.

"Where's T. Barry?" Della asked.

"Asleep," said Frank. "I'll get him."

Della was disappointed but tried not to show it. She turned her attention to Snapper, who was struggling frantically in Marjorie's arms. "Hello, Snapper," she said. "Are you tired, too?" He was a small, kinky-haired dog with stains below his eyes that made him look as if he'd been crying mud. He belonged to a professor in Frank's department, but the man and his family had gone overseas on sabbatical, so Frank and Marjorie had agreed to keep him awhile.

"What kind of dog is it? You said on the phone, but I forgot."

"A peekapoo," said Marjorie. "He's a cross between a Pekingese and a poodle."

"Funny-looking thing," said Della. "I think he wants down."

Marjorie continued to hold him. "He's house-trained. He thinks he's human."

"Poor peekaboo," said Della, petting his head. "My dogs aren't here. They're out courting. Put him down and let him run loose, why don't you?"

As soon as his paws touched ground, Snapper lifted his leg and hiked on Della's marigolds. When he finished, he began to explore the yard with quick, greedy sniffs.

"Look at him go!" said Della.

"I'd better get him. He'll be filthy," said Marjorie.

Frank returned with three more suitcases, one in each hand and an overnight case under his arm.

"Is he awake, yet?" Della asked. "I can't wait any longer. Let me get him." She pulled her sweater around her and started out the walk, but Frank stopped her.

"I'll get him, Mom. He's sound asleep. You'll have plenty of time to spend with him tomorrow."

Della could count on one hand the number of times she had seen her grandson. She often wondered if she would even recognize him if she met him on the street. She knew that before the age of ten, two years can make a big change in a life. "You need to bring the boy out here to see me more often," she said every time she called Frank.

"Road runs two ways," he reminded her.

He was right, Della knew, but the older she got, the less she liked to travel. How could she tell her son, who had half his life ahead of him, that although she was in good health and not afraid of dying, she didn't want to do it in a strange bed, several hundred miles from home?

It bothered her to have a grandchild she didn't know. She had known both sets of her grandparents and thought herself a better person because of it. Such was life these days, she supposed; have children and you cast a part of yourself to the wind. She was grateful to know where the seeds had landed. Was it asking so much to want to watch them grow?

She talked to T. Barry on the phone every couple of weeks, but it was hard to tell much about a person when you asked, "What're you doing?" and he said, "Talking to you." He was going to be whatever he was going to be Della knew, but whatever that was, he hadn't turned into it yet, and in the limited time she was allowed to spend with him, she hoped to have some sort of impact on his life, though exactly what sort of impact she hoped to have was still vague in her mind. It was a selfish, conceited notion, she reckoned, but there were things she wanted to teach him, such as how to be happy by learning to appreciate the little things in life: sitting under a tin roof during a warm summer rain, eating persimmons after the first frost, building a hay house in a barn in winter, or watching bees emerge from the hive on the first warm days of March. She wanted to teach him to avoid the ho-hums, the blahs, and the wearies, that crafty trio that played tricks on a person by appearing years away when really they were not. "Come down off your high horse," she could almost hear Royce saying, and if he'd been there he would have teased her and made her feel starry-eyed and foolish and said something like, "Here you go. Trying to put up detour signs before the bridges are even washed out."

As Frank carried T. Barry through the yard, Della was surprised and a little sad to see how much he'd grown. She planted a kiss on his smooth cheek and held the door open for Frank. "I've fixed a place in your old room. I'll help you tuck him in."

"I wish you wouldn't," whispered Frank. "If he wakes up and sees you, he'll know he's not at home, and I'll never be able to get him back to sleep."

Gently, Della picked up her grandson's bare foot and kissed it, then she stood aside and let them pass. Frank took T. Barry upstairs while Marjorie roamed the yard calling "H-e-e-r-e Snapper, h-e-e-r-e Snapper." Della got a flashlight and helped her look. They finally found him out back in the weeds where Della burned trash.

"Ooooh, stinkie doggie," said Marjorie. She picked him up and swatted his rump.

"He's all right," said Della. "Just got a little soot on him. He's fine."

They took him inside, to the bathroom, and Della helped Marjorie clean off his paws. The dog lay on the edge of the sink, his body limp with resignation. He closed his eyes and assumed an expression Della had seen on the faces of women receiving a manicure.

"My dogs wouldn't hold still for this a minute," Della said.

"It's bred into house dogs," said Marjorie.

Della watched as Marjorie toweled him. "You must be worn out, too," she said. "Let me fix you something to eat. I've got butterscotch pies in the warming oven and a pot of hot coffee on the stove."

Marjorie put her hand over her mouth to stifle a yawn, then checked her watch. "Thanks," she said, "but we never eat after six o'clock."

Della carried the suitcases into the downstairs guest bedroom, unable to shake the feeling she was giving shelter to tourists. While Marjorie unpacked and settled Snapper in his basket, Della headed for the kitchen. She had no rules about when she ate; she ate whenever she was hungry—a bad habit, she supposed, probably bred into her. As she passed through the dining room, she was about to close the inside door that led onto the back porch, but she stopped, surprised to see Frank out there in the dark. The screen door was covered with bugs and moths and millers, beating delicate wings against the mesh. Frank stood, arms folded, leaning against the porch post, and Della was struck by an almost uncontrollable urge to slip out there and scratch his back. She put her hand on the screen door but withdrew it because it occurred to her that he might have gone out there to be alone. What was it like, she wondered, to come home after two years? Did home still *feel* like home, was it a place you were instinctively drawn to, or did you come because you thought you ought to, because the navigator in you happened to remember the way?

At eleven o'clock the next morning, Frank and Marjorie were still asleep. The sun had completed half its arc across the sky, and Della's dogs, two male mongrels, had already lumbered off to find shade. Silvervine, the cat, just returned home from hunting, sat licking her paws and sunning herself on the walk.

Della had been up since five. When she was younger, she used to crave sleep. She dreamed of going to bed before dark and nesting there until noon the next day, but now that she had the opportunity, she had lost the inclination, which was just as well, she supposed, considering she had a grandson to attend to and a turn of light bread to make.

T. Barry sat beside her on the back porch steps, hands on his knees, a wrinkled bag full of hickory nuts in his lap. Della had gathered the nuts last fall from the big shagbarks that lined the road below her house and had stored them in a box on the top shelf of her cupboard until the insides were sweet and chewy, the shells the color of clean sand. She had saved them for this occasion, and at the end of the week, she planned to send what was left home with T. Barry with the hope that each time he cracked one, he'd remember the fun they'd had. She scooped a handful from the bag, tapped one with her hammer, then dropped the kernel into her grandson's open mouth. "So," she said, "Tell me again what the T. stands for. It's Timothy or Terrence or Tutwyler. My memory's not as good as it used to be, you understand."

The boy chewed steadily and looked at Della out of clear, deep-set gray eyes. He was a quiet kid with thick, blond hair cut so his head appeared peanut-shaped and difficult to balance. His arms and legs were remarkably unscarred and new looking, as though he hadn't figured out what to do with himself from the neck down. "It stands for Thurman," he said, shyly. "You know that."

Della nodded and cracked another nut, this time for herself. "Maybe," she said, "and maybe I just wanted to see if *you* did. I knew a man once, a pitiful fellow, who got kicked in the head by a horse and couldn't remember his own name. He went crazy trying to remember it, so they locked him in a corncrib and kept him there till he died."

T. Barry frowned and studied Della's crib. The rock supports at the two front corners had crumbled during the years, allowing the north side of the building to sit down, but the south side was still stable and several feet off the ground. Della liked her corncrib, though she had to admit it was hazardous. It reminded her of the hotrods the young boys drove through town.

"I don't believe that," said T. Barry. "It's against the law to lock someone in a corncrib."

"They abolished that law," said Della." I guess you're not familiar with the Corncrib Act."

Behind them, inside the kitchen, Snapper whined and dug at the screen. Della had walked him earlier and would have let him out to run in the yard, but Marjorie had forbidden it. "Not as long as your dogs are home," she'd said. "Fleas."

T. Barry bit down hard on an unshelled nut. "What's 'abolish'?"

"It means to do away with, to get rid of. Don't worry about it though. I still think you're plenty smart."

"I'm in the E.L.P."

"Sorry," said Della. "I didn't know." She tilted her head and looked at her grandson through her bifocals. "What's the E.L.P.?"

"Extended Learning Program. It's a thing for smart kids at my school."

"Oh," said Della. "Are you smart?"

T. Barry shrugged. "They say I am."

"They say a lot of things," said Della.

"I'm smart enough not to believe everything you tell me. Mama and Daddy say you have a bad habit of making things up."

Della laughed. "I don't know why grown-ups do that."

"Do what?"

"Try to keep things from kids." Della shook her head. "Fifty cents says they'll tell you there's no such thing as the Corncrib Act."

"I'll ask them," said T. Barry, rising.

"Go ahead. I guess I'd better hurry inside and fix their breakfast. But I must say I was having fun sitting out here cracking nuts and talking to you."

T. Barry rolled a nut with the toe of his shoe, then sat down again. "Is it true about that crazy man? I want you to tell me the truth."

"Of course it is," said Della.

"Tell me his name, then."

"Can't do that."

"Why not?"

"If he didn't know it, how do you expect me to?"

The day turned out to be a scorcher. By three o'clock that afternoon, the temperature had reached the mid-nineties, and the cows had wandered off the hills and stood under the apple trees below the house, chewing cuds and flicking matted tails at the flies.

Della's house had no air-conditioning, but she kept fans in most of the windows. On humid days, the only really cool spot on the place was the cellar because it was partially under the hill, and occasionally, Della would pull a chair in there and relax or take a flashlight and admire the variety of colors in her canned fruits and vegetables. Earlier, she had mentioned the cellar to Frank and Marjorie, but neither of them took her up on it, so she assumed they weren't too uncomfortable with the heat. She had also suggested they all get in her car and go for a drive to enjoy the countryside, maybe get an ice cream cone, her treat, but no one had seemed especially wild about that idea.

"Don't think you have to entertain us," said Frank. "You just go on and do your thing, and so will we, and that way we can all relax."

"I *am* relaxed," said Della. "I just thought you might enjoy getting out and seeing the sights."

"I grew up around here, Mom. Remember?"

"Things change," said Della. "You've been gone a long time."

Della stood in her kitchen, rolling and cutting egg noodles. She had the radio on to help pass the time. Frank was asleep, Marjorie was reading, and T. Barry lay stretched out on the living room floor doing his home-work. It was their first full day of vacation, and Della wanted it to be memorable and exciting.

"Homework?" she had said when Marjorie told T. Barry it was time to get his books. "It's summer."

"He takes a test in three weeks when school starts. He has to have a high score if he wants to stay in the E.L.P. That's a program for gifted kids at his school."

Della looked at her daughter-in-law over the top of her glasses.

"He enjoys it," said Marjorie. "At home, he'd much rather be inside reading or fooling with his computer than outside with the other kids playing in the street."

"You think that's normal?"

"What's normal?" said Marjorie.

"Homework," Della said to herself as she picked up a big knife and sliced off sections from the roll of noodle dough. Frank had never done homework during the summer, and as far as school went, he had certainly done all right.

At the moment, he was snoring in the front porch swing. He had eaten his breakfast a little after noon and had gone upstairs and prowled through some boxes of old books. He was asleep again when Della went to check on him at two. The noodles were for him; Della hoped they might enliven him. When he was a boy, his favorite dish had been a concoction of homemade egg noodles and beans. In those days, he liked to fish and hunt, and he spent hours walking the creek banks or just wandering over the hills. Back then, he'd come home with burrs in his socks and a craving for noodles, and Della had wound up fixing them once or twice a week. Now, he insisted they weren't worth the trouble it took to make them. Della loved her son dearly and was proud of his accomplishments, but there were moments when she was struck by the unmotherly thought that, at some point, he had turned into one of the most boring people she knew.

He had done well in high school and had earned a scholarship to the state university. Four years had turned into six, six into ten; more than half his life had been spent in school. He had knocked off all the rough edges, but in the process, something else had been knocked off, too. Though he could tell her there was a statistically significant correlation between canopy tree mortality and drought-induced stress, he could not tell her how to save her wild chestnut trees. And Della was surprised and, secretly, a little disappointed the first time she discovered that, unlike his father, he could not recognize a white oak suitable for veneer from one destined for crossties.

Neither she nor Royce had any education beyond high school, and Royce had always been proud that his son was smart and had done so well at books. "It's the way the world's goin'," he had said when Frank finished his Ph.D. "Gettin' an education is the ticket to a better life." There was a slightly wistful tone to his voice that Della hadn't heard before.

"Oh, I don't know about that," she said. "I don't have an education, and I'm happy with my life." She laughed. "Why, I don't know as I could stand it if it got any better."

Royce smiled, patted her shoulder, and said, "Some are just easier satisfied than others," which caused Della to wonder for weeks whether he knew something about their life that she didn't.

Della lifted the noodle sections, combing with her fingers until the yellow strips unwound and lay like a pile of shorn curls. Through the kitchen window, she had a clear view of Marjorie, who was stretched out in a lawn chair in the backyard. She was a good visitor, really, no more trouble than the cows. She did not hang around the kitchen and get in the way by trying to be useful, nor did she rattle on about the food and interrupt Della's work by asking for recipes. All she wanted was to be left alone with her book, and occasionally, she would look up and inquire whether there was any iced tea.

She was Frank's wife, and Della wanted to like her, but Frank's wife or not, she wasn't very lively, and Della often wondered how she worked up enough energy to pull a tooth. Della recalled having a tooth pulled by a dentist, a Dr. Weeble, when she was a child, and what she remembered most about the experience was not the pain or the blood but the look on Dr. Weeble's face as he rolled up his sleeves, rubbed his hands together, and told her to say, "Aaahhh." It was an eager, alive look, one that said, "I am *passionate* about teeth!" To be good at anything, you had to feel passionate about it, Della had always believed, the way she felt about the people she loved, the way Royce had felt about trees.

"If you had only ten minutes left on earth, how would you spend them?" she once asked Royce, and, without hesitation, he told her he'd go to the woods, lie on his back, and look at trees. At the time, she was hurt because he hadn't said he'd spend his last moments with her. Looking back on it, she thought she recognized a rare, uncalculating honesty and a genuine love of nature in his answer, and she wished he were around to instill a little of that love in their grandson.

When she had finished with the noodles, Della washed her hands and tip-toed into the living room. T. Barry lay on his stomach, studying. Seeing him like that took Della back almost thirty years. He looked so much like Frank from certain angles.

"Psstt," she said.

He glanced up.

"You don't look like you're having much fun," she said. "Are you having fun at Grandma Della's house?"

He wrinkled his nose. "You've got something awful in your carpet," he said, pointing at a dark spot in the pile.

Della knelt and examined it. " That's not something awful," she said. "It's a mashed raisin. Your better brand of carpets come that way."

T. Barry looked skeptical.

"It's true," said Della. "The manufacturers put little pieces of food in there so the people who buy the carpets will have something to fall back on in case of hard times."

T. Barry put his face closer to the raisin and peered at it. "You're making that up," he said. "I bet it doesn't say that in any carpet books."

"Just because it's not written down somewhere doesn't mean it's not true. Grandma Della loves T. Barry. True or false?"

He shrugged. "True."

"See," said Della. "You believe that without reading it." She untied her apron and took it off. "Are you finished with your homework?"

He shook his head.

"Too bad. I was looking for someone to take a walk with me."

"I've got to do my math," said T. Barry.

Della picked at the raisin. "What's nine plus nine?"

He rolled his eyes and looked insulted. "That's easy. Eighteen."

Della held up her hand. "Ding-a-ling-a-ling."

"What's that?"

"A bell," she said. "School's out. You already know more than me."

Della had carefully planned the week. There was so much to do while Frank was home and so little time to do it. On Tuesday evening, she wanted to have a wiener roast, and she had invited the neighbor children, the Peevys. But when she asked Frank to gather wood and cut sticks, she discovered that neither he nor Marjorie nor T. Barry ate wieners anymore because they were leery of the ingredients added to the meat.

Frank pulled a package out of the refrigerator and pointed to the fine print on the label. "Look at this. Sodium nitrite, all kinds of additives. You don't want to eat that stuff, Mom. Don't you know what it can do to you?"

Della listened and shook her head in pretend dismay while Frank went on about the general laxity of the Food and Drug Administration. She waited until he had finished his spiel. "Will you eat chicken?" she asked.

The five Peevy children showed up at six o'clock, bare-footed, carrying a half-empty bag of marshmallows. Della had forgotten to call them to tell them not to come. They sat in the dusty road in front of the house. Della was trying to get supper on the table, and she wouldn't have known they were out there if Snapper, who was locked on the front porch, hadn't barked and scratched at the screen. The oldest boy, Bud, who was T. Barry's age, was standing in the yard when Della went out. He put his hands in his pockets and alternated between looking at the sky and his feet. "We come for the weenies," he said.

Della stretched her mouth into a smile and herded the children around back. She poured each a glass of Kool-Aid, then went back inside to get T. Barry to come out and play. He refused. He stood at the dining room door, hands on the screen, and looked at the Peevys as if he were the one on the outside observing caged animals at a zoo. Della switched the burner on her stove from medium to low so she wouldn't burn the chicken, dumped the mashed potatoes into the Crockpot to keep them hot, stuck the raisin pie in the warming oven, then took off her apron and went outside to entertain her guests.

For the first fifteen minutes, they sipped their drinks and told Della what all they had been doing, and when they grew restless, she let them chase her cat. After a short time, the cat grew tired and so did they, and it became clear to everyone that the fun had peaked.

Bud stood, hands in his pockets, and blushed. "We got to go now," he said. "But I want to thank you for invitin' us."

Della had always admired politeness and guests who knew when to leave. "You are more than welcome," she said. "We'll have to get together and do it again sometime."

Bud rounded up his brothers and sisters and made them say thank you, and Della gave them two packs of wieners and buns and sent them on their way.

Early Wednesday morning, before anyone else was up, Della's brother Harve called to ask if Frank and his family had made it home. Della told him they'd arrived on Sunday night, but as soon as she said it, she began to have doubts because it seemed they'd already been there at least a week.

"I hope it was a good trip," said Harve, and Della said it was.

"No close calls, I suppose. No wrecks or anything like that."

"Not that I know of," said Della.

"That's good," said Harve, "but they still have to worry about getting back. Most people get killed within twenty-five miles of home."

Della sighed. "Is that a fact?"

"It sure is," said Harve, and he tried to remember when and where he's read it. "Getting around to the reason I called," he said. "I wanted to invite you all out to our place this evening for supper. Doris is making a red velvet cake, and Elaine and her kids are coming out. Nothing fancy. Just a little get-together."

Della wanted to know what she could bring and Harve said nothing, and Della said she couldn't just come and eat, and Harve said, all right. "Whip up a gallon of potato salad and stop by the Piggly Wiggly for hamburger," he said. "And if you happen to have some extra charcoal, bring it along. You can help me fire up the grill."

At breakfast that morning, Frank announced that he and Marjorie planned to drive up to the mall in Clendenin to see the new Jack Nicholson movie, and that they wouldn't be back in time. "Seems silly to have to drive to another county to see a movie," said Frank, and Marjorie agreed.

"What you need is a theater in Farlanburg," he said. "It'd give some of those kids you see hanging out at the pool hall something to do."

Della was fixing breakfast, and she was not interested in the hoods at the pool hall. She dropped a hot blueberry waffle onto Frank's plate. "You don't want to waste your time watching a movie," she told him. "You can do that in Oklahoma." She had never been to Oklahoma, and before Frank went out there, she had envisioned it as a desert with nothing for miles but red dust. She had been surprised to discover that the state had a forestry department; the wasteland she had pictured did not include trees. At some point, she had added stores and a post office to her scene, and adding a theater seemed relatively easy compared to the initial adjustments she'd had to make. She put a large pat of butter on Frank's waffle and passed him the syrup. "You've always liked Uncle Harve and Aunt Doris. They'll be disappointed if they don't get to see you."

"They know where I live," said Frank.

T. Barry was still upstairs asleep, and Della was glad because she didn't want him to get the impression that Jack Nicholson movies were anywhere near as interesting or important as a trip to Uncle Harve's farm. She poured another cup of batter into the waffle iron, then turned to Marjorie, who was breaking off bits of sausage and dropping them under the table. "T. Barry would have a such a good time," she said. "He'd get to pet pigs and ride ponies. When does he get a chance to have an experience like that?"

Marjorie wiped her hands on her napkin and looked at Frank. "Not very often," she said, "if he can help it. He's not really the outdoorsy type."

Della broke off a piece of unclaimed waffle and ate it. She threw an equally large piece under the table, which promoted a chain of events that began with toenail action on the linoleum and ended with a teeny-weeny growl. "Don't you want him to appreciate nature?" Della asked.

"He does. We all do. But that doesn't mean we want to wallow in it," said Frank.

Della would have liked to continue the discussion, but she decided not to because she didn't want the day to get off to a bad start. She did, however, risk mentioning the fact that T. Barry might enjoy playing with some other kids. "Elaine and her boys will be there. It would be good for T. Barry to run and romp with them."

"He doesn't particularly like Elaine's boys," said Frank. "Last time we were home, the big one, what's his name, hit him in the head with a rock. Remember?"

"That was probably Roger," Della said. "He's in 4-H camp this week. He won't even be there."

"Neither will we," said Frank.

Della planned to take T. Barry out to Harve and Doris's farm whether Frank and Marjorie went or not, but in the end, she changed her mind. T. Barry didn't seem all that keen on going. She called Harve and apologized and said that Frank was run ragged trying to visit everybody, but that he'd be sure to stop by and see them before he went back.

Frank and Marjorie went to Clendenin to see the Jack Nicholson movie, and Della and T. Barry sat in the living room listening to the metronomic ticking of the clock. "What do we want to do?" she asked him, and he said it didn't matter.

"Of course it does," said Della. "Everything matters," but even as she said it, she had doubts. They sat, side by side, on Della's lumpy couch. "Help me think," she said. "I'll take you fishing, I'll play ball with you, we can go hiking, we can—"

"Watch cartoons," said T. Barry. He got up and flipped on the TV set.

"What's on?" asked Della.

" 'Teenage Mutant Ninja Turtles,' " he said.

Della watched about five minutes, then got her sun hat from the hook behind the kitchen door and followed the path to the garden. She pulled a few weeds from around the tomatoes and checked the cabbage heads for worms. When she finished, she sat down on the wooden stool she used for corn shucking. High overhead, a hawk circled, wobbling a little in flight. Della gazed at the green, wooded hills and at the creek she used to water her plants. She picked up a handful of dirt, letting the loose soil sift between her fingers. "Is this worth nothing?" she asked.

When she went to the house, T. Barry lay in the recliner, half asleep. "Wake up," Della said. "We're going on an adventure."

"I don't want to go on an adventure," he said. He yawned and turned on his side.

"You just think you don't," Della said, trying to rouse him with her cheerfulness. "We're going berry picking. I know a place back on the ridge where there are blackberries as big around as my finger."

T. Barry gripped both armrests and scowled.

Della tried to persuade him by promising to bake a cobbler and when that didn't work, she told him she'd take him to see a haunted house. "Help me a little," she said. "I'm just trying to make sure you have a good time."

"There's no such thing," said T. Barry.

"No such thing as a good time?"

"No such thing as a haunted house. I don't believe in ghosts."

"You might if you saw one," said Della, kindly.

"No one on this planet has ever seen a ghost," he informed her, "and that includes you."

"Seeing has nothing to do with it," Della argued. "The biggest part of what I believe in, I can't see." She scooted a footstool beside the recliner and sat down. "Do you believe in bird lice?"

T. Barry nodded.

"I do, too," said Della. "My eyes are bad now, so I can't see them, but I don't doubt for one minute that they're there. Just like I believe in trolls and witches and elves."

T. Barry laughed. "No you don't." He suddenly frowned. "Do you?"

"I believe in dragons, dead Ed Sullivan, and leprechauns," said Della, "Santa Claus, Jesus Christ, and the Easter bunny. And I believe little boys are little boys until they are big boys and that if they don't run and have fun and climb trees while they can, it will be too late because they'll forget how."

"Think about it," said Della. She picked up his hand and kissed it, then hurried into the kitchen. She packed sandwiches, apples, and cookies in a metal bucket and filled a mason jar with ice water. Her Polaroid was the only thing she lacked, and she found it in the bottom drawer of the china closet.

When she returned to the living room, she switched off the TV and knelt beside the recliner. "Please," she said. "Come with me."

T. Barry hesitated for an instant. He shook his head.

Della winked. "I'll let you have the biggest berries."

"Berries stain my teeth."

"I'll take you to town for a milk shake."

T. Barry leaned over the edge of the chair and picked up a copy of *TV Guide*. "It's too far into town. I don't want to go on an adventure," he said.

Della looked at her grandson. He was already much older than she'd thought. She went to the hall closet to get her purse and returned with a five-dollar bill. "Do you believe in this?"

T. Barry stared at the money.

"Come with me," said Della, "and it's yours."

The dirt road above the house was narrow and followed the creek. When Della was younger, it was well-traveled, connecting two main county highways. But during the years, shorter connectors had sprung up, serving more families, and the road was now used mostly by young boys buzzing dirt bikes and subdivision escapees who needed a place to tear up their Jeeps.

Foot-high weeds ran mohawk-style up the middle between two dusty tracks. Della walked on the left side, carrying her metal bucket, its handle squeaking and clanking with each step. T. Barry followed. He was so quiet that Della stopped periodically to make sure he was still there. "Why don't you walk beside me?" she suggested, pointing to the right track. "That way I can see you. I don't see you often enough." She took the bill out of the bucket. Without a word, T. Barry switched to the right track. She handed him the berry bucket and took his picture.

As they walked, she pointed out various historical sights and places of interest. "This is where your dad caught his first fish," she informed him. "We had a cow die from eating hedge apples over there." At the first creek crossing, they turned left and hiked a short distance until they came to a pile of rotting boards and a sawdust heap at the edge of the field. "This was where your grandpa had his last sawmill," said Della. "He had a mill, an old diesel motor, and a edger he dragged around from spot to spot."

They saw several deer tracks, surprised a quail, and ate their picnic on a mossy spot in the woods. It was almost six o'clock when they headed back. They had no berries, but Della's bucket carried more than a dozen snapshots, proof of the outdoor experience they had shared. The adventure had cost her almost nine dollars, not including the initial five, but she didn't regret the expense. He had waded, skipped rocks, and caught minnows, and she had an especially nice shot of him on a grapevine, looking, if not thrilled, at least pleasant, on his joyless ride through the air.

His last night on the farm, T. Barry was tired and went to bed early. Marjorie had almost finished her book, and she asked if anyone would mind if she went to her room to read. Della washed the supper dishes, then went out on the back porch to spend time with Frank. He stood, eyes closed, head cocked as though listening to something running the ridge tops, moving away from him, almost out of range. Della leaned her head against his shoulder.

"Do you hear it?" she asked.

"Hear what, Mom?"

"Whatever you're listening for. Whatever it is you drove all this way to hear."

"I came home to be with you," said Frank.

Without worrying whether he was too old for it, Della began to scratch his back. You're ruining him, she imagined herself saying, but she could not imagine what good it would do, so they stood, without talking, and watched darkness settle over the hills.

Frank, Marjorie, and T. Barry left at six the next morning. The night had drained away, and a heavy fog filled the hollow. Marjorie carried Snapper from the house to the car, and as she strolled down the walk, he twisted his head as if craving one last look at Della's yard. Della said goodbye to Marjorie while Frank returned to the house to get T. Barry.

"You'll have to come out and see us," said Marjorie.

Della nodded. She rearranged pillows and covers in the back seat.

"I mean it. We've got plenty of room, and we're gone all day. You'd have the whole house to yourself."

"Thanks," said Della. "I may."

T. Barry was asleep when Frank carried him out. Della tucked him in and kissed his cheek. "There's a paper bag that belongs to him in the trunk," she whispered to Frank. He looked puzzled. "Hickory nuts," said Della. "Don't throw them away."

Della hugged her son and over his shoulder, she saw a bright patch of sun burning through the fog. "Don't stay away so long," she said, and Frank promised he wouldn't. As they pulled out of the barn lot, Della waved. For a moment, she thought T. Barry was awake and moving, but when she looked again, it was only Snapper in the back window trying to gnaw his way through the glass.

On Friday night, Della went to the Vacation Bible School Wiener Roast and Parents Program. She had not missed it in fifteen years. She arrived a few minutes before the program began, in time to see the artwork and crafts. In the chapel, she watched the children clap and nod their heads as they sang the familiar songs.

When the singing was over, the crowd moved outside, and Della joined them. She pulled a lawn chair next to the fire in the only open spot, one beside Mary Sue. For a long time, they roasted wieners without talking. When Mary Sue's stick began to burn, Della pointed it out, saving the littlest Peevy child's supper from the flames. "So," Mary Sue finally said. "How was your visit?" She looked tired. Bible School took its toll on the teachers.

"Good," said Della. "Same as always." She gave her roasted wiener to a passing child, then took a couple of marshmallows from the package and fastened them on her stick. "How about you? How'd it go this week?"

Mary Sue put her hand to her temple and shut her eyes. "Considering the fact that we were two teachers short and one of the craft shipments didn't come in, I'd say we did all right."

Della nodded.

Mary Sue gazed at the kids playing in the churchyard. "I don't know," she said. "Sometimes I think we're just wasting our time. Sometimes I wonder whether any of these kids take anything home at the end of the week besides their crafts."

Della watched a group of boys laugh and chase each other with hot marshmallows. The sun sank behind the trees, making it look as if the woods were on fire. "They're kids," said Della. "Maybe that's enough."

Memoria

Louise McNeill

I have never heard them;
I shall never hear—
Still an echo falling
When the night is clear,
In the darkness wakes me
Like a trumpet's call:
Wild swans crying
Southward in the fall.

The Roads
(Appalachia)

Louise McNeill

Where do the roads go—
The ruined country roads flow,
Fern-clogged and weed-bogged, wandering the hills?
Nowhere that I know—by shad-blow and fence-row,
By woods where the lilacs grow,
By the rotted sills.

What can a road feel?
How can this sorrow heal?
Sole mark and wagon wheel passing through the day,
Grain load and apple load creaking down the hilly road—
All of the life that flowed—
Now gone away.

Where do the roads wind?
What do they go to find—
Crossing on the mountain tops and meeting by the shores,
Swamp-locked and briar-blocked, searching for the rib-rocked
Men of the mountain stock,
By their empty doors—

Frost-pocked and bur-docked.
Winding through the passes
Where the dying chestnut trees reach their shriveled arms—
Thorn-crossed and time-lost, through the tangled grasses—
All the little country roads,
Searching for the farms. . . .

Granny Saunders

Louise McNeill

Her ministration was to heal
With pungent herb and bitter peel.
Up in the drying loft she hung
Horehound and sage and blacksnake-tongue,
Wild cherry, spice bush, "penny rorrel,"
Blue monkshood, ginseng, sour sorrel,
Thin twisted stalks, sharp jimpson weeds,
Bloody percoons, hot mustard seeds,
And meadow docks—both broad and narrow,
Rough bone-set, golden thread, and yarrow,
Field balsam, catnip, dittany,
All to be simmered down to tea.

All to be brewed for aches and ills—
Red pepper pods for croup and chills;
Spearmint for phthisic; flax for pain;
Horseradish roots for bruise or sprain;
And for uncertain maladies
The northwest bark of dogwood trees.

The Long Traveler

Louise McNeill

All that I am,
Except the combination,
Was here on earth when tyrannous Rex ruled over—
All my calcium, carbon, potash, et cetera,
But not my particulars;
Not my conglomeration

Still I was here—met myself
Coming, and will meet again,
For I am a long traveler;
A long hunter of one chance circumstance—
Have traveled here from the big bang—
Or, say, my MACL is pacific.
Hair follicle from some old Frank's kingdom—
A wild gene from County Clare,
I have wandered the broom hills of Scotland—
A particle blown on the windy steppes.
I am white milk from a black cow's udder,
Snow crystal—photon of sunlight—
Corn blade, lime rock, lonesome water;
I am very old;
Old mud is in me—swamp black,
The dinosaur tracks in that mud;
I am old Virginia clay,
Connecticut wetland,
A pink moccasin flower that one summer in the Berkshires.
I was here—all of me—
From The Beginning.

The conglomerate breaks—
Hard bone blows to fern spore.
My lips back to the red seed, the rose hip . . .
I am very old
And will be older still
When I wander the plasma fog,
Return, recombining, return and return once more, my
sediment drifting, always returning in brooks,
I can hope—
Falling in silver cataracts through April woodlands,
Seeking to become a Self.

The Road

Louise McNeill

A road of asphalt, silver hard
Runs close by Gauley's cliff-hung shore.
Plymouth and Chevrolet and Ford
Zoom up and down route twenty-four.

Old trucks haul moonshine corn to town.
New trucks haul crates of ten point Schlitz
Smug limousines make haste between
White Sulphur and the New York Ritz.

Busses with greyhound lines and speed
Pass lizzies jerking on their way.
Sedans crammed full of picnic food
Careen upon a holiday.

Red oil trucks, laundry trucks, a hearse—
Police cars snooping after crime—
Slim trailers on their homeless course—
All driven mad by lack of time.

The red men hunt their happy ground,
The pioneers have earthy rest,
Crozet has found his fatherland,
The bison herds have straggled west.

A road of asphalt, silver hard
Runs close by Gauley's cliff-hung shore.
Plymouth and Chevrolet and Ford
Zoom up and down route twenty-four.

The River

Louise McNeill

Now they have bridged the canyon of the Gauley
And built a lock above the Swago shoal
To float the barges past the lazy shallow
With loads of river sand and mountain coal.

Along the shore where passing Mingo warriors
Built drift-wood fires to parch Ohio maize
Cook ovens glare red-eyed upon the darkness
And belch their cinders at the fevered days.

But in the broken rushes of the inlet
Where herons rose with beaten-winged alarm
That autumn evening when an Irish rascal
Knelt by the stream to bathe his wounded arm,
. . . White herons sleep, their folded wings unstained
By all that blood the savage Gauley drained
From pale-faced men whose kindred now possess
The last dark current of the wilderness.

Family Knots

Meredith Sue Willis

*N*arcissa Foy made patchwork quilts. Even when she was a little girl turning frayed bits of feed sack into covers for her dolls, people praised her neat stitching and nice contrasts of color. After she married and moved over the mountain to live with her husband's family, her fame spread in the new community. She would spend the evenings with her patches spread on the bed, trying to get the colors to move a certain way, until her husband Axel came in yawning dramatically. Most people favored her blue-and-pink Grandma's Flower Garden, but her mother-in-law, Mrs. Foy, preferred a Courthouse Steps pattern in shades of lavender and gray.

Narcissa herself liked the crazy quilts best. Years ago, it was explained to her that a crazy quilt wasn't like a lunatic, but crazed like the cracks under the glaze of old pottery. With a planned quilt, you looked for pieces to play up the pattern, but with a crazy, you went off following trails of color wherever they led and then later discovered the shapes that contained your discovery.

Narcissa didn't say this in so many words: she didn't say much, as a rule, but people noticed her. They liked to look at her with her fine complexion. There was something special about her smile, too, something in her eyes, as if she was always looking partly at you and partly up at the clouds. Then there would be a shift, and just for a second, almost in passing, you would have her eyes in your eyes, all to yourself, and you felt warmed, as if she knew your secret beauty, the part of you that was like the mountains and the clouds.

She was a good girl, too—respectful, quiet, cheerful. She wasn't much of a hand to do fieldwork, but the Foys had plenty of men in those days just before the Great War, and women, too, what with Mrs. Foy's maiden sister and the girls. Narcissa always offered to get up from her quilting to make the cornbread or slop the hogs, but her mother-in-law and the others would say, Sit, sit. When she got pregnant so soon, they were all even more solicitous. They wanted her to feel at home and loved, so far from her own relations.

Some said that Mrs. Foy indulged Narcissa, let her do a young girl's chores too long. She collected the eggs, picked the raspberries, beat an occasional white cake for Sunday dessert, and after the baby came, she sat in the big cane rocker on the porch, sweetly nursing, softly singing, looking up over the hills or down into the baby's eyes.

"Mrs. Foy," she said one afternoon, "I never seen a scrap that color, did you? Wouldn't I love a piece that color."

"What color, honey?" Mrs. Foy was snapping beans and dropping them into the big tin pot where they made a substantial clang.

"Sky eyes," said Narcissa. "The baby's got sky eyes."

Mrs. Foy looked up, not altogether sure what made her so uncomfortable: the rhyme, the hint that Narcissa had strange things going on in her mind? "You mean sky blue, Cissy?"

"No, something different from sky blue. It's a change color."

Mrs. Foy snorted. "Babies' eyes don't settle in for a color till they're right big. I wouldn't worry about it."

"I'm not *worried*, I just wish I had a piece that color. I'd make a quilt called Sky Eyes."

Mrs. Foy winked without meaning to. "I expect you'd have to go to silks for a color like that, and you won't find any silk in this house." But she added, "I have some nice blue lawn in the drawer I was saving. If you want to do some kind of fancy quilt, I'd let you have a little bit of that."

They weren't always comfortable with Narcissa's dreaminess, but in those days she was the kind of luxury a mountain family could afford and even show off with pride. The backbreaking and tedious years of clearing the land and carding the wool to spin the yarn to weave the cloth were over. People worked hard but felt compensated for their labor. There was a design to things that everyone could see, and Narcissa was the touch of red against the blue and tan, the berry in the bush. The juice in the berry. She made the commonplace even more comforting.

But times changed. The girls married and left home and Narcissa had more work and more babies. Mrs. Foy and Aunt got older. Narcissa's skin lost some of its resilience and color, and the subtle thinning of her lips made her look more capable of work, whatever she felt inside. She always did what was asked of her, but she managed to keep on making her quilts. When Mrs. Foy complained about the time she spent on her quilts, Narcissa turned out to have the jaw of a bull terrier. She hung on to what mattered to her. It didn't make her sweeter to bite in so grimly, but it made quilts.

Maybe it would have been better if Narcissa had been born a few years later. Maybe it wasn't really quilts she wanted to make. Maybe in another time she would have been a painter, or a performance artist, a field scientist who studied wild pygmy chimpanzees, or the discoverer of the genes that cause the variations in Indian corn. Or perhaps she would have accomplished more with her quilts if she'd borne fewer children. Her fourth labor was fierce; the baby was breech and nearly strangled by the cord, but they saved it, and it immediately grew large and voracious, a night screamer and nipple chomper who nursed for hours at a time. Narcissa's breasts became caked and inflamed, and she cried and whimpered along with the baby, who seemed to thrive on blood as on milk.

The family had no time to sit and hold her hand. They knew it was difficult, but so was harvest season. And, if the truth be told, Mrs. Foy and Aunt, and even Axel, secretly thought that they wouldn't mind a little fever and infection themselves if it meant they could sit on the porch in the overheated beauty of the late afternoons, with the mountains rising directly behind, unutterably green with buzzing and enormous thunderheads in the west and blue. When she had a moment's respite, Narcissa looked up and groaned at the beauty. When the baby rested from its gobbling and gumming, she fell into a feverish nap and dreamed of quadrants of green and lavender, some milky, some bloody, and a ground the color of baby flesh. She dreamed of a quilt the color of her struggle to nourish this baby and the color of the peace she couldn't get hold of. The colors began to trickle and form paths like veins, twisting, weaving, plaiding, bursting open like fireworks or zinnia petals unfurled.

The fever of her inflamed breasts broke with the firework zinnia and the storm. It's not a crazy quilt at all, she thought, watching the sheets of gray rain slash at the hillside, watching the old women hurry in the wash. I'll have to make up some fool name for it, I'll call it the Exploding Zinnia or Shriek of the Wild Cat, just so they'll know it's a pattern and then I can do whatever I want with it.

The quilt should have been a new beginning, a breakthrough. She was all ready to start on it, but then the one thing happened that nobody expected. And Narcissa saw that *this* was a pattern too, the inevitability of the unexpected. Aunt—Mrs. Foy's sister, the maiden, spinster, scrawny fifty-year-old with a stoop—revealed that she had a secret beau and was going to marry him and go live in town. It made Narcissa's peculiarities pale. Aunt asked Narcissa for a red, white, and blue Star of Bethlehem quilt, and Narcissa made the most beautiful one ever, the one that her oldest daughter Lou eventually inherited.

And then Mrs. Foy went to bed with dropsy, her legs swollen and propped on pillows. Narcissa took a step back, saw: Aunt gone; Mrs. Foy in bed; Lou supposed to be free to do her homework because she was so smart; and the men waiting for their dinner. A headache struck the back of her eyes like a blow. This was an old story—the sudden, the unexpected, the demands of living. Narcissa was now the one to start the fire in the morning and set the biscuits to rise. Narcissa to boil the great kettle on Monday morning for the wash, to make pistons of her arms over the washboard. Narcissa to run to the big bedroom and help Mrs. Foy with the chamber pot. Her headache ended, but it was followed by the toothache, and she lost four teeth and whatever was left of the sweetness that used to make people forgive her oddities. She never went bitter about the mouth, but she sealed off something in herself the way Brother's left thigh sealed off a piece of shrapnel. Brother came back from the Great War alive and walking, thank the good Lord, with just a slight limp, but there was a piece of metal in him all the same, and on certain days, he could feel its weight. Thus Narcissa—her quilt.

One day she saw a spider weaving its web in a corner of her quilting frame. It was a beautiful web of exquisite, complex design, and she ripped it apart and rubbed it into the grain of the wall boards.

"You told us spiders eat flies," said Lou, who was supposed to be studying. "You told us spiders do good."

"It was in my frame," said Narcissa. "I was jealous of that spider's web."

That night she prayed for forgiveness for killing the spider. She prayed for strength, and received just enough to stay awake and start piecing the exploding zinnia. What God gave her to see was that if she was going to make that quilt for love or money or glory-be, she had better make it now, because there was no slack time coming. She had the extra bit of energy every night, and sometimes in the day.

Once, she was working on the quilt and didn't get to the tomatoes until they were so heavy they dropped to the ground and rotted. Mrs. Foy couldn't get over it and counted up the number of lost quarts. "It's that quilt, Narcissa," she said. "You're using such little small pieces. It'll take too long to finish."

Narcissa's bull terrier clamped shut. "Mrs. Foy, I'm real sorry, but I have to say, it's only tomatoes. I don't think a peck of tomatoes is all that's standing between this family and starvation."

She had never talked back to Mrs. Foy before, and Mrs. Foy, who didn't know how to take it, had an uncomfortable feeling that it was a bad sign.

"It's the waste, Narcissa," she said. "You know very well it's the waste that bothers me. Just the same as with that quilt. I swear that quilt is going to take forever, Narcissa. All of them say it just has too many pieces."

Narcissa kept her jaw tight. "I'm not making this quilt for all of them. I'm making this quilt—I'm making this quilt—"and she wasn't going to say it was for herself, although it was, because it was also for the family and the neighbors, "I'm making this one for God," she said.

Mrs. Foy snorted and shook her head and said to herself: That Narcissa. That's just like Narcissa. Make a quilt for God. What's she going to do, hang it at church? Mrs. Foy decided then and there she had really better get out of bed and take charge if they were going to have anything put up for winter.

When the quilt was finished, Narcissa decided it wasn't a flower after all. It didn't satisfy her with its dark complexities. Where was that fleshy life color she had wanted? The shapes were crude; the color changes too quick and uneven. People called it unusual. Narcissa called it Family Knots and folded it away in the cedar chest, and started in on some bright cheerful ones that refreshed her spirit. She continued to make up her own patterns, though, including a nice one called Big Zinnia with new cloth Axel bought her as a present.

The cheerful quilt ushered in a good period. Mrs. Foy was better, the boys came back from overseas, and Narcissa got pregnant again. This time it didn't seem like such a burden, though, because they'd sold off the coal and timber rights and used the money for a new washing machine. They stopped baking bread, too, and bought white bread at the store, and sometimes pies in boxes. Lou did more around the house, usually with a book stuck in her apron. She had always been quick with words. And right before the baby was born, Narcissa sold Big Zinnia to some city people for an astounding sum of money.

Some other city people came another time to look at Narcissa's quilts and asked why she didn't do more of the traditional patterns. "Such beautiful work," they said. "So colorful, but what about Dutch Girl and Barn Door? Don't you ever do a Honeycomb or a Bear's Paw or Virginia Reel or Country Squares?"

And before Narcissa could answer, Lou jumped in. "Why," she said, "Don't you reckanize that pattern? All my mama's patterns go back to the American Revolution. That one there is called the General George Washington Dancing Quilt."

Actually it was called Canning Beans Is Hard Work, and she should have shamed Lou for telling people stories, but the city people said, Oh, they hadn't seen it right off, of course it was, and offered her too much money. She took it and mentally changed the quilt's name to save Lou from lying. It could just as easy be called General George Washington Dancing, she thought.

Mrs. Foy was in bed again. "I'm getting too old, Narcissa," she said. "You must start taking over, planning the things."

Well, Narcissa had been planning everything for five years now. "I will, Mrs. Foy," she said, "but you know it won't be the way you do things."

She had meant to pay the older woman a compliment, but tears popped out in Mrs. Foy's eyes. "That's hard, Narcissa Foy," she said. "That's a hard thing for a woman to hear. The day will come when Lou will spit in your face too." But then Mrs. Foy seemed to come to herself. "Now Narcissa," she said. "I never meant anything. You know we all love you like a daughter. We always did. We spoiled you a little in the beginning, but you worked out just fine." She looked out the window and patted Narcissa's hand.

Once, during Mrs. Foy's final illness, Narcissa took out the strange dark quilt called Family Knots and nailed it to a pine strip and hung it in the hall. Axel said, "What's that thing doing on the wall?" And then got so busy sniffing around the kitchen for his dinner he forgot to wait for an answer. Or maybe didn't need an answer, just wanted Narcissa to know he noticed.

Mrs. Foy noticed too, tossed on her pillow and moaned. "You're still trying to convince me you don't have sense to run a house, but I know better, Narcissa, I know better."

Narcissa sat down and followed the complicated flow of Family Knots under bridges and over rapids. She recalled that as she was working on it, she had named the prominent navy blue stream Mother and a series of broken loops in green and brown Father. A deep maroon was Sweetheart Love, and Little Girl and Baby Boy burst out here and there in bright splashes.

Then she went through her chest and found a very old crazy that she had made when she was young, all in robin's egg blue and yellow, and she nailed that one to a pine strip and hung it up too. She was looking for something she had lost or put away. Every few days she would sit down and study those quilts, but when Mrs. Foy died, out of respect, she took them off the wall and laid her out in her favorite, the old lavender Courthouse Steps.

The day after the funeral, she started on the best quilt of her life. It was a variation on Family Knots, somewhat simplified but using sixty different brown and tans and thirty blues and thirty violets and purples.

Unlike the first Family Knots, it had no background proper; everything was foreground, all equal. She called it—feeling fancy because she knew it was a success—Braided Candelabra, even though it was really another Family Knots. She took great satisfaction in that quilt; she laid it on her and Axel's bed and never would consider an offer for it.

After that, her quilts were fewer, but just what she meant them to be, and they took a place in her life as if each of them were a child of hers, or at least a niece or nephew.

Mrs. Foy's boys married and left, and Narcissa and Axel's boys grew big and healthy. Lou became either a schoolteacher or a flapper, it was hard to tell from the way she dressed when she came for a visit. She was taking art courses in the evenings, and she came back with her red mouth going a mile a minute. Why didn't Narcissa realize that *she* was the artist? said Lou. These weren't quilts, these were easel paintings in cloth. Narcissa had all on her own invented Dynamism and the Fauves, said Lou.

"What's Fauves?" said Axel. "Sounds like some kind of purple fox to me," and they all had a laugh, but Narcissa was interested and flattered, and she trusted that in the end Lou would separate out the wheat from the chaff. It was too much, though, when Lou told her to drop everything and come back to the city with her and study at the Art School. "Now Lou," said Narcissa. "Now Lou," as if Lou had told an off-color story.

"It will smother your talent, never leaving here," insisted Lou. "It will just smother you."

Narcissa wondered if she *had* been smothered, and allowed it was possible that something had been, but something else had been made strong. She remembered the baby who chewed her nipples, but couldn't remember which one it was, and she remembered poring over the quilt pieces by kerosene lantern till they burnt into her eyes. She remembered a time when she used to be in her own world and it surprised her when dinner appeared on the table. She remembered, too, that a time had come when they began to touch her, Axel first, then his brothers and sisters and her own babies and, finally, even the old people. And I began to hear them and speak back, Narcissa thought, as if she were telling her own story. And after that, quilts weren't the most important thing anymore, or rather, everything wasn't separate from the quilts. It was the quilts, Narcissa thought, *and* the family. The pattern of people, and I was in the pattern.

In Dubio

Timothy Russell

Smoke plumes coil in the valley
like cavalry dust, and irises
so purple they must ache bloom
in front of the white block wall,
but rescue is still improbable here
where the moon is as likely
to pass behind heated vapors
rising from a boiler-house stack,
as if it were a lemon slice
sinking in some summer drink,
as it is to catch a locust branch
delicate and vaguely Oriental,
lying across it like scrimshaw,
the same hour, the same night
where cardinals nest in the wisteria,
Baltimore orioles in the sycamore,
and sparrows in the air conditioner,
where fresh asparagus is exotic,
and men tend machinery all night
as if it were troubled livestock.

In Aegri Somnia

Timothy Russell

The heat makes it
almost impossible to sleep,
but easy to say the blast furnaces
north of town make me think
saguaro. Sometimes,
I think I'd rather live
in some more temperate zone,
amid less brutal scenery,
where people are familiar
with public fountains, say,
or jazz at noon saturating
the plaza, small round leaves
quivering in the ornamental trees,
but I know this is weakness.
It is this life that makes
any other life possible.
Blast furnaces actually resemble
the great muscles they are,
huge pipes curving around them
like venae cavae, like aortae.
If it takes a desperate mind
to imagine they resemble saguaros,
then I guess mine is.

In Consideratione Praemissorum

Timothy Russell

Seven men sitting on a railroad tie,
ailanthus sprouting like tropical lies
against the blue corrugated sheet iron
behind them, lunch buckets and thermos bottles
open at their feet, all look up at once,
as if by plan. They seem dazed,
or astonished this could happen,
this one open, interminable second.
There is vacancy in their eyes.
They naturally think of home here,
down home, downstate, down "hoopy,"
where they return to hunt or just to touch
the leaves of a familiar bush
or to chase that old emptiness
or to cuss groundhogs or crows
in the corn and come back to tell it,
but right now, this instant,
they all know their break is over.

In Actu

Timothy Russell

Looking back now, I arranged everything:
thirty tracks glinting in the amber light
shed by three high-voltage clusters
perching brightly atop their standards
to illuminate the empty railyard,
and the fringe of forest slipping down
the hill. I knew black bricks formed
jagged black letters on the stack
above the unused incinerator
like separate faces on a totem.
The name of the town had to be there.
The lagoon had to be there behind
the silhouette of bunched trees rising
to escort Harmon Creek away from
the lumber company buildings painted orange,
past the ballfield and its dugouts
behind Kroger's and the Ford dealership.
It was night and streetlights
had to be strung out like constellations
in all the declining neighborhoods.
Two plumes rose and merged
above the hydrochloric-acid plant,
and traffic thumped across the Lee
Avenue railroad bridge, headlight beams
briefly flashing up to escape the planet
before the jolt yanked them back.
The long low buildings, of course,
had to be there, black even in daylight,
lying south to north as if magnetically
aligned. I live beyond them.

I know there is a powerhouse above me now
squatting like a duck on the brow of this hill.
I have seen it from my back porch.
I have seen it struck by lightning.
I have seen it turning purple at sunset.
I have seen it and its green aura at night.
It has to be there as surely as the mermaid
bottle has to be on the dining room windowsill,
just above the Christmas cactus.
In five seconds of climbing though,
it's all gone: the four blast furnaces
standing north of town with pipes
wrapping down around them like aortae,
pigeons that had to roost
by the hundreds at the Open Hearth
and the Sinter Plant,
and the BOP flashing like a brain.
In five seconds the fluorescent
red white and blue gasoline signs
flicker one last time in memory,
then I am gone, climbing this hill
toward the powerhouse on Calico,
then all of it below me, behind me,
vanishes. Everything disappears—
until somebody else who lives there,
or works there, on the railroads, say,
comes along to retrieve it.

from Crum
Chapter One

Lee Maynard

When I was growing up there, the population of Crum, West Virginia, was 219 human beings, two sub-humans, a few platoons of assorted dogs, at least one cat that I paid any attention to, a retarded mule and a very vivid image of Crash Corrigan. At first there were no whores, but later on I got to watch one in the Making.

"Crum—unincorporated" the road sign said at the edge of town. It should have said "unnecessary." The place is located deep in the bowels of the Appalachians, on the bank of the Tug River, the urinary tract of the mountains. Across the flowing urine is Kentucky.

Life in Crum was one gay, mad whirl of abject ignorance, emotions spilling over emotions, sex spilling over love, and sometimes blood spilling over everything. The Korean War happened to be going on at the time, but it was something being fought in another world and, besides, who really gave a damn about all those gooks anyway. Our boys could handle them. Or so they said in the beer gardens. And what the hell were gooks? I had never seen one. Or a nigger. Or a Jew. Or a wop. I had heard those names from some of the men who had been outside of West Virginia, working in the steel mills of Pittsburgh and the factories of Detroit. But I didn't know what the names meant and I had never seen any of those people.

During the winters in Crum the days were long, boring and cold, and during the summers the days were long, boring and hot. In Crum, only the temperature changed. The sad little town lay in a narrow valley, squeezed between the river and the hills, trapped before the floods, baked by the ancient heat of the mountains, awaiting each stagnant winter with all the patience, good looks and energy of a sloth. It was a collection of small houses, an assemblage of shacks, a reflecting pond of tin roofs.

The only paved highway into Crum came from downriver, from the general direction of Huntington. Actually, the road entered the valley by coming over the top of Bull Mountain, a dark and brooding hill that hung over the far ridge, closing off the valley. At the top of the hill the Mountaintop Beer Garden was penned between the ridge and the twisting road. Once past the beer garden, the road dropped into the valley like a dead snake. As soon as the road hit the valley floor it met the railroad tracks, a few miles downriver from the town. The two ran side by side from there on, seeming to be tied to each other, right through the middle of Crum and out the other end. The highway and the tracks stayed together until they were farther away from the town than any of us had ever ridden our bicycles.

If you drove down the highway from Bull Mountain and kept on going through town, the highway and the tracks divided the town into the hillside on the left, and the valley floor, across the tracks, to the right. At the beginning of town a narrow dirt lane led off the highway and crossed the tracks and then followed the rails closely all the way through town, recrossing the tracks at the far end. The few people who lived along the hillside used the paved highway to come and go. The folks who lived on the valley floor used the dirt lane, and the even smaller dirt lanes that left it and ran off between the houses in the general direction of the river.

When the dirt lane first crossed the tracks on the way into Crum, it separated the tracks from the high school football field, with the school building sitting back across the field on the edge of the river bank. That school building was one of the first things you saw when you drove through Crum, and it was one of the places I always went when I was lonely. I could sit on the school steps and watch the cars go by—whenever there were any cars. And I could think about the people in the cars and wonder where they were going. I wanted to find out.

There were only a few houses along the hillside. Yvonne lived there, and so did Elvira. And Parson Piney had his house on the highest spot on the hill, where he could look down on everyone. I'm sure he thought God had ordered it that way. And the tiny house I lived in was there, tucked in between some trees and partially sheltered from view. But mainly the hillside was too steep. Most of the people lived on the flat valley floor, jammed between the triple routes of the highway, tracks and lane to the left and the river on the right. The houses began at the downriver end of the valley, just beside the high school, and continued upriver until they ran out of space, a distance that couldn't have been more than a mile.

Across the river was Kentucky, a mysterious land of pig fuckers.

About halfway through town, to the right of the tracks and just off the lane, was Luke's Restaurant, the only restaurant in Crum. It wasn't much of a restaurant, just a square box of a building with bare light bulbs inside, a few wooden tables and some rough, handmade booths. But it was open at night and it had an old juke box. And a light on the front porch. There was no public lighting on any kind in Crum—"unincorporated" meant there was no public anything, no sewer system, no water system, and no real law except for the constable and now and then when a state police car rolled through town. But Luke's Restaurant had a light out front, and so it just naturally served as a focal point for the kids in Crum. Just a little beyond the restaurant, sitting back at the edge of a small grove of trees, was the town's only church, a lonesome, rickety little building. When you looked at it from the side, it looked as though a truck had run into it from behind, pushing the back of it up and in, the whole building leaning slightly, only we could never figure out in which direction.

After the church there was the tiny post office, and then Tyler Wilson's General Store. There, the dirt lane widened into a larger area so that cars could park in front of the rambling, two-story building. There were heavy wooden benches on the front porch and, at some time during the week, most of the older men would go down to the store and sit for a spell.

The railroad station, looking like a scale model, sat out on the edge of the wide parking area, snuggled right up against the tracks.

At the far edge of Tyler's parking area the dirt lane went back across the tracks and ended at the highway. And that was about all there was to Crum.

In the summer, when school was out, the town died. The teachers, the only people in Crum who could provide diversion and interest, left the town the day after classes ended. Almost all of them lived somewhere else and stayed in town solely because they had been assigned to teach there. For the most part, Crum was the only place the county school board would let them teach. Not because they were bad teachers, but because, for some reason or other, they were out of favor with the school board, usually because they refused to kick back part of their salary to the county political leaders. Of all the teachers in the high school only one or two actually lived in Crum the year round. The rest arrived a few days before school was to begin, rented a small house or a room or two, opened up their books, and taught. When classes ended, so did their stay in Crum. And you really couldn't blame them. The whole place was a mistake for them. The town was a zero. A blank. Nothing. All the cakewalks, the school carnivals, pie socials and church meetings of the year couldn't make up for that. The teachers came and went like migrating birds in reverse, showing up in the autumn and leaving in the spring, but building no nests and sending forth no singing.

No one in his right mind would spend four years in college earning a teaching degree, just to come to Crum and teach. Many of those assigned to Crum refused and many of those who came just walked out after the first month or so. The school itself didn't help much, either. It was a twelve-year school, all twelve grades from elementary to high school in the same building. The halls were hard and hollow and the noise echoed through the rooms in great crashing peals. There was no gymnasium, no auditorium, not even a large meeting room. The library was a tiny, cramped room with two tables, eight chairs, a small desk, a collection of Zane Grey books and for some reason a subscription to the *NEA Journal*.

And there were no indoor rest rooms. Crum High School had what must have been the world's largest outhouses, two of them, thirty yards out behind the school. It was enough to drive you nuts, and it sure as hell drove a lot of teachers nuts. They didn't stay long. They just didn't stay long, and I used to watch then get in their cars and drive away and wonder where they were going and how many other places they had been and why they had ever come to Crum in the first place. God, how I used to wish that I were one of them, that I could climb in a car and drive away.

Crum really was lonely when school was out. The teachers were gone for the summer. Nine out of ten of the kids rode the bus to school and just weren't seen again until the following September. All the buses were taken to Wayne, the county seat, and parked in the school board bus lots until the next school year, row after row of long yellow vehicles sitting in the sun. Almost every autumn, when they were getting the buses ready to go back into use, they would find where some kids had gotten into one or two and done a little drinking and a little fucking. Beer bottles would be lying around in the aisle and on the seats, and a few used rubbers would be hanging from the steering wheel and the rearview mirror.

So action in Crum in the summertime was limited to the few kids who actually lived there. There were Ruby Harmon, Nip Marcum, Wade Holbrook, Cyrus Hatfield, Yvonne Staley, Elvira Prince, Mule Pruitt, Ethan Piney and Benny Musser. And sometimes that sonofabitch Ott Parsons. And a few others, now and then. Some more girls, of course, but the only girl I think I ever cared about was Ruby Harmon. I would get tired of the same people day after day, and I would spend long days by myself, exploring the ridges, playing in the river, foraging in the hills, finding small streams and trying to follow them to their source, locating the hardwoods and the nut trees where I knew the squirrels would be when hunting season came around, looking for deer and wild turkey sign and every now and then discovering a pack of wild dogs. Sometimes it was a good time in the wilderness around Crum and sometimes it was not, but it was always lonely.

I'm not really complaining about being alone in Crum. Most of the time I *wanted* to be alone. I thought most of the kids in Crum were my friends, but there were a few I wasn't really sure about. Ethan Piney was one of those. I don't know how it was that Ethan and I got to want to kick each other's ass so much, but that's the way it always was. If there ever was a line drawn, you could bet that Ethan and I would be on different sides of it.

And there were some kids who weren't my friends, and they weren't my enemies. They weren't anything to me, and I wasn't anything to them. They didn't give a damn if I was there or not, or if they ever saw me again. When school was in session, they were just there, taking up seats, faces in the classroom. I hardly ever saw them when school was not in session. I knew that they lived in Crum and didn't come to school on the bus, but I didn't know where they went or what they did. I didn't know who their families were. Some of those kids just seemed to disappear.

In the summer people busied themselves in Crum by dumping trash on the riverbanks and digging new toilet holes. Early on they planted a few sugar cane patches down on the flats just above the river, hoping that the last high water had come and gone. Along about May, the town's only gas station would pour a winter's collection of oil drippings on the driveway and the oil would seep into the ground, collecting dust and spreading its smell. Little kids played in abandoned cars, using them as forts, houses, schools, cars, whorehouses and a thousand other things, then took stones and broke every scrap of glass out of them. Trains steamrolled through town, throwing smoke and cinders and bringing the town to its knees by the sheer size and sound of their passing. In the summer in Crum the river would go down and the springs would dry up and the people would talk about their wells. With no water system, no sewer system, no systems of any kind, the heat of an Appalachian summer would bring the outhouses to their full ripeness and spread the pungent aroma up and down the narrow Tug River Valley.

Some of the houses had electricity and a few had bottled gas but for the most part they were just a collection of boxes strung up and down the railroad tracks. The hills came down to the tracks, and across the tracks the flat, narrow valley floor spread gently toward the river, then dropped off sharply to the river bottom. And across the river, Kentucky.

My house—on the hill above the valley—wasn't "my" house exactly. I mean, it was their house, the house of my second cousins, Mattie and Oscar, I think, or maybe they were third cousins. I was born in Turkey Creek, a holler up on the north edge of the county. (Those narrow spaces between the ridges and the hills are "hollers"—not hollows, or canyons, or anything else.) Nobody would ever tell me what happened to my parents, if anyone ever knew. They were just gone to their reward. After a while I stopped asking about it. I was handed from relative to relative, from holler to holler, until I was old enough to be sent to Crum where I could go to school. Until I was raised, they said.

My relatives in Crum were an ordinary bunch, for Crum. Mattie was the woman of the house, a large, dark, hardworking woman. During the day, Mattie sometimes worked in Luke's Restaurant, helping Luke cook whatever there was to be cooked that day, and trying to keep Luke's dirty hands out of the stuff that he was going to feed the customers.

Mattie's husband, Oscar, was a miner, and the nearest mine was some distance away from Crum. I don't really know how far. I know that Oscar left the house early and got back late. He would scrub himself at the mine right after quitting time, then come home and go out back and scrub again, trying to rid himself of the grime that collected around his eyes and in the creases of his hands. He scrubbed out back even in the winter.

I thought that Mattie and Oscar were a lot older than my parents would have been. They had a couple of children, both girls, but they were grown and gone from home, both of them having gone off to Williamson a long time ago to get jobs and to live in a town that was bigger than Crum. I used to see the girls sometimes around holidays, but then they got married and Mattie and Oscar would go to Williamson for holidays and I would stay in Crum, alone. In fact, there were a lot of days when I never saw anybody around the house, only the heat from the wood stove telling that anybody at all had been there. But that was okay with me.

After the girls had left home, Oscar and Mattie had moved into a smaller house, tiny, with only one bedroom. It was the house they were living in when I showed up. The house was perched on the upriver end of Crum. A narrow porch ran along the front and around one side, reaching back to the shed that was tacked onto the back of the place, the shed where I slept and kept all my valuables, the shed that was mine. The shed was the only thing they could afford to let me have. But it wasn't their fault; they had already raised their kids, and one day they had been sent another one, one they had never seen before. That's the way things go. All things considered, I was luckier than most kids.

The folks in the house didn't bother me much, and I didn't bother them. They fed me if I was hungry and they made sure that I got to school often enough to keep from being kicked out of the place, but it was not their job to raise me. I was raised already. I was old enough to go to high school.

When I think about it, I guess I never paid much attention to them, and that seemed okay at the time, for all of us. Most of the kids in Crum never paid much attention to the grown-ups, unless they had to because of trouble. Mostly, we just kept to ourselves, doing our things and letting the grown-ups do theirs. We all seemed happy enough with that arrangement.

Summer seemed like the day after Christmas, when you have had something just a little nicer than the rest of the year but now it's over and there is some sort of empty feeling that won't quite go away. And you want badly for it to go away and you work at it but nothing seems to help. Just suddenly it's gone and you don't know why and you are caught up in summer in Crum and it's lonely.

There were a few regular weekly events that seemed to help regulate a town which needed no regulation. There was the weekly arrival of the meat truck form Huntington. It made two stops, then went on its way to Kermit. It seems odd but I never saw the meat truck on its way back to Huntington. I used to watch for it arrival in Crum because it was a sign of outside life and of other people doing things. But after it left for Kermit I never saw it return. I guess it went home by another route, but I knew the road maps by heart and I could never figure it out. We stole a load of meat off the truck once, and the driver never knew how he lost it. We stole so much that it rotted before we could eat it all and we would sit, gorging ourselves, trying to keep ahead of the spreading green rot, only to finally throw most of it in the river.

Another weekly event was the moving picture. There was a building in town that had been a general store, then had been converted into the Masonic Hall. The ground floor was one large room and every week Aaron Mason, who was a teacher and coach at the high school—about the only teacher who lived year-round in Crum—would show a moving picture. Because his name was Mason, we always thought that he owned the Masonic Hall.

The moving pictures were rented and came on the mail train, and the only pictures Coach Mason could afford to rent were the old Westerns. Those were the ones all the kids likes anyway, so there we were, with television taking over the big cities like New York City—only we didn't know that—and we were growing up with Hoot Gibson, Tom Mix, the Riders of the Purple Sage, Ken Maynard, Al Fuzzy St. John, Gene Autry, Roy Rogers, Sunset Carson, the black hats and the white hats and gunfighters who could sing. Autry and Rogers were relative newcomers and not nearly as popular as the other cowboys. During the movies the kids would yell and scream and throw trash at the screen when the villain was doing okay. And everybody believed in everything, particularly the heroes. There was a hero named Crash Corrigan, a big cowboy who could lick everybody in sight and who was one-third of a trio called The Three Mesquiteers. Crash was our local hero. Little kids called themselves Crash and local make-believe gunfights always had a Crash who stood up alone against everybody else.

The only other regularly scheduled event in Crum during the summer was Mean Rafe Hensley's weekly drunk at the Mountaintop Beer Garden. Mean Rafe would get it going on Saturday afternoon and by late Sunday night he would be out in the middle of the highway, shooting a pistol at the moon and challenging all comers. When Mean Rafe went outside, everybody else stayed inside, and when he reeled his way back inside the beer garden, everybody else cleared out the back door. We would stand outside and look in at the greasy tables and dirty floor, the rows of coolers behind the bar. Selling whiskey across the bar was illegal in West Virginia then and if you wanted the hard stuff you had to sneak it in yourself, or buy moonshine from the bartender. The 'shine was served in water glasses, or sometimes in old fruit jars. The bartenders wouldn't sell good whiskey because the 'shine made a hell of a lot more money for them. And besides, it was pretty damn good moonshine. We could see Rafe, a glass of 'shine in his hand, standing dead center in the middle of the floor, laughing and shouting and scaring hell out of everybody. Sometimes he'd go out to the middle of the highway and shoot at the moon. We all hated him. We all wished he would drop dead or get run over by a truck. At least once his pickup truck got hit by a rifle bullet as he drove to the beer garden, but the bullet didn't touch Rafe and he would point out the hole to you as a sign—I'm not sure of what. But all we ever did was stand outside and look in. It just wasn't safe to mess around with Mean Rafe Hensley on a Saturday night.

There were no other regularly scheduled events.

In the summer, the sun beat down on nothing much. It scorched the vegetable gardens that everyone had just outside their houses. It burned the drowsiness into the people and out of the flies. The early morning mists and the sun and the evening light as soft as cotton were a part of most every day.

Sometimes it would rain. There is nothing softer than a quiet summer rain in the mountains, warm, musical and clean, coming from air that has been scrubbed and polished. When I used to feel that I was really closed in, when I felt that I had about come to the end of my string, when I felt that if I had to look at five more minutes of Crum I would just lie down in front of the next train . . . usually when I felt that way, for some reason or other it would rain. The rain would close in my world, bringing it down to a small gray dome that moved with me as I walked through the hills and hollers. Nobody else stirred much in the rain. They huddled against the damp, waiting for the drops to cease their drilling against the tin roofs.

They didn't smell the peculiar smell that you can smell just before the rain. They didn't hear the sounds that can happen between the drops. They never heard a bird sing in the rain. But I did. I loved to prowl the hills and the town in the rain.

In the summer in Crum the world died. I would wait through the long months until autumn brought whatever spark of life there was to bring. Maybe it was the teachers. I like to think so.

Of course, there were a few bright spots during my life in Crum, such as fucking in the cane fields down by the river on warm, sunny afternoons, and the day we robbed the meat truck, and the day that Constable Clyde Prince's outhouse exploded, and beating the living hell out of Ethan Piney. And Ruby Harmon.

Chapter Six

It wasn't long from our coal-collecting experiment to the day that Mule and I decided to rob the meat truck. There was no real reason for it—we weren't hungry, but we'd been handed our asses by those Kentucky pig fuckers and we needed something to make us feel good again. Plus, we needed something to do—the summer days stretched emptily ahead.

The meat truck came from Huntington once a week and made two stops in Crum on its way to Kermit. It dropped over the ridge at the top of Bull Mountain, at the Mountaintop Beer Garden, gear-ground its way down into the valley and made its first delivery at the little store by the bus stop. That store never bought more than a roll or two of lunchmeat and it only took the driver a few minutes. He would get out of the truck, unlock the small doors on the back, take out the meat and disappear inside the store. Soon he would come back out, climb into the truck, drive across the railroad tracks and onto the narrow dirt road that went past Luke's Restaurant and on to Tyler Wilson's General Store. He usually stopped at Luke's place for a quick drink of Nehi Orange. He didn't lock the truck doors again until he came out of Tyler's store.

I said we weren't hungry but I guess in a way meat was sort of valuable to us. Meat, all the meat we could eat, had never been had by any of us. Usually we ate meat two or three times a week—pork sidemeat, bacon, jowl, and whatever other piece of the hog could be had for near nothing. We had an egg or two for breakfast with some bacon, and you could eat a hot lunch supplied by the government in the school's small cafeteria or you could bring your own lunch in a paper sack. At supper, though, it would have been nice to have meat all the time, but we seldom did. It just cost too much. There were days on end when supper was a collection of potatoes, beans and whatever other vegetables that were cheap at the time. Even Mule, whose dad was one of the best pig killers around, mostly ate only the leftover parts of the hog. And we almost never got to eat any beef.

At Mattie and Oscar's house every month or so we did get some beefsteak. We would get the toughest steak that money could buy and then take a hammer—a real hammer—and pound the living hell out of it until it looked, felt and smelled like the aftermath of a slaughter. Mattie would then cook the bloody remains for hours over a low fire in the wood-burning stove. She'd make brown gravy and bring the whole thing to the table in a large pot, the steak bubbling in a pond of hot gravy and sending out a smell that made you hungry enough to eat your belt. There would be potatoes and green beans, sliced tomatoes and cucumbers, biscuits and homemade jelly and pitchers of cold milk from one of the neighbor's cows. And if you were lucky, there would be apple or blackberry cobbler for dessert with more milk and pots of coffee. When you ate it you knew you had eaten something real. You lingered over it until you just couldn't hold any more, and then you just sat and remembered it for a while. That monthly ration of steak was like Christmas. You looked forward to it and when you knew it was *the* day you would hang around the house just so you wouldn't miss any of the smell. The smell from the stove would come straight through into my shed and I would lie there for hours, reading my books and scribbling on my scraps of paper and just smelling that incredible smell.

Mule had never eaten steak until I brought him to the house once for the big meal. I thought he was going to cry. All the Pruitts *ever* ate in the way of meat was pork—after all, Mule's dad was a great pig killer. For months after that all Mule could talk about was how he was going to buy steak when he had the money, buy steak until he was smothered in the red, slimy, raw, bleeding stuff. I guess that was one of the reasons we robbed the meat truck.

We had a clubhouse down on the riverbank. We had dug a huge hole into the clay and sand in the middle of a thicket of brush and scrub trees, had covered the front and part of the top with boards we had picked up along the river, had covered the boards with cardboard and old pieces of canvas, and then had thrown dirt and sand over everything. It made a good clubhouse, but it sure as hell was dark in there. We made candles and we would sit around in the clubhouse talking and laughing in the wavering light and listening to the river gurgle. It always seemed comfortable, no matter how damp or chilly it got. Probably that's because the place was ours and only we knew where it was. We never even told the girls, although actually they knew anyway. In fact, maybe everyone knew, though we didn't know it.

When we decided to rob the meat truck, Mule and I dug another small room at the back of the clubhouse into the cool earth deeper into the riverbank. We planned to hide the meat in there, saving it until we had rested up again and could eat some more. We planned to go up into the hills with part of it and have a big feed up on the hill that overlooked the town, which we called Shit Hill. We also planned to take some of the scraps, swim across river and dump them on one of the trails over there. That way if the law came looking for the meat the trail would lead over to the Kentucky side and put the blame on some of those Kentucky pig fuckers.

Mule and I figured it would take more than the two of us to do it the way it ought to be done, so we got Nip and Wade to help. We thought about Benny, but he'd probably get too excited and screw everything up. Cyrus Hatfield would have been better but Cy was simply too honest. Cy was strong and would fight anybody at the drop of a hat, but he just wouldn't steal.

So we got Wade and Nip and explained the whole thing to them. The plan was simple. The truck would stop at the bus stop and the driver would unlock the doors on the back. After he made his delivery there, he would get back inside, drive the truck across the railroad tracks and head for Luke's Restaurant. The dirt road on that side of the tracks was never in very good condition. No one maintained it and the mudholes and ruts sometimes got so bad that ordinary cars just couldn't make it. The truck would have to go *very* slowly. It was a half-mile to Luke's from where the truck crossed the tracks. As soon as it was across the tracks, one of us would leap out of the bush alongside the road, run behind the truck and climb onto the small platform on the rear. Then, he would unhook the back doors, slip inside, and begin throwing meat out of the back of the truck. The others would be placed along the road ready to pick up the meat. If the driver got wise and stopped the truck, it was every man for himself. We had to get the whole thing done in the first quarter-mile after the truck had crossed the tracks because that was the only place where the banks were high enough and the brush thick enough to hide the operation. Besides, after that, there were houses along the road and it would just be too risky.

Wade volunteered to get onto the truck and throw out the meat. We argued about that, because we thought that Wade wouldn't be able to move fast enough to catch it. In fact, we were surprised that Wade wanted in on the robbery at all, since he hardly ever got his ass out of the chair in front of Crum's one television set, up at the beer garden where he lived. But the thought of all that meat was enough to make even Wade move his butt.

Mule would be the first to pick up the meat, then Nip, then me. Wade would jump off the truck and pick up the last pieces himself. We knew the meat would be in chunks and we were going to pick them up in gunnysacks, each of us carrying whatever was flung out into his area. We would meet at the clubhouse, store the meat, and go up to Shit Hill behind my shed for our first big feed.

On the day the truck was supposed to arrive, the four of us were down by the school, rolling around in the grass on the football field, soaking ourselves in the summer sun. We were there a good two hours before the truck was due. We tried to be calm, talking in low tones, not moving enough to show our nervousness, generally acting as though this was old stuff and we robbed meat trucks every day. But we were all excited and we knew it. Nip was so wound up that he was giggling, rolling around on the ground and making spitting noises between giggles. The closer it got to the time for the truck to arrive, the worse Nip got. Finally, Wade and Mule sat on him, hitting him with their caps and punching around on him until he got mad and settled down.

After a while we just lay there on the grass, watching birds ease their way through the air, listening to the afternoon insects make their particular noises, and getting hungry at the thought of all the meat we would soon get to eat.

Nip saw it first, downriver where the road cuts into the edge of the hills. The truck was on its way to the little store at the bus stop.

We headed for the dirt road, each on a separate route. Wade walked straight through the bush toward the bus stop. Mule dropped about a hundred yards back and hid in a thicket at the edge of a narrow, bumpy spot where the truck was sure to be going very slowly. Then Nip, and then me. We settled down to wait, each of us deep within his own fantasy, each of us dreaming of sides of beef, huge rump roasts and sirloin. I eased out toward the edge of the road. I could peer through the brush and see all the way to the crossing. It really wasn't very far away. I wondered if we would have time to get any meat off the truck. I readied my gunnysack.

The truck thumped its way across the railroad crossing. I could hear the gears chunking and grinding all the way at my hiding place. I watched the spot where Wade was hiding. As the truck passed, Wade leaped out from beside the road and disappeared behind it. The big meat robbery was under way.

The truck crawled toward Mule and I wondered if Wade had been able to get the small doors open. It got to Mule but still no meat was coming out. Instead, I saw Mule jump from beside the road and disappear behind the truck, just as Wade had done. Something had gone wrong.

Mule was supposed to stay where he was, waiting for Wade to fling out the meat. If he got too far out into the road, the driver would be able to see him in the rearview mirror. But Mule jumped right into the middle of the road.

Then I saw why. Back down the road, a few yards from where he had been hiding, Wade was flat on his gut in the middle of the road. He had caught up to the truck okay, but he lad lost his footing trying to swing himself up on it and creamed himself on the little platform on the back. Mule had thought fast and taken over Wade's job. He was determined to get the meat, and Wade could damn well lie there and bleed for all he cared.

As the truck moved forward I couldn't see Mule and I knew he had gotten inside. The truck neared Nip and as soon as the cab passed the spot where Nip was hiding, he popped out into view at the edge of the road, gunnysack in hand, waiting for the meat. It wasn't long in coming.

A flicker of motion at the back of the truck sent a giant slab of bacon sailing through the air. It struck Nip squarely in the chest and Nip and the bacon flew backward and disappeared into the brush. What a hell of a mess. One guy lying bleeding in the middle of the road, another knocked ass over false teeth into the bush with a slab of bacon wrapped around his ribs, one on the truck sailing meat out into the countryside, and there I was, alone, thinking about how the hell I would ever pick all of it up.

The truck was gathering a little speed, now. The road was getting better and the driver was in a hurry for his Nehi. I could see some packages and stuff flying out of the back of it and I tried to remember where most of them landed. As the truck passed me I eased to the edge of the road and waited.

Nothing happened. The doors on the back of the truck were still open and I thought I could see someone inside. If Mule was still in there I didn't know what the hell he was doing, but he didn't have much more time to do it. The truck was nearing the first house.

I forgot about picking up meat and was lost in watching the truck. Suddenly, two figures appeared on the little platform, clinched tightly and lurching with the movement of the truck. One of them was Mule. The other was a full side of beef. The beef must have outweighed him easily, and he had the stuff in a death grip, wrestling it to the edge of the platform. They teetered there for a moment, the truck bouncing down the road nearing the houses, Mule and the slippery meat dancing madly back and forth to the bounces as though they were enjoying the ride in the warm afternoon sun.

But not for long. The next big bounce launched Mule and the meat out into the air and they crashed onto the road. The meat hit first and then Mule hit the top of the meat, bounced off and rolled across the road. He was covered with blood and beef fat and as he rolled he picked up dirt and gravel and dust from the road. You couldn't recognize him.

Mule was up instantly, grabbing the side of beef and dragging it toward the nearest thicket. I knew he wouldn't be able to carry it. We would have to drag the damn thing all the way to the river.

I came out of hiding and began working my way back down the road, looking for meat. I found some almost at once and shoved it into my sack. It was wrapped in shiny brown butcher paper. I couldn't tell what it was but I wasn't going to waste time finding out. I looked back over my shoulder toward the truck. It was still heading for Luke's Restaurant and Mule and his meat were nowhere in sight. It looked as though we had gotten away with it. I went back to my meat gathering. The next thing I found was a bucket with its lid half popped off. The bucket was full of liver. I shoved the thing further into the brush, covered it with some leaves and hoped the dogs would find it. I wasn't going to carry liver all the way back to the riverbank.

A few minutes later I bumped into Nip. He was crawling along the ground, gunnysack in hand, gathering meat with one hand while he kept the other pressed against his chest. I figured he had some cracked bones in there, but he was keeping on with the robbery. I had to give him credit. I peeked out into the road. There was no more meat out there—Mule had flung it all into the brush—and I couldn't see Wade, either. Nip and I got all the meat we could find and took off, half carrying and half dragging the heavy sacks.

It took Nip and me more than an hour to go the half mile to the clubhouse. We crawled in through the tunnel and lit some candles, stashed our sacks in the cold meat storage room, covered up the entrance to it with some boards and settled down to wait for Mule. And for Wade, If he was still alive.

Wade was the first to arrive. He was covered with cuts, and cinders and gravel were sticking to his skin from when he hit and rolled. He had a couple of small packages of meat with him, picked up at the edge of the road before he figured he had better get out of there. I knew where the first meat had come out of the truck and figured Wade must have crawled more than fifty yards through the brush to get it.

We waited for Mule. The sun went down and the air around the river began to cool. The clubhouse was warm from the candles and our sweating bodies but we stayed inside afraid to leave our haul. When a couple of more hours went by we went looking for Mule. We didn't find him on the route we thought he would have taken to get the meat from the road to the clubhouse. We fanned out and looked some more, but wherever Mule was he didn't want to be found and so we didn't find him. A little later we gave up and went home, agreeing to meet back at the clubhouse for breakfast the next morning.

I was back on the riverbank before the mist had time to clear off the water. I came down off the hill where my house was, headed straight for the river, then turned upstream after I was sure that no one had seen me. I made my way through the brush, drifted trash, cane fields and low-hanging trees. As I got closer to the clubhouse I slowed down and crept forward cautiously, thinking that maybe someone found the meat and was staking us out. But all I found was Nip and Wade, glancing nervously up and down the riverbank.

"Man, you guys sure must have got up early," I said.

"Yeah, we wanted to check the meat and find Mule. We went by his house and looked in his window. He wasn't in his room and nobody else in the house was up," Nip said. He looked worried. Nip liked Mule and sort of looked up to him.

"Did you check inside the clubhouse? Did you look in the meat room?" I was a little stung by Nip's concern. I guess I was jealous.

We crawled single file into the clubhouse, Nip first, then me, then Wade. Wade hadn't said anything much, just kept pulling his shirt away from the wounds on his chest and fingering the cuts on his face. When we got inside, Nip lit a candle and held it around the cavelike room. There was nothing in there but our junk, but some of it had been knocked aside, shoved up against the wall, and there was a deep groove down the middle of the sandy floor. The groove led straight from the tunnel to the meat room.

We just stared at it. Then Wade got up the nerve to pull back the boards that covered the entrance to the meat room. As he removed the last board, Nip move in closer with the candle. As the light edged its way into the dark hole, a huge, naked form flashed out of the blackness and tackled Wade. The two of them fell into the middle of the clubhouse with a thud that made the roof leak some of its sand and dirt. We knew then that Mule was okay. Sometime in the night he had made it back to the clubhouse. Wade had been clobbered by Mule's side of beef.

Four days later we were still eating on that meat. Every day we would spend some time down on the riverbank, building fires and trying our hand at cooking it in every possible way. And Mule was the biggest eater, even bigger than Wade. He would stuff that meat—especially the steaks—into himself until he could hardly breathe. The juices ran out the corner of his mouth. Gulping sounds accentuated his chews. Sometimes, when all of us were eating at the same time, we created a kind of music out of the sounds we made, a sort of rhythm of gulps, belches, smacking, chewing, ripping, hiccupping, snorting and farting. Sounds seemed to blast from every opening in our bodies as the meat slid down our throats.

The four of us ate meat until we literally were sick at the sight of it, and even so we hardly made a dent in the pile. We got picky, choosy about what we would eat. We fished through the packages for choice pieces, for spicy sausages and thick strips of bacon, tiny little round things of tender beef, the ribs that hung together in slabs, anything we could drive a stick through and hold over a fire, anything that we knew would be tender and juicy.

Nip found some pieces of liver wrapped in with some other cuts, and he was about to throw them into the river when he suddenly changed his mind. He got a piece of old rope out of the clubhouse. He found some sort of stringy, springy tree right at the edge of the water, climbed it until it bent toward the bank, then used the rope to tie the top to a small stump. He took the liver and carefully placed it on the top of the bent tree, making sure that the liver was properly balanced. Then he cut the rope. The tree swooshed upward and the liver was launched far out over the river, the bloody mass sailing into the bright air and gaining altitude as it headed toward Kentucky. It disappeared into some trees on the Kentucky side and we could hear it breaking small branches. A liver bomb. We talked about how some Kentucky pig fucker would be walking along a path over there and would get hit smack in the face with a load of liver. He would have a hell of a time explaining that! We laughed until we almost threw up.

Mule kept hacking away at the side of beef. Wade poked through everything, toasting a tidbit here, selecting a morsel there. We felt like Robin Hood just after he had slaughtered one of the king's deer. We also began to feel pretty sick.

We were always too filthy for anyone to notice the new juice stains on our clothes, but, just the same, we were pretty careful around town. We didn't know what would happen when the driver missed all that meat. We thought for sure that he'd notice the loss when he got to Tyler's store, but we never found out. The next time the truck came through it was a different driver—we heard Tyler ask him what happened to the other guy—but he wasn't much for talking, just mumbled something about company orders.

So the great meat robbery went unnoticed: That was hard for us to take—nobody talked about how neat the job was, how smart the robbers were, how they must have been professionals to pull it off like that. Nothing. Not a word. That was really hard to take.

At the end of the first week after we robbed the meat truck the meat began to spoil. Parts of it turned green, other parts just stiff, so we cut them off and threw them in the river or launched them over into Kentucky. Soon, however, the green was spreading too fast for us to keep up with and more meat was going into or over the river than was cooking over the fire. We couldn't eat the good meat fast enough to keep ahead of the rot and in the end at least a third went into the muddy current.

I've thought a lot about that meat and how we stole it. And I've thought a lot about Mule and Nip and Wade sitting on a damp riverbank eating rotten meat in the near light of a fast evening. The fire and the smell of cooking meat are still with me. Years later I saw another meat truck in another town far away. And there was a kid standing there looking at it. And I wondered if he had a couple of buddies and a clubhouse down by the river.

Aunt Anna
For Lyda Tuberville
1880-1965

Llewellyn McKernan

Aunt Anna, greatest aunt of all,
come home again. I'll give you
the henna rinse you always wanted,
bob your hair in the back like the
Shaker women in east Kentucky, make
soybean meatloaf for supper, give you
the richest soil in the kitchen garden
for your Concord tomatoes. Aunt Anna,

Weltschmerz has come for a visit.
Remember how we used to laugh and
welcome him: a spot of beer for
the peptic ulcer, his favorite chair
by the kitchen table, and how he'd talk!
"Ah, love," he'd say in a throaty whisper,
"God is dead, what's left is self, poetry
is all." Taking another draw on his beer,

he'd repeat himself endlessly, his large
brown eyes like a gentle dog's, liquid
and melancholy. But you weren't having any!
You'd pull his red-veined nose and call him
a "durn furriner," you'd shower white lilacs
on his head and shoulders, while I looked
up long words in the dictionary like alcohol
and infantile colic, maniac, choler and quack
to fling at him. He always flung them back.
And afterwards we'd laugh. But now he sits

on the three-legged stool, staring for hours
at the old gas flame without calling me
any names at all. The lilacs in his hair
have silvered. Oh, Anna, you can have the
star-burst quilt I made for Momma so long
ago. It's blue and red, remember? And
the feather bed you wanted so badly I
put in the attic but it's yours forever.
Great-Aunt Anna, come home again.

The Peaceful Kingdom
For my sister, JeNell, 1939-1989

Llewellyn McKernan

When I dream of the Second Coming,
it always unfolds in silence.
According to St. John, all God's big guns
   will go off, but I won't
   be there, I know it.

I'll be strolling down a country road,
squinting drowsily up into the sun, or
I'll be back home in West Virginia, leaning heavily
   against the side of the house where I was born,
   vomiting up the breakfast of champions.

Afterwards I walk to the middle of the yard
where tiger lilies tiffany the air: one small,
one large, and one just the right size to slip
   inside my palm, where I inhale its perfume,
   rinsed white in the laundry.

As the sun continues to rise (the porthole
of a ship through which I look, saying, "Well,
that's interesting,") I turn and walk back, my dress
   shriven to a mirror
   where in riotous confusion

red tulips, green grass and light
glancing off windows ricochet from left to right.
In one of these windows my mother is sewing
   a coat of many colors. In another my father
   is butchering a fatted calf.

My German shepherd, the one who died,
solders the earth, muzzle resting on paws.
Opening one eye, he gives me the once-over
    and then goes back to sleep,
    apparently satisfied.

My sister, already a child, takes off
her red wig and mascara. She sits at a small white
table, serving up tea and crackers to all those who
    join us in the sweet By-and-By.
    Such tiny cups and saucers!

They glow
like Noah's eyes when the dove returns
and the ark runs aground, anchored at last
    in a world
    without a drop of darkness in it.

The Only Old Timer
In The Neighborhood

Llewellyn McKernan

is Jimmy J who lives
across the alley from me.

He walks on stilts, his bald
head tilts as he see-saws

down a bottle of RC. He's
survived more floods than Noah.

In the Big One in '37 he floated
down the Ohio on a grand piano.

At Buffalo Creek, he crawled
bare-assed up the neck of

a chimney, and clenching a Jew's
harp between his teeth and a cat

between his knees (she spat,
rosy-eyed in the darkness), he

nested for hours with rats, bats,
spiders, moths, and a cardinal

with a broken wing, popping out
of the top like a black-face

vaudevillian when he heard
the all-clear signal: "Coo-eee!"

And when the Big Sandy rose one
spring — pressed down, shaken

together, and running over — and
hives of yellow jackets went

on a spree, he lost everything:
all his tools for making imitation

antiques. The Bible where in
fading blue ink was listed

the birth and death of every
person on his family tree. Both

his legs down from the knees.
Now he collars everyone — his

brothers, sisters, strangers,
neighbors, me. His left ear

wiggles, his Adam's apple jiggles
as he tells the same old story

that like the ancient mariner's
ends with just one moral:

"Everywhere I go," he says,
"I bring water!" In his eyes

unholiness gleams as he speaks
of the imminence of the second

holiest flood in history.
Pausing for effect, he says,

tensing his neck as if
there were a crick in it:

"IT'S GONNA BE PRETTY BIG!"
I stare at the pocket of snuff

tucked inside his lower lip
(it bleeds). I look into the eyes

where with one apocalyptic blink
the whole city of Hunter sinks

like Atlantis to the bottom of
the Ohio, the windows of every

house burst and darkend by
the weight and wonder of the river.

Catfish scale these jagged glass
peaks, nibble the gray glue of

wills and deeds, losing all their
whiskers as they nose their way

forever through dense arcades
of mud and fresh water weed.

In Spring

Llewellyn McKernan

4-Pole crooks
a careless arm around the southside of Hunter.
Tumbling and
sprawling between green thumbnail banks,
it rushes down from
Ruby Springs west to Harveytown, twisting and
turning like the Balm
of Gilead on a hot skillet. Severe as prayer,
fierce as an ax, it doubles
back on itself, see-sawing between the hope of
heaven and earth's
royal shadows as it sticks to one truth: "WATER,
WATER,"

it cries over
and over until precious little is left to add, only
that as we walk
the seasoned edge of an endless circle, it rises
and falls, embracing
the dark that turns into light and the sounds that
burst from the noise
that constantly bombards us—say, the cardinal's
clarinet solo
as it makes a clean sweep of the water, the sun's
high C that shatters
the still perfect stream, or the wind's Hallelujah
Chorus,
or the creek itself,
rising to its greatest oratorical heights when rain
wrestles the earth
to a standstill, and nothing is left but the operatic
howl if its tenor.

Rondal Lloyd
from Storming Heaven

Denise Giardina

*E*arliest thing I recall from when I was a boy is daddy coming in from the mines and taking his bath. It always scared me when he came in. It would be way after dark, and I'd be asleep with Talcott and Kerwin in the bed in the front room. Most nights he'd come in quiet, just lay himself down, coal dust and all, on a mat behind the cookstove in the kitchen, so as not to track dirt into the rest of the house. He would be back out before dawn anyway, so there was no need to bathe. But on Saturday, Mommy boiled water, rattled coal in the buckets to throw on the fire, pulled out the Number Three wash tub. I could never sleep through the noise. I always lay on the side of the bed next to the door, so I could hang my head over the edge and watch her. Daddy would stomp onto the back porch, peel off his boots, and bang them against the steps to knock off the crusts of mud and coal dust. He stripped off his clothes and left them in a heap for Mommy to wash the next day. She never washed his mine clothes with the rest of our things. Then Daddy came inside. His face and hands were black and shiny; the rest of him was pale and waxy like lard. The whites of his eyes were vivid. He tossed his pay envelop on the kitchen table.

"Snake again," was all he would say, meaning he hadn't been able to mine enough coal to pay off the bills at the company store, that he still owed for food and doctoring and his work tools and blasting powder, that his paycheck had a single wavy line where the money figures should have been. But I learned about those things later. At that age, I thought he meant he had seen a copperhead, and that was why his eyes looked so wild and frightful. I lived in terror of snakes.

Daddy sank slowly into the round tub of hot water, moaning as he went down. The tub was just large enough for him to sit in if he drew his knees under his chin. The edge of the tub scraped his backbone just above his fleshless buttocks. Mommy stood over him pouring water from her pots and kettles. She scrubbed his face like he was one of us babies but never got all the coal dust off. His face was gray on Sundays like a newspaper photograph.

We lived in Winco, West Virginia, once our homeplace. American Coal Company owned our house. Richmond and Western Railroad owned our land. Mommy never talked about the old days, but Daddy told me how it used to be. Our cabin had set on the same piece of ground as the company store, which was three stories high, wood painted white with black trim, with stone steps trailing up to plate glass windows. "American Coal" was painted in gold on the glass door. Daddy said the cabin used to creak when it was windy, but the company store stood firm and unyielding. The railroad track, its ties oozing tar, ran through Mommy's vegetable garden. Most of the houses were built around the hill where the cow and sheep had grazed.

"The creek was clear as glass, and we used to git trout outen in, and bullfrogs," Daddy said. "You aint et till you had frog legs. Now the creek wont run clear till kingdom come, I reckon. We let it git away from us."

We never ate trout or frog legs, but mostly beans, biscuits, and gravy. The creek water was black with mine drainage and raw sewage, and acid stained the rocks orange.

On Sundays in the spring, Daddy and Mommy took us for walks up around the mountain, searching for wild mustard, poke, and creasy greens for supper. Mommy carried Kerwin on her back. She had broad cheekbones and brown hair pulled back in a bun so that the top of her head appeared flat. We followed the road the company had gouged out of the mountainside. Mommy said there had only been a path there once. The Negroes lived in the houses on that road. Their houses were tinier than the small ones the company provided for white people. Each Negro family was crammed into two rooms of a four-room double house. The company never painted these houses, and so they were streaked with black. In summer the windows stood open and faded pink or green curtains flapped out in the breeze. The colored people had no porches, so they hunched on their front stoops when they wanted to take some air. Their outhouses were not built over holes, but hung out over the hillside. One night a man broke his arm when white boys toppled over the privy while he was inside.

Skinny yellow dogs barked and lunged at us as we trudged by those houses, and the colored people watched us silently from their stoops. Mommy always walked with her head down, never speaking, for she didn't like the colored people. Daddy said they never would have come if the coal company hadn't brought them in.

When we were past the colored houses, we'd start gathering greens. Talcott and I took turns holding the paper poke. Sometimes we went farther up the mountain to the Lloyd family cemetery. Daddy carried a scythe and cut away the weeds from the graves.

One day we climbed to the cemetery but were stopped by a gate and barbed wire fence strung across the road, and a sign which read, NO TRESSPASSING. PROPERTY OF AMERICAN COAL.

We never went to the cemetery again.

I attended the Winco School and did well. When I was in the third grade, the teacher, Miss Radcliffe, invited the ten best students to her apartment for oatmeal cookies. She lived in the clubhouse, a building most of us had never entered. It was reserved for the unmarried teachers, nurses, and bookkeepers of the company.

Miss Radcliffe, tall and gray-headed, led us single-file up the stairs and ushered us into her rooms with the air of a genie revealing a treasure. We tiptoed across a rug Miss Radcliffe said was oriental and settled in miserable silence upon her purple-striped sofa and chairs. Miss Radcliffe smiled proudly as we craned our heads to take in the high cherry bookcases with glass doors, the purple-flowered wallpaper, the grandfather clock with gold trim on the door.

She served the cookies on bone-white china, and we had hot tea served in delicate cups with handles so small that even a child could not get a proper grip without being burned. Miss Radcliffe talked about the importance of an education, about how we had the obligation to raise ourselves above our parents and save our mountain people from ignorance. She reminded us that Abraham Lincoln had been as poor as we were. Then she gave us our assignments for Class Day, when our parents would visit the school. I was to memorize the first two paragraphs of the Declaration of Independence.

Cookie crumbs kept falling down the front of my overalls and I couldn't fish them out without spilling my tea. I was afraid they would drop on Miss Radcliffe's carpet when I stood up, and she would call me "slovenly," one of her favorite terms of disdain. When the grandfather clock struck four, we escaped. I wrapped three cookies in my bandana to share with my brothers after supper, and ran down the hill to our house. When I went inside, I smelled grease. Mommy was scraping the bacon leavings in the iron skillet for gravy. I scuffed my bare feet across the gritty wood floor, sprinkled with coal dust despite Mommy's daily scrubbings. Yellowing newspapers plastered the wall to keep out the cold.

Talcott and Kerwin wrestled on the bed in the front room.

"Yall lookee here," I said. "I got a surprise treat for after supper."

When they reached for the bundle I held it high above my head.

"After supper," I said.

I stuck the cookies beneath my pillow, dared them to touch it. Then to show I was not so strict, I hugged Talcott to me and tickled his belly. He wriggled and laughed. The back of his neck smelled of dried perspiration, sweet like a field in summertime. I sighed, lay back on the bed, and was glad to be home.

Our house was one of three that sat in the bottom beside Trace Fork. A narrow strip of grass and a fence of wood and wire separated the houses. Daddy put up a swing on the front porch where Mommy could sit of an evening and shuck the beans that she grew in the company garden. Ivy grew on one end of the porch, and flower boxes full of red and white petunias lined the bannisters. Coal dust speckled the flowers. Each day Mommy splashed the petals with water and gently wiped them clean with a dry cloth.

Daddy didn't work on Sundays. He would have liked to, because he was paid by the ton and would make more with an extra day's work. But the mine owner, Mr. Davidson, who was an Episcopalian, said the miners owed the Lord a day of rest. At first Daddy slept on Sundays, but as I grew older he spent most of the day drinking.

Sometimes C.J. Marcum, a friend of our family, paid the train fare to bring Talcott and me to Annadel. Annadel was seven wooden buildings put together so poorly they all leaned in opposite directions—Ermel Justice's store, stable and smithy, three private dwellings, and two taverns. The main town straddled the forks of Blackberry half a mile from the Justice farmhouse. C.J. and his mamaw, Missouri, still lived at the farmhouse at that time.

Talcott and I loved to play with Isom Justice and his sister Pricie. We climbed the mountain behind the Justice farm to a cave overlooking the railroad cut. Inside, we crouched together, the rough stone wall chafing our backs where we leaned. Isom told haint stories. When he stood close to the cave's mouth, framed by the sunlight beyond the darkness, the ridges and peaks of his curly mop of hair formed a silhouette like a miniature mountain range.

"Who-o-o!" he cried at the climax of the story. He rolled his head upon his neck and waved his arms. Pricie would scream with fear and delight. But Isom could never match the shrieking of the trains that roared through the cut and blew their whistle on the approach to Annadel. These were like the cries of evil fairies Mommy sometimes warned us about, the henchmen of the Unseelie Court seeking lost souls. Even I was frightened of the trains, but we couldn't bring ourselves to abandon the cave above the tracks.

Often we would swing across the fifty-foot precipice on grapevines. The vines, gray and scaly, creaked like an old wooden floor as they bore our weight out over the cliff. We launched ourselves from a moss-covered root, and if we misjudged our return, our bodies slammed into the broad oak that harbored the vine. Too shaken to swing out again, we must wait to be hauled up to safety.

I helped with the blacksmithing, taking turns with Isom cranking the blower. The blower kept the fire roaring, the fire where Ermel laid his slender lengths of black iron. The hot irons glowed orange and appeared fragile and clear as glass. Ermel plucked a length of iron with his tongs, laid it across the anvil and tapped it into a graceful curve with his hammer. Then he dipped it into a tub of cold water where it sizzled and spat before surrendering in a cloud of steam. A line of finished horseshoes hung beside the tub.

"You remember, boys," Ermel said, "anything will bend if you put enough fire to it. You remember that."

Sometimes C.J. and Ermel took us squirrel hunting. Isom and Talcott were better shots than me. Talcott, Ermel claimed, was the best he had seen. Besides the squirrels, we shot rabbits, and possums for baking with sweet potatoes. I would take some dressed back home to Mommy. It was the only meat we got except bacon and an occasional chicken or ham on holidays.

I loved to hunt, to tramp through the woods with my friends, to climb the mountains far away from the coal camps and wonder which mountain my Uncle Dillon lived on. But I didn't like to shoot the squirrels, though I was ashamed to admit it. Isom always whooped when he hit one. Sometimes I would have a squirrel in my sights and remember what it would look like dressed out, naked and long limbed like a skinny little man. I would miss on purpose and the others would tease me for being a bad shot. Then I would be mad and go out of my way to shoot another one, never wavering as I pulled the trigger, then feeling a wave of remorse when I retrieved the warm body. I dressed my squirrels quickly and cut them into pieces, for then they were not something that had lived, they were meat that would feed Mommy and put color in her cheeks.

We always ate a big supper before we went back to Winco, and we played music afterwards. I took my banjo that Uncle Dillon made me before he went off. Garmon Tackett taught me to play, and Isom learned the fiddle from Ermel. We liked especially to play, "Sally Ann." But the first song we learned was "Boil That Cabbage Down," because it was easy. Talcott, not yet big enough for the guitar, sang along. Isom sawed the fiddle hard, elbow flying to and fro. I learned to flail and drop my thumb. *Boil that cabbage down, bake that hoecake brown.*

I took my banjo to school one day and picked and sang "Cripple Creek" for Miss Radcliffe. I hoped she would let me pick instead of reciting the Declaration of Independence. But she only said "How nice," and pressed her lips tightly together.

C.J. Marcum used to come visit on Sundays, sit on the front porch with me and sip iced tea he brought up from Annadel.

"One of these days . . ." he was always saying. "One of these days we'll git that land back. One of these days you'll go off to school and come back and help your people."

C.J. and Miss Radcliffe were the only ones who talked about "my people." I wasn't sure who "my people" were. Were they my kin, most of them scattered when the land was lost? Were they the old-timers who had been around before the companies came in? What of the Italians and the Poles and the Hungarians and the Negroes, hauled in by the trainload to dig the coal? Were they my people, too?

I studied the Italian children in my school. They were different from me, talked different, smelled different. While we brought biscuits spread with sorghum for our dinner, they ate hard white bread soaked with olive oil. Their skin was darker, their hair shiny and thick like a groundhog's coat. They wore garlands of garlic around their necks, instead of asaphidity bags, to ward off colds. They were bigger than we were, for their difficulty in understanding English caused them to be held back in school. Big Italian boys beat me up on several occasions.

I asked C.J. if they would be returning to Italy "one of these days." He rubbed his square chin.

"I reckon they's land enough for all," he said after a time. "I like to think we can live together ifn we have to. Hit wont never be the same, but we'll have to do the best we can."

C.J. hated the coal camps, had as little to do with them as possible. He rarely went to Jenkinjones, at the head of the Pliny, although it was only two miles from Annadel. He passed through Felco, then the largest camp, on the train, and only came to Winco to see me. He usually brought a newspaper with him, the *Justice Clarion*, or the *Charleston Gazette* when he could get it. He said there were things going on in the world I would never learn in a coal operator's school, and was always pointing out stories about revolts in the Philippines or strikes in Massachusetts.

"I fret about you growing up here," he said. We sat on our porch swing. "Company runs everything, makes all your daddy's decisions for him, even gits his mail. Hit's like Russia with that there Czar. Your daddy aint a free man. He's like a slave."

"Aint nothing he can do about it," I said defensively. I didn't like to think I came form a cowardly daddy.

"Aint nothing he is doing about it except drinking," C.J. said.

I shushed him, afraid Mommy might be listening and send him away. "Hit eases his back," I whispered.

C.J. pushed back and forth hard with his legs. I looked anxiously at the ceiling to see if the swing would hold. C.J. was a big man, over six feet tall and two hundred pounds, and his end of the swing tipped lower than mine so that I was jerked back and forth each time he pushed off.

"What you learning in school these days?" he asked.

"I'm a-memorizing the Declaration of Independence for Class Day. Can I practice on you? 'When in the course of human events . . .' "

I spoke proudly and confidently. I had already practiced before the class and Miss Radcliffe said I had "presence."

I stopped breathless with "the pursuit of happiness" and waited for his praise.

"That it?" he asked, like he was disgusted.

I nodded, hurt.

"Aint it just like them," he said. "Where's the rest of it? Where's the part about overthrowing the government?"

"I don't know nothing about that. Miss Radcliffe just wrote this here out for me on a scrap of paper."

"Declaration of Independence says we got a right to overthrow the government when it gits worthless," C.J. said grumpily. "I'd like to hear about that there sometime."

I wanted to hear that I had presence, but C.J. was in a bad mood the rest of the day. His parting words were a vow to bring me a copy of the complete Declaration to read.

In fact, his visits became less frequent after that. A company policeman told him he came too often; the company did not like outsiders to be such regular visitors. He was welcome only once a month, and then he must tell the police he was there.

C.J. tried to save me from the mines. It was like him to think that he could. Daddy started taking me with him when I was ten. The law said you had to be fourteen, but the company looked the other way. Daddy thought if I helped, he might get out of debt to the company store. C.J. came down to argue with him.

"They aint never going to let you out of debt," he said. "The bastards is weighing you light as it is. They'll keep right on no matter how much coal that boy loads."

"It will help," Daddy insisted. "Denbigh says hit could mean as much as fifty cent more a day. And he's taking Talcott on as a breaker. We'll do a lots better."

"What about Rondal's schooling?"

"What about it? He cant eat them books."

"He could be a lawyer or a doctor someday."

"Someday. You're a-talking twenty year down the road about something might as well be a fairy story. Boy aint smart enough for that."

"That boy is plenty smart. You just aint around to see it. They got you stuck in that hole so you don't know what's going on in the world."

"Damn it, C.J., I know what it takes to live. Look at my woman. She aint nothing but skin and bones. She don't eat no supper half the time sos the younguns can have some. Schooling takes money, and I aint got none. Have you?"

My heart sank when C.J. shook his head.

"No, I aint got it right now. Maybe in a couple years. Ermel talks about setting me up with a store in Annadel."

"Then tell me about it in a couple of years. Right now, I cant see wasting no more time on schooling when they'll just be teaching the boy what that boss wants him to know anyhow. Hit's got nothing to do with us that I can tell."

I didn't sleep that night, and hid under the bed the next morning when I heard Daddy get up. I hoped he would think I had run away. But Talcott was awakened by Daddy's swearing and said, "He was just here. The bed is still yet warm." Daddy looked all over, went out on the front porch and hollered, stuck his head under the house and rousted out the dogs. It was Mommy found me and dragged me out from under the bed. Daddy took the belt to me.

"Later we git started, longer we got to work. Otherwise theys one less biscuit on the plate. You git that through your head, boy."

I went to the mines with a sore back from his strap. I had on my first pair of boots. They were too large and rubbed blisters on my heels before we even reached the tipple. I told Daddy and he said, "We'll tell your mommy to put you on two pair of socks next time."

An early morning rain fell as we walked past the outbuildings—the engine house, the supply house, the blacksmith's and new powerhouse, all built of solid brown blocks of stone with high windows of thick cloudy glass. Daddy and I held Talcott's hands. We took him to the breaker boys' shed. Here the chunks of coal came trundling in on conveyor belts, and Talcott would sit beside the moving line and pick out pieces of slate to be discarded. The shed was drafty and the roof leaked. Drops of water left hissing round craters in the coal dust on the floor. Some of the boys were already at their places, hunched on wooden boxes beside the conveyors like they had been working all day, even though the coal hadn't started to run yet. The boss man paced back and forth, a stick in his hand, ready to strike the shoulders of any boy who missed a piece of slate.

"He's going to hit me with that there stick," Talcott whimpered. He was only eight years old.

"You just do what the man says." Daddy sat him down on a stool. "Don't you back talk him. Mommy put a piece of dried apple pie in your dinner pail, special for your first day. Don't let nobody else git a holt of it."

We left quick before Talcott could commence to crying. Soon after we walked into the drift mouth, we passed the underground mule stable.

"Can I pet one of them mules?"

"Hell, no. We aint got time to pet no mules. This is the coal mine, this aint Ermel's damn farm. Besides, them mules is mean. They'll take your hand right off."

One mule was led out in from of us and I gave its flank a furtive pat. Its hair was sticky with sweat and dust. The skinner saw me and yelled, "Git back fore you get your head kicked in!" Daddy grabbed my arm and pulled me along behind him.

"Git offn that track. You got to git in the habit of watching out for cars, or you'll git run over."

I shrank against the ribs of the tunnel, walking so close that I kept bumping into the wall and staggering. I was afraid some invisible force would drag me into the path of an oncoming coal car. Once I looked back. The drift mouth was small, a milky gray circle that promised the dawn.

"Say goodbye to the light," Daddy said. "Hit will be dark when we come out of here."

It wasn't really light outside. But the weeds had smelled strong and green in the spring dew, mourning doves and meadowlarks had cried for the sun to rise, and a breeze ruffled the fine hair at the nape of my neck. Now there was no movement of air except the unnatural breath of the trap doors opening and closing in the tunnels. The smell was like the inside of our coal stove, but damp and decaying. Ahead of us, lamps bobbed like monstrous lightning bugs. Here and there an arm swung free from the darkness and disappeared again. I felt the mountain hunkered over us, pressing down, and it was hard to breathe.

"Daddy, I cant do this."

"Other younguns do it. You aint nothing special. You'll git used to it."

I knew there were other children in the mine. Boys at my school were always dropping out to go to work. I would lose sight of them for weeks, then they would reappear on a Sunday afternoon, some with chaws of tobacco bulging in their cheeks, looking hard and wise like little old men. I felt ashamed when I thought of them. Daddy was right. I was due no special privileges.

I knew the boy on the first trap door we came to. He was an Italian who went to first grade with me. His job was to pump the trap door all day long, keep the air moving. He had to open the door for the mule trains too, and keep out of the way so he wouldn't be run down. When the light from my cap reached his door, I saw he had been writing on it with slate. DO NOT SCARE THE BIRDS, he had scrawled, and beneath that a picture of a canary with fancy swirls on its wings. I raised my hand to him. He nodded briefly as he hauled on the door.

We walked almost two miles in. It was low coal so that Daddy and his buddy must always crawl, but I was short for my age and could walk if I bent over. I was called on to fetch and carry the tools, the auger, rod and black powder. Daddy stretched out on his belly and showed me how they would work.

"This is called our place and that there is the face of the coal. We drill in there with our auger and then we tamp in the powder and dirt and the needle. Tamp it in tight as a virgin's ass. Then we pull out the needle and stick the squib in the hole and light it. Then we git for cover on our hands and knees. You stay put out of the way while that's going on. You'll help is load the coal after it blows."

Daddy's buddy, Joe Kracj, crawled in and was listening but not understanding a word. He was a foreigner. I couldn't see his face in the dark because of the carbide lamp on his head, and it occurred to me that I might work with him all day and never recognize him outside the mine.

"You git down when the coal starts to blow," Daddy said. "Put your head down. You'll know hits a-coming when I holler out like this."

He leaned back and yelled, "Fi-i-i-yah! Fire in the hole!" He laughed. "I allays do the hollering cause hit just dont sound right when ole Joe does it."

I went back where Daddy showed me to wait while they drilled. I tried not to think of the mountain pushing down on us. To distract myself, I bobbed my head up and down and watched the light from my lamp skitter across the ribs and timbers. It was quieter than I had expected. Puffs of coal dust danced in my lamplight. I heard a steady plopping of water, like a banjo played with only one note. My eyes were heavy with the darkness. I longed to see the mine lit just once, to possess a magical eyesight that could see the men all at their places; Daddy crawling on his belly in the number four coal; others drilling upright in the number five; the skinners driving their mules; the trappers opening and closing the trap doors. I felt them trying to breathe together as one, in unison with my own heaving chest. The air was still and our breathing could not move it. The mountain pressed down, uneasy at the violation of it entrails. Daddy hollered. The air blew apart. I bounced onto my belly, covered my ears with the heels of my hands. The earth stroked my chest, my thighs.

Daddy emerged from a billowing black cloud.

"Come on, boy, time to break it up and load it."

I jumped up and hit my head on the roof.

When we left the mine at the end of the day I was so weary from shovelling coal that I could not walk very fast. When we came for Talcott, he could not stand up, but sat hunched over on his bench. Daddy picked him up and he cried out.

"Dont worry, son," Daddy said. "You'll git toughened up."

I heard Mommy crying in the kitchen that night before I slept.

"What an I supposed to do? I'm a-scairt to hug my own babies for fear of hurting them. I seen bruises all over Talcott's back where that boss man hit on him. Aint no mother supposed to let such things happen to her younguns."

"Shut up!" Daddy said. "I can take care of them boys."

I closed my eyes.

The pain in my body settled into a dull ache. I went on. For the first time in memory, I spent time with my daddy. I came to realize that he was glad to have me with him. He had few ways of showing it. We seldom spoke underground. We were too busy with our picks and shovels, straining to load as many tons as we could, for the more we loaded, the more we were supposed to earn. But when we left the mine, Daddy sometimes pulled off my cap and gently rubbed his knuckles back and forth across the top of my head. He could never bring himself to touch me with the fleshy palms of his hands. But I knew he loved me.

It was Mommy I missed now. I only saw her on Sundays, except for a few moments in the early morning and late at night. Even on Sundays she seemed more distant. She went to church and stayed all morning, or worked in the garden and told me not to come bother her.

One Sunday when she was outside, I got the idea of reading the newspapers covering the walls. I missed C.J.'s visits with the *Justice Clarion*, missed the books at school. The newspapers were new; Mommy had put them up that very week. I brought a wooden chair from the kitchen and set it by the front door, lit a kerosene lantern, and stretched on tiptoe to read the headlines near the ceiling. When I had read halfway down the wall, I got down and stood on the floor, then hunkered down to study the articles near the baseboard. I worked my way around the room, even removed the calendar with the picture of Jesus given out by Ermel Justice's store so I could read beneath it. I was wedged in tight behind the black pot-bellied stove, my rear end pressed against the pipe, engrossed in an account of how European companies would soon be mining coal in China, when there came a sizzle and pop and a burst of acrid smoke. The heat from the lantern's chimney had set the wall on fire.

I squirmed from behind the stove, ran outside to the rain barrel, returned with a bucket of water. I dashed the water against the wall. A gaping black-edged hole was left in Mommy's clean newsprint wallpaper, but the flames were dead.

I went to find her in the garden.

"What you doing down here?" she said. She was clearing a patch for fall planting.

I told her what I had done. When she didn't answer, I said, "You going to switch me?"

"Why should I?" She chipped at the ground with her hoe. "You done gone in the mines. Aint no switch going to faze you none. Your daddy done made a man outen you. I cant do nothing with you now."

I wished she would whip me about the bare legs with a briar switch, like in the old days, then weep at the sight of the scratches, hug me and feed me an apple butter biscuit. But I was left lonesome to chastise myself.

One of my jobs in the mine was to keep an eye on our canary. We were always in danger from black damp, an odorless poison gas that collected in pockets where we blasted. We kept the bird in a small wooden cage at our place. If we hit a pocket of black damp the bird would fall over dead, and we would know to run. It didn't take long for black damp to kill a man.

I grew fond of our bird, and named him Butterball. He was a sooty gray color from the coal dust, but I could ruffle his feathers with the tip of my finger and reveal tufts of yellow down. I began taking his cage with me to the dinner place where we met other miners to eat our bait. The other boys teased me at first, but then they started to bring their birds too. We argued about whose bird was the best.

One of the Negro boys, Antoine Jones, had the biggest bird of all. He named him Tiger. The others agreed Tiger could lick any bird in the mine. But I wasn't so sure. Butterball was small, but he jumped around con-stantly and had a bald spot on his scalp from hitting his head on the top of the tiny cage. I pointed this out to the others.

"He's like a banty rooster," I said. "He's born to fight."

"My daddy raises fighting birds," Antoine countered. "He aint lost a cockfight in years. And he taught me a lot. Your bird couldn't beat Tiger."

Tommy Slater proposed a fight. The loser would have to give the winner his bait to eat. I was reluctant because bird fights were supposed to be to the death. But I couldn't back down since I'd done too much bragging. We unlatched the doors, stuck the cages together and shook them sideways until Butterball was coaxed into the bottom of Tiger's cage. He fluttered his wings and pranced nervously in one corner.

"Git up on the perch!" Antoine urged. "Get up there and fight, you coward!"

"He aint no coward!" I protested. "Tiger don't know what to do neither."

Tiger sat on the bar and craned his head.

All the boys started yelling. "Come on! Fight, you cowards! Sic him, Tiger!"

The birds just sat.

"We got to make them mad," Tommy Slater said. He picked up the cage and shook it. Tiger clutched the wooden perch and Butterball flew against the bars in a panic. "Come on! Fight!" Tommy shook the cage harder, up and down.

"Stop it!" I jerked the cage away from him. Tiger stood up in the bottom of the cage, wobbling like he was drunk. Butterball lay still, his head twisted sideways.

"He's dead!" Antoine shouted. "Your bird is dead! Tiger wins!"

He opened my dinner pail, sorting out the biscuits and side meat. I didn't care about the food. I reached into the cage and picked up Butterball as gently as I could. His head fell across my finger. I wrapped him in my bandana, concentrating hard on being neat so the others wouldn't see me cry. When they were busy talking, I slipped back to Daddy's place to be alone.

That night I took Butterball down by the creek to bury him. But I decided it would be cruel to put him back under the ground, so I made a pyre out of twigs, laid the stiff body upon it, and set it on fire. It burned quickly. A breeze bore away the gray flakes of ash.

The next day we went into the hole after we shot the coal, on our hands and knees, Joe Kracj first, then me, then Daddy. Like we always went in. Suddenly the air cracked; Daddy gripped my ankle and dragged me backwards; thunder filled my ears and a steaming slab of rock sat where Joe had been. I screamed. Daddy kept dragging me backward. I screamed again and again.

I sat beside the prop while they dug for Joe. Daddy sent me away but I crawled back in to see if I could help. A gritty fist stuck out from beneath the slab of rock. They broke the rock up and lifted it away. His arm was mashed flat and spread wide like the body of a frog run over by a wagon wheel. Daddy turned away, cussing, and saw me.

"Jesus God! Didn't I tell you to git?"

"Take him on home, Clabe," someone said.

He carried me out. The women had heard the whistle blow and gathered at the tipple to learn who was killed. Mommy was there. She came forward, her face wild.

"What are you doing down there?" She shook me. "I done lost you. Coal mine will git you sure. You're bound to git kilt. I seen it coming."

She kept shaking me. I tried to cry out for her to stop, but no words would come. Daddy carried me home, undressed me, bathed me and sat me before the stove. He paced up and down.

"It happens," he said. "Hit's one of them things. Joe's number was up, that's all. When it comes, you cant stop it, no matter where you are."

I opened my mouth to speak but still I could not. I was mute for three days. My tongue felt like it had swelled to twice its normal size, and it pained me to swallow. Talcott crept to where I sat beside the stove, plucked at my sleeve.

"Why cant you talk none, Rondal?"

I shook my head and concentrated on breathing, afraid that if I didn't think about it, I would stop.

C.J. heard what happened and came to see us.

"I'm setting up my store next month," he said to Daddy. "Drug store. Let the boy come to me. He can go to school, work the store in the afternoons, send the money back to you."

"What do you think, Vernie?" Daddy asked.

"I don't care," Mommy said in a flat voice.

"He's still yet my boy," Daddy said. "He don't want to leave home so young. Besides, I need his help. He cant make as much in no store."

"Twenty-five cent a day," said C.J. "Hit's something anyhow. Ask him. Ask him what he wants to do."

"He cant talk," Mommy said.

"Ah-h," I said. "Ah-"

They all looked at me.

"Ifn that boy leaves," said Daddy, "I'll take Talcott in. Hit comforts me to have my boys around."

C.J. walked to the door. "You got to talk, Rondal. You got to say what you're going to do. Hit's your choice."

I motioned for a pencil to write with.

"No," C.J. said. "You got to say it."

So I tongued the words as though speaking a new and exotic language.

"C.J." I said. "C.J. Take me."

Talcott ran away from home the day after I left. Daddy found him below Felco and wore him out with his strap.

The Burlap Bag

Davis Grubb

*T*he room of the house was warm, for the Christmas morning itself was unseasonably warm. Liza fanned herself with a cardboard fan from the undertaker's establishment they had visited the day before. She stared out the window by the scuffed, warped door at the melting expanse of snow which stretched to the river.

She wore five petticoats, three sweaters from the relief people, army socks and a heavy pair of man's work brogans. Yet, as was she, her clothes were immaculate as she tilted to and fro rhythmically in her rocker.

On her old face was all of her past. Wars had been fought, won and lost, battles and sieges had raged across the contours of that face, leaving it trampled some, shell-scarred a bit and rutted with the wheels of life's jostling caissons. Yet there was still upon the face fortitude, even merriment, which was unvanquished, even virgin, a face still capable of bristling outrages and incontinent and outrageous joys. Snows seemed to have fallen on the territory of that face, too, snows of yesteryear drifted in her piled white hair.

She stared now across the poorly furnished room at her latest sorrow, her daughter Lovey's stillborn infant. The dead child lay like a small, translucent figurine cast in beeswax, in a cheap, small, pine coffin which rested upon two sawhorses, the legs of which were wrapped in pale, blue satin bunting.

It was all for the best, the old woman mused, rocking all the faster, for Lovey—like her sister Dovey, who was knifed to death by her lover in a speakeasy called the Blue Moon—was a whore in a Baltimore Street whorehouse, and, had the child been born alive and kicking, the relief people would surely have taken it and put it Lord knows where. Liza flung her face around to regard the dead baby for an instant and then, unable to endure the spectacle any longer, rose and stole to the wall where her dulcimer hung, fetched it back to the rocker, laid it across her knees and began playing and singing in a young, high, keening voice:

> Oh, my lover he roves, he trips the groves
> He trips both groves and valleys,
> Scarce in the dew, there could I view
> The tracks of my loved Molly!

The irrelevancy of the lyric to the occasion, Death or Christmas either one, troubled her not the slightest. And with no further glance at the infant's coffin, cheap yet somehow as elegant as a satin lined candy-box, she went on in her clear, sweet voice:

> Last night I made my bed so wide
> Tonight I'll make it narrow:
> With a pretty baby by my side,
> And a dead man for hits father!

Attracted by her singing, for she sang less and less these days, the two little boys of the dead Dovey came into the room for they gloried in her songs, so full of gypsies and kings and gore.

It was a large country boardinghouse they lived in, down the Ohio River a mile from Glory. Somewhere from afar in the upper recesses of the great ragged building came the drunken laughter of one of the boarders and the crash of a festive bottle against the wall.

Twins seemed to run in that family. Wilfred and Pretty Boy, he had been christened that in memory of the poorboy Floyd, were five. They were, oddly enough, considering their parents, reasonably bright and curious and mischievous. They came now to the woman's side, resting their small fingers on the wicker of her old rocker and breathing in her clean smell of camphor and arnica and the rose petal sachet bags she stitched and filled every autumn and packed among her things.

"Grandma," asked Pretty Boy. "Sing us the Cherry Tree Ballat."

Liza shook her head and fetched from the unfathomable deeps of her skirts and sweaters and petticoats a small can of snuff.

"The Cherry Tree Ballat," asked Wilfred. "Hit's Christmas, Grandma, and you done sing hit ever' year since we was borned."

"But this Christmas," said the old woman, "hit's not the same, children. With that poor dead child yonder in its pine coffin. And Lovey sleepin' off a bad drunk in that house on Baltimore Street."

She shook her head fiercely, not smiling and then abruptly smiling: that smile which is the vainglorious reflex of the poor.

"What kind of Christmas morn is this!" she cried out then, laying the dulcimer on the carpetless floor beside her rocker. "Lovey off drunk and whorin'! That poor stillborn baby yonder in hit's coffin, and she'll not show up when the county and the preacher come to take it this afternoon. And what's worstest of all, not a Christmas toy in sight for you two younglings!"

She smiled at the children.

"Fetch me my burlap bag from the pantry," she said. "Hit's like as not about to turn afreezin' tonight for there's a west wind from across the river. And I must go up and gather coal on the railroad tracks for the stove."

The burlap bag meant a great deal to her. Fright trains, swaying and clashing past along the river route spilled goodly sized lumps from the high heaped hoppers and these were the family's sole means of warmth and fuel for cooking. Now the children paid her no mind.

Pretty Boy snuffled his runny nose and sleeved at it.

"How come we never got no toy this year, Grandma?" he asked candidly. "Was we bad this year gone by?"

"No, lambs, no," cried the old woman, ruefully. "You been angels the livelong year!"

She let her gaze stray then into the snow, pristine and unsullied, beyond the window glass which was so old it was wrinkled.

"There warn't no money for toys," she said. "Because ever' penny of the Christmas relief chick hit went to buy that poor dead babe hits little coffin and a gown and a bit of fancying cloth and them two saw horses hits coffin rests upon."

She thrust her rough brogans hard against the floor and set her bulging wicker chair rocking faster than ever. The children wandered off. Liza was heedless of them now: her griefs and shames had overtaken her now and for an instant she was a little mad, like an ancient Ophelia, and then she rallied: flung her head back again: still a little mad, yet stubbornly fending off her feelings and chanting into the hushed air of the stuffy, sealed room.

> Last night I made my bed so wide
> Tonight I'll make it narrow!
> With a pretty baby by my side—.

Then she stopped and coughed, wheezing a little with her asthma like a sound from a broken concertina, and settled back in her rocker for a little nap before she fetched the burlap bag herself and went into the cold and gathered the coal along the rocky ballast of the railroad tracks. Sorrow and misfortune always made her either furious with outrage or drowsy, and the thought of the dead infant and no toys for Dovey's bastard younglings, this was all too much. She slept now in her chair, heedless of them, dreaming of her beauty and youth at Raven's Rock.

Pretty Boy, the bolder of the two children, sidled over to the small, garishly ruched coffin and looked at the motionless infant. Wilfred came presently to his side, full of the same thought.

Liza was deep asleep now, and snoring like a paper nest of wasps in the eaves of a stable, and Pretty Boy had the dead infant out of its coffin now and fetched it off to a place that was warm by the black iron stove, for the room was growing chilly as the coals in the fire clinkered down. His twin witnessed this audacity with envious awe. One finger was sucked guiltily into his lips.

"Grandma she'll git awful mad, Pretty Boy, if she waked and catches us," he said. "And what if Aunt Lovey was to come home unespected?"

"She's in that house on Baltimore Street," Pretty Boy said. "A-whorin'."

Pretty Boy glared back stubbornly, holding the dead infant tight in his grip, its long white burial gown draped over his arm.

"I don't aim to harm it none," he said. "Scuff it up or git it dirty. I just want to play with it for a while."

"How come?" asked Wilfred.

"You don't see no other toys around this Christmas mornin', do you?" he whispered savagely, resentfully.

He pondered it a moment, ferreting out better reasons.

"In some ways," he observed. "Hit's better than a fake play-toy. This here baby doll—hit's real."

Wilfred still sucked on his finger, the only clean one, full of awe and admiration and many other emotions for the boldly brother. He watched as the latter attempted to stand the dead child on its tiny bootied feet and ended by propping it against the wall.

"When we git done playin' with it a spell," he said, "We'll put it back. And neither Grandma nor Lovey need never know."

He scowled thoughtfully, inventively, at the object.

"We could play store with it," he said. "And sell it things. If we had somethin' to sell."

Wilfred, emboldened now, approached a few feet closer to Pretty Boy by the stove and the dead infant propped against the soiled, mildewed wall. He had propped it hastily so that it tilted a little drunkenly to leeward. Wilfred, halting in his emboldened approach, thought of a fresh objection, with a sidelong and uneasy glance at the snoring old woman, the mute dulcimer by her side.

"Playin' with hit thisaway, Pretty Boy," he said. "We'ns might catch somethin' from hit."

"Catch what, if I may ask?"

"I don't know. Catch hits—its deadness."

Pretty Boy scoffed and seized the dead child up again.

"Hit never died at all," he said. "For hit was born dead. It never even breathed nor cried nor caught a sight of the sun. So there couldn't be nothin' to catch."

Pretty Boy propped the long-gowned corpse against the wooden box where they kept the coal. Wilfred grew more uneasy by the minute and gasped when the dead child, abruptly, slipped from its erect posture and fell, striking the harsh, scrubbed floor with a muffled thump. Liza murmured a snatch of a ballat in her sleep at the faint and distant disturbance.

To the dismay now not only of Wilfred but of Pretty Boy the shock of the fall had opened one blue eye so that it stared up at the boys. This development so unnerved Wilfred that he sat down suddenly, cross-legged, on the floor, as though his legs had failed him. He sucked on the one clean finger again.

"Jist look, Pretty Boy," he said. "Like hit war awatching us. Knowing. Thinking. Wishing a curse onto us maybe."

Pretty Boy snorted contempt at this thesis, fetching the body up from the floor, brushing off some coal dust and carrying it to the bench by the front door. With some effort he bent the tiny legs at the hips and set it upright there. The open eye seemed more acutely cognizant and indicting than before. Yet Pretty Boy ignored this. Wilfred felt the gathering coldness in the room as the glowing cinders in the coal stove dwindled and diminished. The one open eye seemed to give to the face a kenning and arcane knowing beyond the understanding of either of the children.

"There now," Pretty Boy commanded. "You jist sit there, baby, and don't you dasn't move. I'm the county health doctor and I come to make you well."

He pondered this, staring, and came up with a more appropriately ecclesiastical improvisation.

"No," he said. "I take that back. I hain't the county doctor at all. Set there like a good baby while I tell you who I really am."

His voice fell to an earnest and in no sense blasphemous whisper.

"I'm Lord Jesus," he said. "And you're Sir Lazarus, the Knight, and I done come to raise you from the dead."

Wilfred, a child of more secular leanings, found no consolation in this.

"Do me a big favor, Pretty Boy," he said then. "Either make that one eye be closed again or else open the other one. Hit just plumb gives me the willies with that one astarin' at usns thataway."

Pretty Boy endeavored to comply. The lid of the other eye only opened halfway and would fall back halfway when he pulled it all the way open. The adjustment worsened matters considerably.

"Now!" said Wilfred in a harsh whisper. "Now you done it."

"Hit's better. And hit war your idea anyways, dern you, Wilfred!"

"Lordy, if Grandma don't ever give us both a hiding now!"Wilfred whispered, tears of terror glittering in his eyes. "We went and done it now, Pretty Boy."

"We'll get it straightened out and back in hits coffin ere she ever wakes," Pretty Boy said, calmly. "You know how sound Grandma's little naps are."

"That's just it," said Wilfred. "Her naps. They're little. You never know when she'll wake up spritely as a fox!"

"She's good for another five minutes," Pretty Boy said, appraising the old woman with a measuring stare. "We still got time to git it fixed up proper."

Wilfred got to his legs now and went and sat on the saltbox with frayed carpeting tacked on it that served the room as a stool. Pretty Boy glared at him, forlornly. And there was a glitter in his erstwhile cynical eye now, too.

"Hit's better," he sobbed, "than no playtoy at all, hain't it? Well hain't it, damn you? This hyere—hit's Christmas morning."

Wilfred ignored this sentiment, his gaze mesmerized by the one open eye and the half open eye, both seemingly fixed on him.

"One eye all wide and starey," he murmured. "And the other one sort of squintin'. Looking it was about to make us both be dead like hit is, too."

Pretty Boy waved his hand, having gotten a grip on himself again.

"Hit don't think nothing'," he said. "Dead things they can't think, you derned fool."

Wholly skeptical of this, Wilfred picked his nose, defeated now by the whole dilemma.

Wilfred was by no means the more adventuresome of the two.

Pretty Boy, himself a little unnerved now, struggled desperately with the lids. He got the left eye shut again—almost, let us say. Yet the right eye, the staring one, was now slightly crossed. The dead child's countenance had now assumed an expression beyond mere malevolence or necromancy; it seemed more than a little crazed, as though its mind had been unbalanced by what they were putting it through. Without a moment's more of hesitation Pretty Boy seized up the disarranged body and staked stealthily back to the coffin with it. But it didn't quite fit now. The small legs under the cheesecloth gown were crooked and stiff at the hips and resisted Pretty Boy's panicked attempt to straighten them. A tiny soft bone cracked somewhere within. And the body was even more resistant to its resting place in the Long Home. Pretty Boy with moist, trembling hands seemed now to be struggling in even combat with the tiny body, and losing. At last he turned and crossed the room and sat on the bench, staring at Wilfred.

"See if you can fix hit," he whispered, hopelessly, knowing better than to ask.

"In a pig's ass I will," said Wilfred. "I'm shed of the whole thing."

"Well, what'll we do then?" Pretty Boy sobbed. "Grandma'll wake directly. Lovey she might come home. The people from the welfare and that preacher from the Salvation Army acomin' this afternoon. Jist look at that thing, Wilfred. Hit's plumb ruinet. And we—."

"We, hell," whispered Wilfred furiously. "Hit was you idea and I never had nary a hand in a bit of hit."

Wilfred, if the truth be told, was radiant with mean and scurvy righteous-mindedness that he had had no part in the cosmetic havoc his brother had wrought upon the hapless infant body. Pretty Boy sat still on the bench, as if striving to rid himself of visions of unspeakable eventualities. He spat upon the floor and glowered out the window at the virgin snow that stretched down the slope to the railroad tracks and beyond that to the river banks.

"We jist got to think of somethin'," he sobbed, trembling as if in a fever, the sweat standing in beads on his forehead though by now the room had grown quite chilly.

"I don't mean to brag nor nothin'," Wilfred said at last. "But I got the whole fishing line untangled."

"How? What—?"

"Grandma's burlap coal bag," Wilfred said.

"What about it?"

"We take the baby out of the coffin," Wilfred said. "Put hit in that bag—weight hit down with them four big heavy chunks of coal yonder in the coal box, tie hit at the top with a piece of rope—."

"You don't mean go drop hit in the river?" Pretty Boy whispered.

"Sure," Wilfred said. "Like Aunt Lovey did that litter of kittens oncet."

"Well, then what will we tell them when Grandma wakes up and they all come and the baby hit hain't there?"

"We'll tell them Gypsies come sneaking in," Wilfred said. "Ever'body knows Gypsies loves roasted babies."

Pretty Boy considered this.

"How come them Gypsies never woken up Grandma?"

"Gypsies is soft tredden'," Wilfred said. "And they held knives at our throats to keep us quiet whilst they made off with the poor little body."

Pretty Boy considered this.

"Grandma'll sure raise a ruckus," he said. "She puts a lot of store in that burlap coal bag."

"She can easy get another one."

"Yeah, but you know her. She gits somethin' and hit's the only one in the world. Nothin' can replace hit."

There was no further contention. Pretty Boy fetched the burlap bag from the pantry, carried it to the coal box, took out four or five heavy lumps, dropped them in the bag and carried it to the coffin. Then, wholly lacking in decorum or solemnity, he tucked the dead child in. They found a length of clothesline, cut off a yard and tied the bag at the top. Then, creeping across the old and squeaking wood of the floor, opened the front door softly, left with their burden and made their way down the snow which, having fallen in the night, bore, as yet, no footprint. On the way Pretty Boy almost lost his grit.

"Grandma," he said. "She's sure to suspicion us when she finds that burlap bag gone. I tell you she puts a lot of store in that bag. Fetches coal home in it every day."

"I'll think of something to tell her," Wilfred said. "I thought of this didn't I? Don't you reckon I can figure out a fib about the burlap bag?"

"Couldn't we just save the bag?" inquired Pretty Boy, still apprehensive. "And just dump the body in the river?"

Wilfred stared at him contemptuously.

"Pretty Boy," he said. "Sometimes I suspicion you're as simple-minded as Lovey."

"Well, could we—?"

"Sure," Wilfred said. "And have some of them shanty boat trash down river see it floating past and drag it in with a gaff and fetch it back to the house in worse shape than you got it into now. Or maybe have it float all the way down to Dam Number 20 and have the lockmaster find it. And fetch it to the county courthouse."

Pretty Boy pondered still.

"Don't dead things sink just natural?"

"Hell no. Now come on. Get some sand in your craw. Let's get this done and over with and be up in our rooms when Grandma wakes."

They came to the river's edge, where the cattails grow in the spring and the catfish leap on moonlit nights like dark dolphins in some Silurian ocean which once that land had been. Pretty Boy wasn't up to it. It took Wilfred to haul off and fling the burden as far as he could out into the deeper part of the river, beyond the shoals, and both stood watching as it disappeared, a few bubbles bursting as they rose from it, and then the river moved on unruffled and unrevealing.

From afar then, from the town of Glory now, came the clear clarion of bells from a dozen churches, each a different timbre and voice, each praising the day and the child and its mother, Maid Mary; their stumbling, bronze and iron chanting telling the hushed, expectant air of the approaching Magi and the star and the Mother—Maid Mary—and the speaking beasts of stable and stall, and poor bewildered Joseph, cuckold of God as the old ballads irreverently yet reasonably infer. They were back in the big room by then and Liza was awake. She smiled at them. And the distant, unbridled ecstasy of the chanting bells set her off. She flung back her face, sang out loud:

> Lulee Lulay! Lulee Lulay!
> The Babe hit is born this Christmas Day!

Conscience can be conquered. Rationalized. Stifled. Forgotten. But seldom in the minds of children. It was Wilfred who, weeping as hard as Pretty Boy, came forth to the old woman's chair to make the fearsome confessions. When he was done the old woman was unperturbed, indifferent. She seemed not even to hear them.

"Whilst I was nodding in my rocker," she said. "I had a dream. No—hit war more than a dream, darlings. Hit war a vision!"

The children waited.

"I dreamed—I seed it—Maid Mary acoming down to take up poor Lovey's stillborn babe from hits coffin," she said. "And she stood there whilst she made it whole again and quick again—not dead. And bore it with her like moonbeam through the ceiling."

She sighed.

"Lord, she was purty," she said. "And I seed her—feeling not fittin'—but I purely couldn't take my eyes away. Golden hair clean to her bare heels and a long gown of dark blue with the crescent moon beneath her little bare feet and stars, like fireflies, shining through her gown."

She looked at the boys and smiled.

"Now what's all this folderol you two been tellin' me about takin' the dead babe from hits coffin yonder and playing with it like a playtoy till hit war all bent out of shape and soiling its poor cheap little burial gown and then dropping hit in the river."

"Hit's gospel truth, Grandma." Pretty Boy, not crying now, having gotten it out of him and ready for whatever chastisement lay ahead.

The old woman smiled radiantly, a countenance behind whose flesh seemed to stand the unwavering flames of waxen tapers, whiter than snow, whiter than the moon, somewhere burning deep behind the life-scarred, yet translucent and uncannily youthful flesh of the ancient and embattled face, the face of one of those, His despised poor. She poked each of them in the ribs with a gnarled forefinger.

"Now no more sich blathering nonsense," she said. "I've got to git me down there on the railroad track and get the big lumps afore them shanty boat trash down in the cattails along the shore beat me to it. Now git! This room's like an ice house."

The children grew stiff as marionettes. Presently Liza grumbled and was off out the front door by herself.

In an amazingly short while she was back with the bag bulging with chunks of good bituminous coal. She went to the stove, emptied the bag into the coal box, tossed it back onto the pantry stool, chose a few goodly sized lumps to lay upon the still glowing clinkers. Then she fetched, from its stone jug, a half a tin cup of coal oil, sloshed it in, and shut the black iron slotted door. She turned and looked at the children an instant before she hobbled across the room and sank into the self-shaped comfort of the creaking wicker rocking chair.

"You can't understand now," she said. "What done come to pass this strange Christmas day. Maybe when you're growed you will, maybe. And then again maybe it will never be made manifest to you. But I tell you true—hit war no dream. I seen Her plain. Heard the dead babe turn quick and commence to cry for the breast of Her."

And she clapped her old hands thrice and snatched up her dulcimer from the floor by the chair and thrumming it merrily began to sing the younglings' favorite, "The Cherry Tree Carol."

Abruptly she stopped her singing and turned her luminous face upon them.

"God save us each!" she cried. "Hain't it a mercy and a goodness to know in our hearts that hit was us'ns Maid Mary chose to fetch a playmate to the lonely, little Lord?"

Yet neither child took heed nor hark to song nor words from Liza. They stood again, having crept there once more, timorously, to the pantry door and stared at it on its stool. The same one. The only one in the house. Liza's coal sack. And beside it the length of clothesline they had bound it with at the top. And both rope and bag bone-dry.

Ruins In Reverse

A. E. Stringer

In holes dug deep in a March
hillside, this dream of home begins:
stones, mortar, more stones.

Come summer, undergrowth will
overlay them. No matter now,
snowy sheet thawed away,

they lie abed, easy to find.
Day upon day, the woman
wears down her spine,

lifting and setting the chosen
into column after column.
Her handiwork is never done.

She can see the future house
override the slope, roof a tin kite
aloft in her eye. Nine months.

The site like a forest of stone,
these piers, trees without branches
or leaves, reach for the floorplan

yet to come. Each one
tilts another way from true.
If she could stand inside one

she would know which vectors
move her, which hold fast. One
August night asleep, her backbone

realigns. Rain runs the grown up
ruins down, carries them
toward the river, last grain first.

Listen

A. E. Stringer

Moon glare. The lake takes
stock. Deer approach the shore,
thirst come down to laps
and airy murmurs.

In rippled sheen that scores
the underleaves of beech
and maple, the water clarifies
its identity with light.

At bottom, the blood of the bass
cools into slumber. A stone
prays to join the circle.
Minuscule bubble

rises toward
the surface of the moon.

My Friend Told Me

A. E. Stringer

When he came upon the family cat
convulsing, chin bubbled with drool,
he recognized the signs of another
poisoned cat, great dry heaves
unmistakable since childhood.

He wrangled the hopeless form
into a pillowcase and pushed it into
a sinkful of water and held on until
the writhing went still. How
cruel are mercy's demands.

He buried it. He washed his hands.
When his children pretty soon asked
after the cat by name, he told them
he had found it already gone. And here
is the grave, he showed them,

as his own father had done.
It is my friend who teaches me
love's requisite dissimulations.
Father to no one, I believe him, place
my life in his children's hands.

The Wars Of Heaven

Richard Currey

*L*isten. Hear me talking to you. Rockwell Lee Junior remembering the glow in your kitchen, Mama, the light that was a mix of gold and blue on a winter's night and the way our talk drifted around like big slow birds in the warm air and Oh what I wouldn't give for one more day in the sweetness of what I didn't know back when, the days before, when I was just a grinning boy in a dirty white shirt, an innocent yes indeed. Or the afternoons sitting at your kitchen table when you'd make me a mug of your coffee, Mama, and sweeten it with clover honey and color it with goat's milk. Always liked your coffee, you know that I did, even when I was a kid I'd ask you for a taste and you'd let me sip from your cup and Daddy grinning at me from across the table. I remember the little circle of heat that would come up from your cup, touch my lips, and what I wouldn't have given for a cup of your coffee, trapped as I was in that icehouse of a sky full of snow where any direction I looked and as far as I could see it was white, whiteness in the trees, humped up against the mountains, whiteness. At least the wind had died down, that was the morning of St. Valentine's Day, at least I could say that because that's what kills you, that's what steals the air out of your lungs, steals the light straight out of your eyes, if anything can do that it's the wind in winter across a field of snow bearing down on you like a ghost train out of nowhere. Early that morning the wind passed off to the north, I could nearly see it go, so God was merciful and I thanked God for that. I dropped to my knees taking care to keep my rifle butt-down and upright leaning against my left shoulder, and I prayed. Thank you Jesus. No wind today. No wind to freeze what life I got left, to steal the light out of my eyes. Thank you Jesus. One more day of life. And Mama, you might ask how it was the condemned man still prayed to his God in the wilderness, you'll say What could I have to say to God and Jesus out there on the run Where could I be going that was any salvation at all after what I done. Maybe this is all I really wanted, a chance at rectitude, restitution by myself and alone and in a place of my own choosing. A simple place where what dreams I might still have harbored could die a tranquil death, lonely as time itself and peaceful as light. And you know the sheriff's posse caught up to me here at Judson Church so there may be a justice in this, an understanding. You know you always said that dreams were made of water and human desire, that dreams went no mortal place at all, they were only man's way to confuse himself and convince himself that a fire was lit at the heart of things. You always said it was nothing but cinder and ashes and now I don't know, the way I walked out there in that whole world of snow with that posse surely on my trail, I don't know, I swear I can't be sure. When I shot that girl you know I saw her fall down right there on her daddy's porch, fall down like a puppet whose strings got cut and I swear I saw the life drawing out of her like light coming out of a window at night. And I was not the man you knew. In that instant I was not the man you ever knew. I was that skeleton engineer on the phantom locomotive in that scare-story you told when I was a kid, I was just one headlong scream into oblivion I swear. At the moment she fell down like an empty sack and I knew what I had done I was lost as I am right now up here in the hills in the snow. Now that it's all too late to think you were wrong, Mama, I think that there is a light down somewhere in the center of things and that if a man knew that for a solid fact he could go down to that place and warm his hands on a cold night. Because how could I be so desperate and finished and on the run and see everything so beautiful and transfixing and everlasting, everywhere I turned was like looking forever, like a picture up on somebody's wall so I had to stop and stand and look into the world for the first and last time, wondering why I never saw it before.

When I got to Judson Church there was enough wood to light a fire and I hung my coat and warmed myself over that stove and thanked the Lord there was no moon that night, no moonlight to let any sheriff's posse see my smoke. No moonlight to show my footprints walking across the snowfield and right up to the church steps. I'd been on the move at night, hiding in tumble-down houses all day with my rifle up and ready and afraid to sleep, and I had my time to think, reflect on things, see where it had all gone bad, and Mama, you know I think it was losing Daddy that did it to us, both of us. It was losing Daddy that took the life out of you, took your own life away from you, that made you so hard and tired and unforgiving. That let your own bitterness rail against you inside like a snow-wind of the very heart and soul I swear, that made you turn away in your loss and violent mind. Mama, I think you died on that old covered bridge with Daddy, I swear I think you did. Daddy was the true anchor, he was the root our lives were growing from when he died only we didn't know it, we were innocents, the two of us. So you claim you know Daddy's killer, that you'd know the face of the devil if you looked straight into that face, and maybe so. But I don't know. All we know is Daddy's body was found on that bridge with his watch and money gone, that's all we really know, and it could have been anybody, it could have been a neighbor or a stranger and we'll never know and that's a fact.

So it's a terrible strange thing that I came to be the very one that killed Daddy for a pittance in the cover of darkness. For we are all of one bad wind, you know that, Mama, all of us robbers and murderers are one evil man split down into a hundred wild boys, all doing the cruel biding of some kind of master within. I had heard that before and now I know it to be true but I never once thought about it, what was happening to me, I never once saw it all coming as I should. I could have turned back a hundred times but I didn't, I was a man on a spooked horse, riding straight into the eyes of a fire and just hanging on for dear life.

You could say it was friends or circumstance or some of both but I can now feel now it was simply Daddy going out the way he did, lost the way he was in some terrible whirlpool of time and I swear I was nothing but a useless boy hanging on a spike thrown this way and that, born under a bad sign, condemned to howl at the moon, to preach to the wind, and I drifted like a rotting boat cut loose on floodwaters after a hard rain, beating from one tree to another until I was out in the main current and running. And that's the way it goes, out there in the deep water with some other power under you and driving you, keeping you whole until finally you hit the rapids and go over the falls.

That's how I came to be in on the robbery of Strother's Store over in the mining camp. The other boys wanted to do it, claimed old Strother kept a mint under the floor behind the cashbox, and I said Well okay. When we got over there I felt no fear, I still cannot explain how I walked right up on the porch and butted my rifle right through the plate glass and opened the door and walked inside like it was my store and not Strother's, but let me tell you it inspired a measure of confidence in those boys that went inside behind me, yes indeed. And you know the strange thing is, I walked into that store holding my rifle up like I was looking to shoot something, walked in and straight back past them tables all laid up with can-goods and linens and bottled water, right back to the rear wall where Strother had all his bridles and reins hung up, and I turned around to face front, leaned against the wall and just stood there. I didn't want a goddamned thing. I didn't care about money, or the things worth stealing in that store. I felt then as I did ever since. I felt mad with temper, and like I could just keep it under my skin if nobody pushed at me. And so goddamned afraid. Afraid of what I've never been truly sure, but I know if the sheriff walked into the middle of that robbery or any other one and shot us all down I wouldn't have much cared, that's the kind of feeling I'm speaking of. And I felt that way until the day I hit Judson Church and looked back on what had gone before, and knew I had to wait in that little house of the Lord, wait there for my redemption in whatever form it was coming and at least I was in a sanctified place.

So I just stood there in Strother's Store while the boys whooped it up and made a mess of the place, and Bob Hanks came back to me, said Rocky what's the matter? And I said I'm just fine, Bob. You just go on and do what you came to do, that's all. And Bob looked at me strange a moment but went on back to work, and when the boys was still and quiet and standing in the doorway with their bags full up I walked over to where they stood and past them and out the door. I stepped down to the road and got in behind the wheel of your truck, Mama, started it up. The boys all filed down and got in, climbed onto the bed, and nobody said a word to me.

They had found old Strother's money pile and split it five ways. Three thousand dollars and change. Everything Strother had in the world and Bob Hanks came over to me with six one-hundred-dollar bills saying This here's your share Rock. And I said Thank you kindly and Bob drew on the whiskey bottle he'd been carrying around and grinned at me. Well sir, he said, you're quite welcome.

And you know, Mama, it was all my plans after that, the branch back over in Federalsville, the general store out to Middle River, right down to the night I shot Betty Shadwell dead on her daddy's front porch and knew I had become the man who speaks to you now in the sure voice of death, dead in the ice, you might even say in the frozen waste of time. Out here in the snow it is surely the end of the world. I could hear the sound of my breath setting up against the air like a rasp: the end of the world I swear.

Outside the church it was going to sunset, the day's light drawing down to that twilight filled with fire-color that burns on the snow before it proceeds to die right into the night. I stirred the wood on the grate and was thankful for that bit of stove heat, wrapped my coat around me and tried to lay down on a pew and saw it wasn't going to work. So I went on and laid down on the floor up against the back wall of the church with a Philadelphia hymnal under my head and the Winchester right there in easy reach. But sleep wasn't about to come. No ma'am. I just lay there, listening to the mice scrap and itch around the floorboards, thieves like me, looking for what isn't there, for what will never be there, and you know how your mind goes into a kind of trance when you're too tired to sleep, how you think crazy things, think the moon moves faster than it does? I lay there on the floor of Judson Church and lived in that half-a-dream, and I saw your face, Mama, and I saw Daddy's, and I saw Rita Clair's face too, it was Rita as I saw her the last time up in the hill over town, sitting on a blanket with that man's workshirt on over nothing, her dress and underwear laid to one side on the grass. We made love up there on that hill, squatting down on that old blanket and moving together and the bees moaning around us and crickets working, every now and again a hot breeze come to rustle in our hair. I had my hands up under that shirt, all over her like I wanted to be more than just inside her, I wanted to melt into her. As if I could just disappear and become part of that one moment, forever, lost in it, outside of this voice that speaks to you now. I raised my face to the sky and the sky was blue as I had never seen and there were clouds as white and soft and eternal-looking as you can imagine and I swear it was as if me and Rita were being raised together into that sky, lifted up, me holding Rita and her in my lap, the both of us panting and wheezing and crying out. We went up in the air floating right out over the brow of that hill, then we started to come down like we were stones settling to the bottom of a slow river, coming down through green light and silence, our ears filled up, our eyes covered over and I thought then, That's right, we're just like rocks thrown into a river. You don't know where you come from or where you're gone, you just get picked up and thrown. But you can have one little moment, yes sir, you can have Rita Clair's sweet fine body on a hill in the middle of a hot summer so as to have a glimpse of what might have been, like looking through a little crack into the future or the past and not knowing which way you're looking, but seeing it all filled up with light and the smell of honey. I laid there, Mama, remembering everything I tell you now, Daddy going the way he did, you turning away from me in your grief, having that little taste of Rita Clair, that little glimpse of heaven and knowing I wasn't fit to have no more than that, and the way I went to stealing and could hate myself so bad and still be so calm, standing at the window of the church and seeing the sheriff and his deputies out there at the treeline like I knew they would be, just shapes out there in those long coats and big hats and the straight black lines of their rifle barrels up against the snow.

There was a thin light seeping into the church, that watery first light you get on a winter dawn. I stood up and shook out of my coat and went to the window and there they were, standing out there looking at my trace across the snowfield, the way it ended right at the church steps.

I turned away from the windows, sat down in a pew. They wouldn't just walk up to the door and knock. No sir. Not with a man like me inside.

Sheriff'd try to get me to come out peaceable, lay down my gun, throw it out in the snow. But he'd be prepared to shoot me.

I got my rifle and went to the window on the other side of the church, unlocked it and slid it up. The stained-glass face of Jesus rose up in front of me and then I saw the snow stretching down to Rucker's Creek and I leaned out and propped my piece against the outside wall of the church, let myself out and down to the snow, waited. I heard nothing. I knew they wouldn't come across the pasture, not with the risk of me being inside the church. They'd be fanning out just inside the treeline, trying to surround me. I started for the trees thinking I could at least get into the woods myself. The snow was frozen over, a crust my boots dropped through an inch, and I saw they'd track me anywhere I went but I had to go, there was nothing else to do. I was halfway to the treeline when I heard my name called out, hollow, booming around in the air. I turned and it was Steward McCarty standing under the stained-glass window I'd left out of with his scattergun trained down on me. *Mr. Lee,* he called out, *just stand where you are real still and put down your rifle.* I could see the smoke of is breath. I raised my Winchester and fired, hit Stewart somewhere above the waist and he grunted, slammed back against the church and slid a red streak down the wall, flopping around in the snow. I turned and ran for the trees.

I could hear the sound of the creek and a man I thought looked like Roy John stepped around in some birches up to my right, and then I knew it was him when he yelled to me *Rockwell Lee, give yourself up now. No use in running no more.*

I turned to the direction of his voice. New snow started to fall. His shape moved back and forth in the trees. *Roy,* I called out. *Roy, help me. What happened, it was an accident.*

Roy John came into full view, aiming his rifle at me. I thought I saw movement behind him. Snow filled the air.

Roy, I said. *Roy, you know me. You know my mama.*

I know what you done, Rock. You're gonna have to come home with us.

The peculiar thing is that I had no intention of killing anyone at the Shadwell place, there or any other place, we just meant to get on out of there with the silver because Bob Hanks knew where the old man kept it in the house. If the old man hadn't come out of the house firing his pistol. I just meant to let go a warning shot, blow out a front window, I swear I didn't even see Betty there on the porch, what was she doing there anyway? You answer me that. I didn't even see her till she fell. Rockwell Lee Junior may have been a robber but he was no murderer. That was a pure accident. It was never meant to be. No sir. So when I lifted my rifle with the intent to throw it down and give myself up and tell my story, Roy John blew off my left shoulder.

The force of it shoved me back and I stumbled, and I had the strangest feeling of surprise but I stayed on my feet and kept hold of my gun. Blood and bone and muscle had sprayed out over the snow like a mist, I could look right down into the hole in my coat where my shoulder had been, an awful burning and the falling snow melting in the wound, steam wisping up out of the hole and my shoulder looking that way got me angry, mad with temper all over again and that terrible fear and I raised my Winchester over my head with my right arm yelling *Goddamn you, Roy, look what you done.*

The second shot was a shotgun, catching me square in the chest, I went off the ground, legs kicking and the force of that shot knocking my right boot off. Damn if I was going to let them take me laying on the ground, I got up again and don't you know I was an awful mess, I looked like the mouth of hell, blood everywhere and my coat hanging on me in rags.

I swayed there in the falling snow. My breath was hard to come by, I could hear air sucking right in through the holes in my chest and the whole lot of them come out of the trees then, the sheriff, Roy John, the rest of the deputies just coming up around me and looking at me and I could see it was Stewart McCarthy who fired the shotgun round. He was back on his feet under that Jesus window and at first I thought I had been shot by a ghost but then I knew I had only wounded him. My eyesight began to go on me then, frayed around the edges in all that whiteness and air filled with snow like an old sheet hung out to dry and coming apart in a heavy wind. Roy John walked up to me and took off his long coat and put it around me. The sheriff came up behind Roy to handcuff my wrists together and standing there half-dead for sure I heard the sound of bells, out in the distance of that snowy air, out in some reach of that wild snowy air there was the slow music of bells and I looked out to the hills and clouds trying to see where that music came from and why it was coming to me. Roy John looked at me and said What is it, Rock?

And I said *Roy, don't you hear 'em? Like church bells.* I raised the handcuffs, my hands clasped together in a fist pointed west, and said *Out there.*

I turned back to Roy John and my knees went to plain water, I fell straight down in the snow on my knees, like a man about to pray, a man calling for mercy. And that is one thing I did not want to be, a man calling for mercy. I did not want to ask for anything, not food or water, not rest, not even for my own life, and I said Roy. *Help me up, now. Don't let me stay down here.* The sheriff stood beside Roy, his shape as big as a tree, the two of them lifting me up, one on either side, and the sheriff said *Let's go, Roy*. And they led me across that snow-covered meadow with the rest of the posse behind us, me with one boot gone and walking short-legged in a sock the same meadow I'd walked across the night before to get to Judson Church. The treeline moved up on us as if the trees were sailing in from a long way off and I could see the sleigh and the two roans snorting and blowing wet smoke in that air and I hope you're happy, Mama, because this is the first and last time you will ever hear this story, your only son shot at Rucker's Creek not five miles from his place of birth, his blood running over the ice like oil and into the water to cloud up colored like a rose and swirl away. I've always heard it said the wars of heaven are fought on righteous ground, Mama, and the godly man shall be the victor. So Roy John helped me up into that sleigh and threw a saddle blanket over me and I laid where I lay, an end to my so-called life of crime, nobody to know how lost I truly was, the man who built his own gallows in the snow, out behind the house of the Lord. I am the man who sought restitution by himself and alone in a place of his own choosing. I am the man who surrendered with one boot gone on St. Valentine's Day, the year of our Lord nineteen hundred and thirteen, with the smell of salt and woodsmoke and gunpowder in the air.

The last of this Lee family is gone now, Daddy crossed over, Rockwell Junior the robber and murderer shot down at Judson Church, and Mama, you know you died with Daddy on that covered bridge and are as gone as me and him, yes you are, sad and gone, and we have suffered for what we didn't know back when and what we couldn't find, and for what we didn't even know we'd lost. And now we are gone, we are history. We are stories nobody tells, Mama, we have disappeared back down to the bottom of that river once and for all.

Ours is the testament of snow. We are in the company of time.

On The Edge Of Highway 10 North

John McKernan

In a deep orange twilight beneath the leafless gingko
        on a tarpaulin of yellow leaves one
mile south of the ghost town Melissa West Virginia

Randolph Gunnoe's red '58 Ford Econline flat-
        bed lugging a dozen junked cars smashed flat
idles in the blue haze of it 30-weight Valvoline

motor oil Hank Williams riding shotgun in nicotine
        air of Country nine-owe-three "It's Bubba
to all you my friends"   Randolph is excited talkative

but his lean daughter Cynthianna is mute "She don't
        want any your help or mine Most she would
take from you right now might be a pair of leather work

gloves so she don't break off her orange and blue sculpted nails
        Cost her foolish twenty dollars downtown"

■ ■ ■ ■ ■ ■ ■ ■ ■ ■ ■ ■ ■ ■ ■ ■ ■ ■

Randolph tells me she'll have the tire changes "in the whisper
        of an eyelash" As I watch her cat-like
moves tap a twenty-pound maul on the lug wrench to loosen

six rusted chrome lug nuts and he talks "This road here
        is a barrel of worms drunk on epilepsy
juice   But the Lord'll straighten it out"   He tells me and then

"What do you think of the Lord?" he asks   I stare at him
            in dazed silence "Just remember" he winks
"I know your deed and thoughts I know you are neither hot

nor cold I wish you were hot or cold.   Because you are
            lukewarm and neither hot nor cold I will
spit you out of my mouth"   I am happy that Randolph

is not doing the spitting here Happy to see he's
            not chewing tobacco   Happy to see
he's not dipping snuff   Happy to see he does not have

a cut-in-two empty R C can or any white
            styrofoam cup or an Ashland coffee mug
Tiny broken blood vessels dipped in and rode out of

the deep creases in his gaunt tanned cheeks   His face blue
            shadow His skin soft thick silk-like Each eye-
lash red tar   Bald skull   When he closed his eyes to lift both

hands to the nude gingko in the failed blue sky I stare
            at his eyes moving up to unseen stars
beneath those translucent eyelids Smashed cars tilt light

in gusts of November air lugging a lost dog's   hill-
            side bark downgrade to riverbed   Auto
wheels pried off   Layer upon squeaky layer the geology

of Detroit rises in rust moonward on the flatbed back
            of Gunnoe's battered Ford Hudsons like green lilies
A crow-blue Buick Century   Even a rice-pink

fish-tailed Cadillac El Dorado   Two white Studebakers
            laced with green mold   A dramatic red and
black   Yes! It is an Edsel A few bits of green glass

still imbedded in solid black plastic   One '38
            Willys—still shiny—Its twin headlights larger
than the moon   In the calm air   I walk slowly around

what must be the thin-foiled fury and rage of two-
            million miles of gravel asphalt concrete

174   *John McKernan*

and dirt Over rivers and mountains The geography

of America Our almanac of the elsewhere
          To touch any part of this is to feel
the cold damp iron mines neat Hibbing Minnesota

■ ■

I circle again slowly the truck "See this" he says
          and points to what seemed dark tarnished aluminum
foil but on inspection proves to be a single shallow

iris-yellow layer of rusted car flowing like
          a thread from front to back "This here is your
Rolls Royce limousine Used to be owned by your Governor

Marley who ended up drunk driving a Yellow Cab
          in Chicago. Just looking at this you
know for sure the wages of life is rust and bilge" His

now musical daughter whistled as the tire iron
          clanged on the concrete berm and the truck
wrestled its jacked weight earthward Four-cornered springs

twittering at the slice of bent moon White neon hood
          in the anthracite starless night "If you're
not in I'm gone Dad" Her voice growling from the truck's front

In the side-panel rear-view mirror her face glowed
          radiant in the torch of a cigarette
lighter Her eyes held their twin dabs of light Nothing

at all like tears The old man's hand waved His
          wizened face drew back into his
highway "Keep praying Buck" he screeched "Buck?"

Trilobites

Breece D'J Pancake

I open the truck's door, step onto the brick side street. I look at Company Hill again, all sort of worn down and round. A long time ago it was real craggy and stood like an island in the Teays River. It took over a million years to make that smooth little hill, and I've looked all over it for trilobites. I think how it has always been there and always will be, at least for as long as it matters. The air is smoky with summertime. A bunch of starlings swim over me. I was born in this country and I have never very much wanted to leave. I remember Pop's dead eyes looking at me. They were real dry, and that took something out of me. I shut the door, head for the café.

I see a concrete patch in the street. It's shaped like Florida, and I recollect what I wrote in Ginny's yearbook: "We will live on mangoes and love." And she up and left without me—two years she's been down there without me. She sends me postcards with alligator wrestlers and flamingos on the front. She never asks me any questions. I feel like a real fool for what I wrote, and go into the café.

The place is empty, and I rest in the cooled air. Tinker Reilly's little sister pours my coffee. She has good hips. They are kind of like Ginny's and they slope in nice curves to her legs. Hips and legs like that climb steps into airplanes. She goes to the counter end and scoffs down the rest of her sundae. I smile at her, but she's jailbait. Jailbait and black snakes are two things I won't touch with a window pole. One time I used an old black snake for a bullwhip, snapped the sucker's head off, and Pop beat hell out of me with it. I think how Pop could make me pretty mad sometimes. I grin.

I think about last night when Ginny called. Her old man drove her down from the airport in Charleston. She was already bored. Can we get together? Sure. Maybe do some brew? Sure. Same old Colly. Same old Ginny. She talked through her beak. I wanted to tell her Pop had died and Mom was on the warpath to sell the farm, but Ginny was talking through her beak. It gave me the creeps.

Just like the cups give me the creeps. I look at the cups hanging on pegs by the storefront. They're decal-named and covered with grease and dust. There's four of them, and one is Pop's, but that isn't what gives me the creeps. The cleanest one is Jim's. It's clean because he still uses it, but it hangs there with the rest. Through the window, I can see him crossing the street. His joints are cemented with arthritis. I think of how long it'll be before I croak, but Jim is old, and it gives me the creeps to see his cup hanging up there. I go to the door to help him in.

He says, "Tell the truth, now," and his old paw pinches my arm.

I say, "Can't do her." I help him to his stool.

I pull this globby rock from my pocket and slap it on the counter in front of Jim. He turns it with his drawn hand, examines it.

"Gastropod," he says. "Probably Permian. You buy again." I can't win with him. He knows them all.

"I still can't find a trilobite," I say.

"There are a few," he says. "Not many. Most of the outcrops around here are too late for them."

The girl brings Jim's coffee in his cup, and we watch her pump back to the kitchen. Good hips.

"You see that?" He jerks his head toward her.

I say, "Moundsville Molasses." I can spot jailbait by a mile.

"Hell, girl's age never stopped your dad and me in Michigan."

"Tell the truth."

"Sure. You got to time it so you nail the first freight out when your pants are up."

I look at the windowsill. It is speckled with the crisp skeletons of flies. "Why'd you and Pop leave Michigan?"

The crinkles around Jim's eyes go slack. He says, "The war," and sips his coffee.

I say, "He never made it back there."

"Me either—always wanted to—there or Germany—just to look around."

"Yeah, he promised to show me where you all buried that silverware and stuff during the war."

He says, "On the Elbe. Probably plowed up by now."

My eye socket reflects in my coffee, steam curls around my face, and I feel a headache coming on. I look up to ask Tinker's sister for an aspirin, but she is giggling in the kitchen.

"That's where he got that wound," Jim says. "Got it on the Elbe. He was out a long time. Cold, Jesus, it was cold. I had him for dead, but he came to. Says, 'I been all over the world'; says, 'China's so pretty, Jim.' "

"Dreaming?"

"I don't know. I quit worrying about that stuff years ago."

Tinker's sister comes up with her coffeepot to make us for a tip. I ask her for an aspirin and see she's got a pimple on her collarbone. I don't remember seeing pictures of China. I watch little sister's hips.

"Trent still wanting your place for that housing project?"

"Sure," I say. "Mom'll probably sell it, too. I can't run the place like Pop did. Cane looks bad as hell." I drain off my cup. I'm tired of talking about the farm. "Going out with Ginny tonight," I say.

"Give her that for me," he says. He takes a poke at my whang. I don't like it when he talks about her like that. He sees I don't like it, and his grin slips. "Found a lot of gas for her old man. One hell of a guy before his wife pulled out."

I wheel on my stool, clap his weak old shoulder. I think of Pop, and try to joke. "You stink so bad the undertaker's following you."

He laughs. "You were the ugliest baby ever born, you know that?"

I grin, and start out the door. I can hear him shout to little sister: "Come on over here, honey, I got a joke for you."

The sky has a film. Its heat burns through the salt on my skin, draws it tight. I start the truck, drive west along the highway built on the dry bed of the Teays. There's wide bottoms, and the hills on either side have yellowy billows the sun can't burn off. I pass an iron sign put up by the WPA: "Surveyed by George Washington, the Teays River Pike." I see fields and cattle where buildings stand, picture them from some long-off time.

I turn off the main road to our house. Clouds make the sunshine blink light and dark in the yard. I look again at the spot of ground where Pop fell. He had lain spread-eagled in the thick grass after a sliver of metal from his old wound passed to his brain. I remember thinking how beaten his face looked with prints in it from the grass.I reach the high barn and start my tractor, then drive to the knob at the end of our land and stop. I sit there, smoke, look again at the cane. The rows curve tight, but around them is a sort of scar of clay, and the leaves have a purplish blight. I don't wonder about the blight. I know the cane is too far gone to worry about the blight. Far off, somebody chops wood, and the ax-bites echo back to me. The hillsides are baked here and have heat ghosts. Our cattle move to the wind gap, and birds hide in caps of trees where we never cut the timber for pasture. I look at the wrinkly old boundary post. Pop set it when the hobo and soldier days were over. It is a locust-tree post and will be there a long time. A few dead morning glories cling to it.

"I'm just not no good at it," I say. "It just don't do to work your ass off at something you're not no good at."

The chopping stops. I listen to the beat of grasshopper wings, and strain to spot blight on the far side of the bottoms.

I say, "Yessir, Colly, you couldn't grow pole beans in a pile of horseshit."

I squash my cigarette against the floor plate. I don't want a fire. I press the starter, and bump around the fields, then down to the ford of the drying creek, and up the other side. Turkles fall from logs into stagnant pools. I stop my machine. The cane here is just as bad. I rub a sunburn into the back of my neck.

I say, "Shot to hell, Gin. Can't do nothing right."

I lean back, try to forget these fields and flanking hills. A long time before me or these tools, the Teays flowed here. I can almost feel the cold waters and the tickling the trilobites make when they crawl. All the water from the old mountains flowed west. But the land lifted. I have only the bottoms and stone animals I collect. I blink and breathe. My father is a khaki cloud in the canebrakes, and Ginny is no more to me than the bitter smell in the blackberry briers up on the ridge.

I take up my sack and gaff for a turkle. Some quick chubs flash under the bank. In the moss-dapples, I see rings spread where a turkle ducked under. This sucker is mine. The pool smells like rot, and the sun is a hardish brown.

I wade in. He goes for the roots of a log. I shove around, and feel my gaff twitch. This is a smart turkle, but still a sucker. I bet he could pull liver off a hook for the rest of his days, but he is a sucker for the roots that hold him while I work my gaff. I pull him up, and see he is a snapper. He's got his stubby neck curved around, biting at the gaff. I lay him on the sand, and take out Pop's knife. I step on the shell, and press hard. That fat neck gets skinny quick, and sticks way out. A little blood oozes from the gaff wound into the grit, but when I slice, a puddle forms.

A voice says, "Get a dragon, Colly?"

I shiver a little, and look up. It's only the loansman standing on the creekbank in his tan suit. His face is splotched pink, and the sun is turning his glasses black.

"I crave them now and again," I say. I go on slitting gristle, skinning back the shell.

"Aw, your daddy loved turtle meat," the guy says.

I listen to scratching cane leaves in the late sun. I dump the tripes into the pool, bag the rest, and head up the ford. I say, "What can I do for you?"

This guy starts up: "I saw you from the road—just came down to see about my offer."

"I told you yesterday, Mr. Trent. It ain't mine to sell." I tone it down. I don't want hard feelings. "You got to talk to Mom."

Blood drips from the poke to the dust. It makes dark paste. Trent pockets his hands, looks over the cane. A cloud blocks the sun, and my crop glows greenish in the shade.

"This is about the last real farm left around here," Trent says.

"Blight'll get what the dry left," I say. I shift the sack to my free hand. I see I'm giving in. I'm letting this guy go and push me around.

"How's your mother getting along?" he says. I see no eyes behind his smoky glasses.

"Pretty good," I say. "She's wanting to move to Akron." I swing the sack a little toward Ohio, and spray some blood on Trent's pants. "Sorry," I say.

"It'll come out," he says, but I hope not. I grin and watch the turkle's mouth gape on the sand. "Well, why Akron?" he says. "Family there?"

I nod. "Hers" I say. "She'll take you up on the offer." This hot shadow saps me, and my voice is a whisper. I throw the sack on the floor plate, climb up to grind the starter. I feel better in a way I've never known. The hot metal seat burns through my jeans.

"Saw Ginny at the post office," this guy shouts. "She sure is a pretty."

I wave, almost smile, as I gear to lumber up the dirt road. I pass Trent's dusty Lincoln, move away from my bitten cane. It can go now; the stale seed, the drought, the blight—it can go when she signs the papers. I know I will always be to blame, but it can't just be my fault. "What about you?" I say. "Your side hurt all that morning, but you wouldn't see no doctor. Nosir, you had to see that your dumb boy got the crop put proper in the ground." I shut my trap to keep from talking like a fool.

I stop my tractor on the terraced road to the barn and look back across the cane to the creekbed. Yesterday Trent said the bottoms would be filled with dirt. That will put the houses above flood, but it'll raise the flood line. Under all those houses, my turkles will turn to stone. Our Herefords make rusty patches on the hill. I see Pop's grave, and wonder if the new high waters will get over it.

I watch the cattle play. A rain must be coming. A rain is always coming when cattle play. Sometimes they play for snow, but mostly it is rain. After Pop whipped the daylights out of me with that black snake, he hung it on a fence. But it didn't rain. The cattle weren't playing, and it didn't rain, but I kept my mouth shut. The snake was bad enough, I didn't want the belt too.

I look a long time at that hill. My first time with Ginny was in the tree-cap of that hill. I think of how close we could be then, and maybe even now, I don't know. I'd like to go with Ginny, fluff her hair in any other field. But I can see her in the post office. I bet she was sending postcards to some guy in Florida.

I drive on to the barn, stop under the shed. I wipe the sweat from my face with my sleeve, and see how the seams have slipped from my shoulders. If I sit rigid, I can fill them again. The turkle is moving in the sack, and it gives me the creeps to hear his shell clinking against the gaff. I take the poke to the spigot to clean the game. Pop always liked turkle in a mulligan. He talked a lot about mulligan and the jungles just an hour before I found him.

I wonder what it will be like when Ginny comes by. I hope she's not talking through her beak. Maybe she'll take me to her house this time. If her momma had been anybody but Pop's cousin, her old man would let me go to her house. Screw him. But I can talk to Ginny. I wonder if she remembers the plans we made for the farm. And we wanted kids. She always nagged about a peacock. I will get her one.

I smile as I dump the sack into the rusty sink, but the barn smell—the hay, the cattle, the gasoline—it reminds me. Me and Pop built this barn. I look at every nail with the same dull pain.

I clean the meat and lay it out on a piece of cloth torn from an old bed sheet. I fold the corners, walk to the house.

The air is hot, but it sort of churns, and the set screens in the kitchen window rattle. From inside, I can hear Mom and Trent talking on the front porch, and I leave the window up. It is the same come-on he gave me yesterday, and I bet Mom is eating it up. She probably thinks about tea parties with her cousins in Akron. She never listens to what anybody says. She just says all right to anything anybody but me or Pop ever said. She even voted for Hoover before they got married. I throw the turkle meat into a skillet, get a beer. Trent softens her up with me; I prick my ears.

"I would wager on Colly's agreement," he says. I can still hear a hill twang in his voice.

"I told him Sam'd put him on at Goodrich," she says. "They'd teach him a trade."

"And there are a good many young people in Akron. You know he'd be happier." I think how his voice sounds like a damn TV.

"Well, he's awful good to keep me company. Don't go out none since Ginny took off to that college."

"There's a college in Akron," he says, but I shut the window.

I lean against the sink, rub my hands across my face. The smell of turkle has soaked between my fingers. It's the same smell as the pools.

Through the door to the living room, I see the rock case Pop built for me. The white labels show up behind the dark gloss of glass. Ginny helped me find over half of those. If I did study in a college, I could come back and take Jim's place at the gas wells. I like to hold little stones that lived so long ago. But geology doesn't mean lick to me. I can't even find a trilobite.

I stir the meat, listen for noise or talk on the porch, but there is none. I look out. A lightning flash peels shadows from the yard and leaves a dark strip under the cave of the barn. I feel a scum on my skin in the still air. I take my supper to the porch.

I look down the valley to where bison used to graze before the first rails were put down. Now those rails are covered with a highway, and cars rush back and forth in the wind. I watch Trent's car back out, heading east into town. I'm afraid to ask right off if he got what he wanted.

I stick my plate under Mom's nose, but she waves it off. I sit in Pop's old rocker, watch the storm come. Dust devils puff around on the berm, and maple sprigs land in the yard with their white bellies up. Across the road, our windbreak bends, rows of cedars furling every which way at once.

"Coming a big one?" I say.

Mom says nothing and fans herself with the funeral-home fan. The wind layers her hair, but she keeps that cardboard picture of Jesus bobbing like crazy. Her face changes. I know what she thinks. She thinks how she isn't the girl in the picture on the mantel. She isn't standing with Pop's garrison cap cocked on her head.

"I wish you'd of come out while he's here," she says. She stares across the road to the windbreak.

"I heard him yesterday," I say.

"It ain't that at all," she says, and I watch her brow come down a little. "It's like when Jim called us askin' if we wanted some beans an' I had to tell him to leave 'em in the truck at church. I swan how folks talk when men come 'round a widow."

I know Jim talks like a dumb old fart, but it isn't like he'd rape her or anything. I don't want to argue with her. "Well," I say, "who owns this place?"

"We still do. Don't have to sign nothin' till tomorrow."

She quits bobbing Jesus to look at me. She starts up: "You'll like Akron. Law, I bet Marcy's youngest girl'd love to meet you. She's a regular rock hound too. 'Sides, your father always said we'd move there when you got big enough to run the farm."

I know she has to say it. I just keep my mouth shut. The rain comes, ringing the roof tin. I watch the high wind snap branches from the trees.

Pale splinters of light shoot down behind the far hills. We are just brushed by this storm.

Ginny's sports car hisses east on the road, honking as it passes, but I know she will be back.

"Just like her momma," Mom says, "racin' the devil for the beer joints."

"She never knew her momma," I say. I set my plate on the floor. I'm glad Ginny thought to honk.

"What if I's to run off with some foreman from the wells?"

"You wouldn't do that, Mom."

"That's right," she says, and watches the cars roll by. "Shot her in Chicago. Shot hisself too."

I look beyond the hills and time. There is red hair clouding the pillow, blood-splattered by the slug. Another body lies rumpled and warm at the bed foot.

"Folks said he done it cause she wouldn't marry him. Found two weddin' bands in his pocket. Feisty little I-taliun."

I see police and reporters in the tiny room. Mumbles spill into the hallway, but nobody really looks at the dead woman's face.

"Well," Mom says, "at least they was still wearin' their clothes."

The rain slows, and for a long time I sit watching the blue chicory swaying beside the road. I think of all the people I know who left these hills. Only Jim and Pop came back to the land, worked it.

"Lookee at the willow-wisps." Mom points to the hills.

The rain trickles, and as it seeps in to cool the ground, a fog rises. The fog curls little ghosts into the branches and gullies. The sun tries to sift through this mist, but is only a tarnished brown splotch in the pinkish sky. Wherever the fog is, the light is a burnished orange.

"Can't recall the name Pop gave it," I say.

The colors shift, trade tones.

"He had some funny names all right. Called a tomcat a 'pussy scat.' "

I think back. "Cornflakes were 'pone-rakes,' and a chicken was a 'sick-un.' "

We laugh.

"Well," she says, "he'll always be a part of us."

The glommy paint on the chair arm packs under my fingernails. I think how she could foul up a free lunch.

Ginny honks again from the main road. I stand up to go in, but I hold the screen, look for something to say.

"I ain't going to live in Akron," I say.

"An' just where you gonna live, Mister?"

"I don't know."

She starts up with her fan again.

"Me and Ginny's going low-riding," I say.

She won't look at me. "Get in early. Mr. Trent don't keep no late hours for no beer drinkers."

The house is quiet, and I can hear her out there sniffling. But what to hell can I do about it? I hurry to wash the smell of turkle from my hands. I shake all over while the water flows down. I talked back. I've never talked back. I'm scared, but I stop shaking. Ginny can't see me shaking. I just walk out to the road without ever looking back to the porch.

I climb in the car, let Ginny kiss my check. She looks different. I've never seen these clothes, and she wears too much jewelry.

"You look great," she says. "Haven't changed a bit."

We drive west along the Pike.

"Where we going?"

She says, "Let's park for old times' sake. How's the depot?"

I say, "Sure." I reach back for a can of Falls City. "You let your hair grow."

"You like?"

"Um, yeah."

We drive. I look at the tinged fog, the colors changing hue.

She says, "Sort of an eerie evening, huh?" It all comes from her beak.

"Pop always called it a fool's fire or something."

We pull in beside the old depot. It's mostly boarded up. We drink, watch the colors slip to gray dusk in the sky.

"You ever look in your yearbook?" I gulp down the rest of my City.

She goes crazy laughing. "You know," she says, "I don't even know where I put that thing."

I feel way too mean to say anything. I look across the railroad to a field sown in timothy. There are wells there, pumps to suck the ancient gases. The gas burns blue, and I wonder if the ancient sun was blue. The tracks run on till they're a dot in the brown haze. They give off clicks from their switches. Some tankers wait on the spur. Their wheels are rusting to the tracks. I wonder what to hell I ever wanted with trilobites.

"Big night in Rock Camp," I say. I watch Ginny drink. Her skin is so white it glows yellowish, and the last light makes sparks in her red hair.

She says, "Daddy would raise hell. *Me* this close to the wells."

"You're a big girl now. C'mon, let's walk."

We get out, and she up and grabs my arm. Her fingers feel like ribbons on the veins of my hand.

"How long you in for?" I say.

"Just a week here, then a week with Daddy in New York. I can't wait to get back. It's great."

"You got a guy?"

She looks at me with this funny smile of hers. "Yeah, I got a guy. He's doing plankton research."

Ever since I talked back, I've been afraid, but now I hurt again. We come to the tankers, and she takes hold on a ladder, steps up.

"This right?" She looks funny, all crouched in like she's just nailed a drag on the fly. I laugh.

"Nail the end nearest the engine. If you slip, you get throwed clear. Way you are a drag on the fly'd suck you under. 'Sides, nobody'd ride a tanker."

She steps down but doesn't take my hand. "He taught you every-thing. What killed him?"

"Little shell fragment. Been in him since the war. Got in his blood . . ." I snap my fingers. I want to talk, but the picture won't become words. I see myself scattered, every cell miles from the others. I pull them back and kneel in the dark grass. I roll the body face-up, and look in the eyes a long time before I shut them. "You never talk about your momma," I say.

She says, "I don't want to," and goes running to an open window in the depot. She peeks in, turns to me. "Can we go in?"

"Why? Nothing in there but old freight scales."

"Because it's spooky and neat and I want to." She runs back, kisses me on the cheek. "I'm bored with this glum look. Smile!"

I give up and walk to the depot. I drag a rotten bench under the broken window and climb in. I take Ginny's hand to help her. A blade of glass slices her forearm. The cut path is shallow, but I take off my T-shirt to wrap it. The blood blots purple on the cloth.

"Hurt?"

"Not really."

I watch a mud dauber land on the glass blade. Its metal-blue wings flick as it walks the edge. It sucks what the glass has scraped from her skin. I hear them working in the walls.

Ginny is at the other window, and she peers through a knothole in the plywood.

I say, " See that light green spot on the second hill?"

"Yeah."

"That's the copper on your-all's roof."

She turns, stares at me.

"I come here lots," I say. I breathe the musty air. I turn away from her and look out the window to Company Hill, but I can feel her stare.

Company Hill looks bigger in the dusk, and I think of all the hills around town I've never set foot on. Ginny comes up behind me, and there's a glass-crunch with her steps. The hurt arm goes around me, the tiny spot of blood cold against my back.

"What is it, Colly? Why can't we have any fun?"

"When I was a young punk, I tried to run away from home. I was walking through this meadow on the other side of the Hill, and this shadow passed over me. I honest to god thought it was a pterodactyl. It was a damned airplane. I was so damn mad, I came home." I peel chips of paint from the window frame, wait for her to talk. She leans against me, and I kiss her real deep. Her waist bunches in my hands. The skin of her neck is almost too white in the faded evening. I know she doesn't understand.

I slide her to the floor. Her scent rises to me, and I shove crates aside to make room. I don't wait. She isn't making love, she's getting laid. All right, I think, all right. Get laid. I pull her pants around her ankles, rut her. I think of Tinker's sister. Ginny isn't here. Tinker's sister is under me. A wash of blue light passes over me. I open my eyes to the floor, smell the tang of rain-wet wood. Black snakes. It was the only time he had to whip me.

"Let me go with you," I say. I want to be sorry, but I can't.

"Colly, please . . ." She shoves me back. Her head is rolling in splinters of paint and glass.

I look a long time at the hollow shadows hiding her eyes. She is somebody I met a long time ago. I can't remember her name for a minute, then it comes back to me. I sit against the wall and my spine aches. I listen to the mud daubers building nests, and trace a finger along her throat.

She says, "I want to go. My arm hurts." Her voice comes from someplace deep in her chest.

We climb out. A yellow light burns on the crossties, and the switches click. Far away, I hear a train. She gives me my shirt, and gets in her car. I stand there looking at the blood spots on the cloth. I feel old as hell. When I look up, her taillights are reddish blurs in the fog.

I walk around to the platform, slump on the bench. The evening cools my eyelids. I think of how that one time was the only airplane that ever passed over me.

I picture my father—a young hobo with the Michigan sunset making him squint, the lake behind him. His face is hard from all the days and places he fought to live in, and of a sudden, I know his mistake was coming back here to set that locust-tree post on the knob.

"Ever notice how only blue lightning bugs come out after a rain? Green ones almost never do."

I hear the train coming. She is highballing all right. No stiffs in that blind baggage.

"Well, you know the Teays must of been a big river. Just stand on Company Hill, and look across the bottoms. You'll see."

My skin is heavy with her noise. Her light cuts a wide slice in the fog. No stiff in his right mind could try this one on the fly. She's hell-bent for election.

"Jim said it flowed west by northwest—all the way up to the old Saint Lawrence Drain. Had garfish—ten, maybe twenty foot long. Said they're still in there.

Good old Jim'll probably croak on a lie like that. I watch her beat by. A worn-out tie belches mud with her weight. She's just too fast to jump. Plain and simple.

I get up. I'll spend tonight at home. I've got eyes to shut in Michigan—maybe even Germany or China, I don't know yet. I walk, but I'm not scared. I feel my fear moving away in rings through time for a million years.

Fox Hunters

Breece D'J Pancake

*T*he passing of an autumn night left no mark on the patchwork blacktop
of the secondary road that led to Parkins. A gray ooze of light began to
crest the eastern hills above the hollow and sift a blue haze through the
black bowels of linking oak branches. A small wind shivered, and sycamore leaves chattered across the pavement but were stopped by the
fighting-green orchard grass on the berm.

The opossum lay quietly by the roadside. She had found no dead
farm animals in which to build her winter den; not even a fine empty hole.
She packed her young across the road and into the leaves where the
leathery carcass of another opossum lay. She did not pause for sniffing or
sentiment.

Metalclick. She stopped. Fire. She hunkered in tight fear against the
ground, her young clutching closer to her fur. Soft, rhythmless clumpings
excited her blood, and she sank lower. With day and danger advancing, fear
was blushing in her as she backed cautiously into higher brush. From her
hiding, she watched a giant enemy scuffling on the blacktop, and a red
glow bouncing brightly in the remnant of her night.

Bo felt this to be the royal time of his day—these sparse, solitary
moments when the rest of the world was either going to bed or not up yet.
He was alone, knew the power in singularity, yet was afraid of it. Insecu-
rity crawfished through his blood, leaving him powerless again. Soon he
began a conversation to make the light seem closer to the road.

"Coffee, Bo," he said to himself.

"Yeah, and Lucy, toosie," he answered.

"And putin*tane.*"

"Yeah," and he quickened his pace, imitating a train.

"*Put*intane, *putin*tane, put*n*tane, p'*tane*, woooo."

The opossum crouched lower. Her unready, yet born, offspring clung
to her belly, nudging to nurse.

His pace lagged back. Maybe Lucy was a whore, but how in the hell would he know? He liked the way she leaned over the grill, showing slip and garters, and knowing it, still, acting vaguely embarrassed. He liked the way she would cock her head to the right, nod solemnly, brows pursed in wrinkled thought, while he talked about cities he had seen on TV. Or about his dad, who sucked so much mine gas, they had to bury him closed-coffin because he was blue as jeans. Bo would live out a reckless verbal future with Lucy. She listened. Occasionally she advised. Once he was going to run off to New York and get educated. Just chuck it all, leave his mother, and get educated in New York. He had felt silly and ashamed when Lucy said to finish high school first. Times like that, he left the dinette convinced Lucy was a whore.

From up the road, he could hear the rumble of Enoch's truck. Instinctively, he jumped over the embankment, slipped into the brush, and squatted. A hiss came from within the brush. Bo turned to see a gray-white form in the fog beside him. It looked like a giant rat with eyebrows. They stared, neither wanting any part of the other—the opossum frozen between acting dead or running, Bo crouching lower as the headlights neared. It was only two more miles to Parkins, but if Enoch saw him he would stop; then Bo would be "crazy boy" at the garage for another week because he would rather walk than ride with his boss.

The truck clattered by, its pink wrecker rig swinging, erratic pendulum of pulley, hook, and cable.

Bo unzipped his pants and pissed with frozen opossum eyes looking on. Steam rose from the puddle, and he shuddered as it drifted to intermingle with the blue mist. He began wading leaves up the embankment.

As he trampled the orchard grass at the berm, another truck could be heard up the road, and he fought the urge to slide back down the slope. He could not explain why he wanted to walk, nor was he certain he wanted to walk anymore. He stepped onto the pavement feeling tired and moved a few paces until headlights flooded his path, showing up the highway steam and making the road give birth to little ghosts beneath his feet.

The truck thundered up behind, then let three high-pitched whines pierce the road spirits of the morning. Bo waited for the truck to stop. When it did, a voice called: "Git in er git ober."

Bo whirled to look at the driver but found his eyes drawn to the white oblivion of the headlights. "Bill?" was all he was able to say as his eyes made red and purple dots appear in the lights.

"Hell yes. You blind?"

Bo looked to the gray hills to drag his attention from the lights, and slowly remembered every detail of Lucy's body as it disintegrated into his brain. Breast hair. Jesus Christ, how long had he stood in that light like a fool? Bill would tell everybody that Bo Holly was out of his goddamned mind. He groped the truck, rubbing the red dots into his eyes with his hands.

"Git in," said Bill, while his eyes explored Bo with the same scrutiny he had once used to search a two-headed calf for stitches around either head. Bo gave a little sigh as he climbed into the truck's cab, and Bill pounced with the question: "You sick?"

"Just not awake yet," Bo lied. He felt professional about lying, and once started, would not stop. "Momma overslept. Got me up and out without coffee and half dressed. Said I was late to work. What time is it, Bill?" Questions and complex sentences, Bo had learned, were the great shield of liars. Bill studied his wristwatch, then sneered at the sky as if *The Black Draught Almanac* had been two days off on its sunrise schedule.

"Ten abter seben," he growled, pounding his hand against the wheel.

"Shit," Bo yelled, watching Bill jump a little. "But Enoch probably ain't there yet. He's always late. Didn't come in last Saturday till eleven."

"Ain't none of *my* biz-whacks," Bill snapped. "By god, I mind my own biz-whacks." But Bo knew Bill would remember this as a gossip gift to a bored wife.

"I's talkin' to Larry up to the Union Hall," said Bill, experimenting shamefully, "an' he says yer faberite song's that damn 'Rockin' Riber.' "

" 'Rollin' on the River'?" Questions don't give offense, he thought, besides, the song's "Proud Mary."

"Stupid song, Bo. You oughta know better."

Bo said nothing.

"Son' like that's ber a riber town. We ain't got no riber in Parkins."

"Got the Elk in Upshur. Watch this pothole." The truck jolted twice. "Guess it's eat up the whole road." Bill had to think to remember where he had left off. Elk?

"The Elk ain't nothin' to sing about," he cackled. "Now, Merle Haggard, he can tell ya . . ."

"S'matter, Bill, ain't you proud to be a West Virginian?"

"Sure, goddammit, but a song like that's ber eberbody eberwhere. You just don't listen to no good stuff, do ya?"

Bo settled back in his seat, stuck his feet under the heater, and once they were warm enough to feel cold, decided why he liked Lucy: she was a genuine person.

In the silence, the opossum thawed, and was carefully slipping up the bank, sniffing after the danger once so close. It paused in the sycamore leaves and wet orchard grass, then scuttered across the blacktop and back into the woods the way it had come. It was almost morning.

When Bill's truck topped the final grade into Parkins, the sun had already begun to ricochet from the western slopes, and the eastern hills cast a gray shadow over the town. From that grade, Bo could see who was up and who wasn't by the position of yellow squares of light on the houses. Lucy was in the kitchen of her boardinghouse, her tenants in the bathrooms. The two Duncan sisters, who did nothing, rose early to get on with it. They gossiped about their neighbors, mostly about Lucy. She ignored them. Bo thought she liked to be talked about.

Brownie Ross was opening his general store near the railroad; turning on lights, raising blinds, shoveling coal into the stove. Bo wondered why Brownie opened so early—Enoch, too. Brownie never sold anything bigger than a quarter-sack of nails before noon, and if your car broke down, you'd have to walk to Parkins for a phone.

Bill worked for the railroad—station manager—and Lucy boarded the few men the reopened mine demanded, so both had to be up and going by six. Enoch opened early because Brownie did, and Brownie was just old. Mornings changed very little in Parkins.

"Just let me off at the boardin'house, Bill. I want a cuppa coffee."

"Ain't none of *my* biz-whacks," Bill snapped as the truck stopped beside the laughing yellow bear Brakes-and-Alignment sign. Out of the truck, Bo turned to thank the driver, but "Ain't none of *yours*, neither" was fired back at him. The truck jumped forward, and Bo let the lurch shut the door. He walked to the garage-door window and peeked in: the yellow night-light was still burning, the workshop bench still scattered with tools and parts from the night before. The green Dodge was gone.

Musta done somethin' right, he thought, they drove her away.

Neither Enoch nor wrecker were in sight. The portent of Bill's attack hit home: Enoch was up to tricks again, but only the men were supposed to know. "Not even the angels in heaven shall know the hour of his coming." Bo laughed as he entered the oppressive smell of red clay, grease, and gasoline. He straightened the tool bench, washed, locked up, and headed for Lucy's.

The boardinghouse was ugly. It loomed three stories straight up from the flat hollow-basin, as plain and ponderous as the great boulders Bo had seen on TV westerns. Noise echoed through its walls; sounds of plumbing malfunctions and boarder disagreements. On the back, a lean-to had been converted into a dinette.

Inside, Bo rediscovered the aromas of breakfast. Ten miners were eating; Lucy was packing their lunches in arch-topped tin boxes. Bo swaggered to the jukebox, punched F-6 in defiant remembrance of Bill, and sauntered to the counter. But nobody had watched as he thought they would have. Ike Turner's bass voice chanted the rhythm; Tina whispered in.

Lucy coldly asked if he wanted coffee. He did not answer, but got his coffee anyway. The miners left and the straw bosses came down. Unlike their men, who whispered labor and safety secrets, the straw bosses ate alone and silently.

Bo, withdrawn, watched them. He wondered why he could not claim kin to men by tolerating their music, their cards, their fox hunting, but he knew a scab of indifference to keep away sociability.

When the foreman left, Lucy refilled Bo's cup. Too many color treatments had left her hair the same red as a rusty Brillo pad. She wore only a hint of green eye-makeup, and her skin was the texture and color of toadstools. On each hand she wore a diamond engagement ring. Bet ya can still throw'em, Bo thought.

"How's goin', Bo?" She meant it, and that was appealing.

"Ain't too clear on it, Lucy. Bored, I guess."

"Try a different song tomorrow."

"Tomorrow's Sunday. 'Sides, I ain't bored with my song."

"How old are you again?"

"Sixteen, last count."

"Took sixteen years to bore ya?"

"Took that long to take effect."

Lucy laughed. Bo watched her face contort, wondered if she was laughing with him or at him, decided that was why the other men called her a whore, and smiled.

"You look hell-bottom low. Somethin' eaten' at ya? Yer momma sick er somethin'?"

"Nobody wants to talk to me, Lucy."

"Quit cryin' in yer coffee. You ain't old enough to be a blubberin' drunk."

"Well, it's the truth."

"Got a girl?"

"Had one this summer. Her daddy moved off to Logan. We wrote, only I don't hear much since school started up again."

Lucy remembered growing up. "Yer okay. Just growin' pains."

"I guess it's just I don't say nothin' worth listenin' to."

"Bo, listenin's worth more to the listener."

He would remember to look for meaning later; he sought another avenue of talk, but Lucy was too quick.

"Case of the lonesomes, huh?"

"Yeah."

"Must be pretty bad if your best talker's a whore."

Bo hung his head and waited for the roof to fall. When it didn't, he slowly added support.

"You ain't that," he said, looking as serious as he could without looking stupid.

Lucy searched for hand business, and found ten seconds in turning off the grill and wiping up a drop of coffee. "I like it . . . you sayin' that. Yer the only one to believe it. Could be right good for ya. Could be dangerous. Don't go talkin' it around, hear?"

Bo shrugged. "Sure, Lucy," he said, withdrawing to his scab and his coffee. He watched her clear the straw-bosses' tables, showing bits of garter each time she bent. He rubbed his finger around the rim of the empty cup.

"How about another, Lucy?" he asked, as she bent long over a table to get at the corner. She smiled in a vague, sleepy way as she tugged her skirt down from her hips.

"Sure, Bo," she said, moving behind the counter for the pot, and added, "Past time for work," as she poured. "When the cat's away . . ."

"Cat's been doin' some playin' on his own."

"Huh?"

Bo gave Lucy the dime, then placed a quarter under the saucer. Nobody tipped Lucy, which compelled Bo to do it. The tip was a game between them, a secret. All the coffee Bo could drink for thirty-five cents.

As he slid from the stool, Lucy asked, "What's the rush? Tired of talkin'?"

"Need to look through the junk pile. Parts for my car. Gonna break out like gangbusters."

"Take me with ya."

"Sure," he said for the sake of play, and stepped out into the creeping shade of morning. Somehow he thought of how fine he felt in a new way, a knowing way.

It was nearly nine when Enoch came in. Bo lay on a crawler under Beck Fuller's Pontiac, draining excretions from the crankcase and twisting a filthy rag around the grease tits to remove warts of clay.

"Be a damn sight easier on the lift," Enoch grumbled. Bo avoided the hole. He was forbidden to use the lift.

He scooted the crawler into the light, shoved his welder's beanie back, and studied Enoch. Everything in the man's posture had slipped to the lowest support. His jaws drooped, dragging the scalp tight on his close-cropped head. His belly pulled the same way against whatever power was left in his shoulders. All of this converged on his khaki pants, making the cuffs gather in little bundles at his feet.

"Don't mind the work. Only thing doin' all mornin'. Where ya been at?"

Enoch lit a cigarette. "Checkin' out a wreck. Dawn Reed and Anne Davis went off the road up by French Creek Church. Car rolled int' the creek. Found 'em dead 'smornin'." He smiled at Bo, but Bo did not smile back. "Wasn't they 'bout your age?" he sputtered.

Bo stood up and brushed his jeans. "Jesus, yes. I go to school with 'em. Drunk?"

"Don't know yet. They was full of water. All scrunged up like raisins."

"Hey, her car was an Impala. I dropped it up to my house till the state cops are done with it. I'll sell ya parts real cheap. It ain't the same year as yours, but you could—"

"No thanks." Bo's stomach contracted, his nose, ears, and hands felt cold. Enoch cocked his head in wonder, took another draw from his cigarette, and turned away.

"Yer crazy," he said, turning back. "Just nuts. *They—are—dead*. Got that? Don't need no car no more." He turned again to ward off fury. Bo traced a stick figure in the Pontiac's dust with his finger, then wiped it out again. Another preachin', he thought.

"I come in here 'smornin' to get that miner's Dodge out," Enoch said. "Them tools was ever'where. You wasn't nowhere. Sleepin'? Sleep more'n ya work. Snuck in t' put 'em away while I's down to the station. Figger Bill wouldn't tell me you's at that whore's house?"

"She ain't that," Bo whispered, looking for something to throw at Enoch.

"She ain't, huh? Well, how do you think she got that boardin'house? Bartram didn't give it to her—she blackmailed 'im for it the way she done them other guys in Charleston. You stay clear of her, Bo, she'll ruin' ya."

"Don't tell me what to do," Bo shouted.

"I gotta watch out for my interests. You work for me, you stay outa that house."

"I quit!" he shouted so loudly his throat hurt. He threw his rag in the barrel for effect, adding, "I got enough on you to earn my keep without workin'." Half out the door the lie frightened him; he wanted to turn back, blame Lucy, and keep his chance to leave forever. You blew it, something whispered, but pride pointed his way outside.

Inside, Enoch worried. Bo was probably lying. But what if he knew about him and the boys and Dawn? He looked up the road, but Bo was walking too fast to catch on foot. Enoch ground the wrecker to a start and whirled off up the road.

As the wrecker pulled up beside him, Bo set his jaw in silence. He looked at Enoch, and the flabby jaws said, "Git in, Bo, we gotta talk." Once he had Bo inside, Enoch let the subject of blackmail sleep, and went on with his sermon:

"I know'd your daddy. That's why I give ya this job. You're a good mechanic, but you proved you ain't no man by walkin' out on me.

"I tried to be good to ya. Let you use my tools on yer car, even teached you how to be a mechanic . . . but I can't teach ya how to be a man."

"Try treatin' me like one," Bo hissed.

"All right. You want to work? Your daddy wouldn't want me to let ya after the way you acted. I'm sorry to his memory, but I'll let you come back."

Bo looked out on the broom-sedge slopes. He could swear his daddy's ghost answered, "Yech."

"All right," said Enoch. "Tonight we're goin' fox huntin'. I figger yer daddy woulda took ya by now."

Bo hated fox hunting, but nodded and smiled. He wanted his job; he'd need a stake.

When he had finished servicing Beck's car, Bo washed his hands, lit a cigarette, and waited to become hungry. Enoch had said he would be back, but Bo was glad to be alone.

Dawn and Anne were dead. He boiled memories of them in his mind. Dawn was chesty and popular. She was dumb, but smart enough to act smart. Bo respected and spoke to her. Anne was built so slightly she always wore white blouses so onlookers could tell she had a bra, and therefore something to hold up. Her only friend was Dawn, her only beauty was in her eyes. She'd never stare down a husband, Bo thought, so maybe it's best. Dawn brushed against him a lot, not always so he would notice, but enough to make him wonder what she had meant.

Bo leaned his head against the red battery-charger and closed his eyes on Dawn's memory, while a vision of Lucy rocked smiling in his brain.

He saw a clapboard house, worn silver by weather, now glistening in the sun. He felt the intruder-sun on his head and the power he loved coax him toward the cool shade of the house. He saw movement up the moss-green sandstone steps, across the grooved porch-floor, and through the screen door. In the cool dampness of the linoleum living room, his cousin Sally stood; her hair pressed in ragged bangs on her forehead, the rest pinned loosely behind. Little chains of grime made sweaty chokers around her throat, but she looked cool and remote as she moved toward him and took his hand. "I don't love you," he said, viciously. Images soon ran together in flesh tones, and he awakened.

The dream had excited him as the cold August rain blowing through a porch might break the monotony of heat and pleasure-chill his blood. He searched for a reason for the dream. Maybe, he thought, I made it up. Maybe it happened.

Hunger drove him beyond Enoch's Law, and he ran quickly to the dinette. The door was locked, so he dragged himself to Brownie's, where he bought cheese, crackers, pork-rind snacks, and two Big Orange drinks.

"Dolla-fourtee." Bo handed the old man the money, tore into the cheese and Big Orange. "Don't eat it here," Brownie added, bagging the lunch.

Bo sat outside the garage in the cold sun and ate. He watched the Duncan sisters as they sat by their windows and watched him with peeping sparrow-eyes. When he had drained the last Big Orange, he felt a wickedness rise in him as he chucked the empty bottle at the Duncan house, and he smiled to see them retreat behind their curtains.

Enoch returned at two-twenty, found Bo asleep against the battery charger. Cuffy had suggested cutting Bo's throat, and now was the time, but Cuffy was not around, and Enoch was not a cutter of throats.

"Wake up, Bo, goddammit, wake yourself up."

"Wha?"

"Look, I'm goin' to get the dogs. You lock up at three, an' be on the road afront of your house by six. I'll get ya there."

"Who alls comin'?" Bo yawned.

"Cuffy an' Bill an' Virg Cooper."

"Cuffy an' Bill don't like me," he warned.

"Don't be a smart-ass an' they will. Dress warm, hear?"

Bo nodded, thinking, son of a bitch.

He waited until Enoch's wrecker silhouetted the grade and passed over, then he locked up and headed for Lucy's. She sat alone reading a magazine and looking day-worn. Maybe she caught a man, Bo thought, but he threw her back. Over coffee he poured out his roil of sickness, hate, and confusion. Soon they were wrestling with the go or don't go of the hunt.

"Bo, ya drive people off an' dump 'em. Go ahuntin' —they're just tryin' to be good to ya."

He looked up sternly. "You don't kick a dog in the ass then give 'im a bone."

Then with a sudden fervor: "Maybe I could take Daddy's forty-five automatic."

"Can't shoot foxie, Bo," she warned. "Be nothing left to chase."

"I know," he said, as if a veteran of hunts. "I just want to show 'em I can shoot. You know, plug some cans."

"Make damn sure them cans ain't got legs," she grinned.

He gulped his coffee and left so quickly he forgot to leave his tip.

The clay trail from the secondary to Bo's hillside house was worn a smooth red in the center, bordered with a yellow crust. He followed the path into the perpetual dusk and sweet-chill of a pine grove. There the path forked, one toward the garbage pile, the other into a clearing where the house stood, rudely shingled in imitation-brick tar paper.

The clearing was scattered with pin-oak and sugar-maple leaves lodged in fallow weeds. The sugar maples blended their colors to camouflage the undying plastic daffodils his mother had planted around the porch.

Bo panicked when he saw the shedded skin of a copperhead on the porch steps, then laughed at the dusty suggestion, bounced on it daringly, and up to the porch. He opened the whining screen door, burst the jammed wooden door open, and heard his mother: " 'Sat you, Bo?" He remembered how she used to call him her "only Bo." As a boy he had liked it; now it made him shudder. But it didn't matter; she no longer called him in that fashion.

"Yeah, Momma."

As he washed his hands at the sink, he looked out the kitchen window at the heap in the backyard. It was slowly becoming a '66 Impala again. "Like gangbusters," he had said to Lucy, then asked himself, "When?" Turning his attention to his soap-lathered hands dissolved the question, but another sprang in its place: Why not use Dawn's car as a parts department?

He tried to find peace in cooking, but while he chopped potatoes and onions into the skillet, he heard his mother stirring in the bedroom. The aroma of pork grease had reached her, and she shouted, "Smells good." Instead of answering, Bo turned to sawing chops from a whole loin. These he fried also, not turning them until the blood oozed out and turned gray in the skillet.

His mother slipped into the kitchen with short, uneasy steps and dropped into the cushioned chair by the table. She had been resting. The doctor told her to rest eight years ago, when her husband died. Miner's insurance paid her to rest until the rest sapped her strength.

She leaned a tired, graying, but still-brown head of hair against the wall, and let her eyelids sag complacently. She wore two print cotton dresses—one over the other. Two-dress fall, Bo thought, means a three-dress-and-coat winter.

Bo put the food on the table and was about to shovel pork into his mouth when his mother asked for her medicine. "It's in the winder above the sink."

"Has been for eight years," said Bo, scooting his chair out. As he gathered the bottles of colored pills, his glance went once again to the car. The tires were flat.

"I need my medicine," said his mother, while mashing her food into a mush between the fork prongs. She spoke over a mouthful: "When you gonna junk that thing like your Momma ast?"

"Never," he said, setting the bottles and himself at the table. "Probably die workin' on it. Enoch's got . . ." He did not want to mention the wreck at supper.

"Enoch's got what?"

"Got some parts, but I need more."

"It'll get snakes next spring."

"It al's gets snakes, and I al's run 'em off. Now will you leave my car be?"

"TV movie looks like a good 'un tonight," she said in penance.

"Gotta date at the dance in Helvetia."

When the supper dishes were finished, Bo dressed quickly while his mother rested from the walk back to the bedroom. Once wrapped, he slipped to the hall closet and took the .45 from its hatbox. He checked the clip: it was loaded with brightly oiled brass shells. The gun even smelled good. Shoving the weapon into his pocket, he shouted, "Night, Momma," and heard her whimper instructions as he closed and locked the door.

The sun was not setting, nor was it seen. It hid behind the western slopes so only a hint of sun rose upward, firing the ridges with a green fire, and leaving everything in the hollow a clean, cold shadow. Bo knew a freeze was coming. It was too cold to snow. He would have to go now.

Bo watched the trees and houses go by as he only half-listened to Enoch's chatter about his two blueticks, Mattingly and Moore.

"Now Matt, he knows how to run, but Moore can figger if a fox is throwed the pack and he knows just where to look for him."

Bo thought: "I shoulda stayed and watched that movie. Wish Spanker hadn'ta run off. Couldn't stand to be tied up, though."

Houses and tales drifted by. Bo looked back at Matt and Moore, wobbly legged and motion sick.

"I was younger'n you the first time my daddy taked me ahuntin'." Enoch shifted down, and the transmission rattled like a bucket of chains. "Got drunk on two spoons of shine an' half a chew. Man. That was a time. Sittin' back . . . listen to them ol' honkers, and sittin' back. I growed up quick. Had to to stay alive. You ever know my daddy?"

"Nope," said Bo, thinking, wonder what that movie was.

"Your daddy knowed 'im. Meaner'n a teased snake. Got me laid when I's eight. Took me t' a house in Clarksburg —ol' gal said I couldn't come in—so he left me in the car an' went back with a tire tool—then he come an' got me an' showed me that ol' gal an' her man conked out on the floor."

"Musta been some excitement," Bo said, looking at the patterns trees threw against the sky as the truck passed.

"Yeah, an' that ain't all. He taked me t' this room an' busted in on this gal an' made her lay real still till I's finished. Then she called Daddy a SOB cause all he give her was fifty cents, an' he knocked her teeth out."

Enoch laughed wildly, but Bo only smiled. Old Man Enoch was dead, but the rumors of strangers' graves found in pigpens still grew.

"When'd ya git yer first?"

Bo told the afternoon dream as a fact, adding color and characters as he went until he was only inches out of shotgun range when "the sweet thing's old man cut down on me with his sixteen-gauge."

"Damn, who was she?"

"Think I'd tell you so's you could go an' tell on me an' get me killed?"

"Just never figgered you for the type. Guess I been takin' you all wrong." Enoch added in consideration: "Yer pretty slick."

Once they topped the hill, small slashes of light broke through the trees; enough to see rabbits and the road without headlights. Bo was about to mention his gun, but they pulled so quickly off the timber trail, he forgot it. The truck rumbled into a small room in the forest: it was walled with trees, hearthed by a pit of cold ashes, and furnished with broken car seats. Now, Bo thought, climbing from the truck. Now loose. Alone. Smell power in the air—smells like good metal in temper. Dawn never brush against me again. Alone.

"Git some firewood," Enoch ordered.

Bo swung around. "Look, I work for you from the time I git there till when I leave. You want somethin' t'night, better ask like a friend."

"Cocky, ain't ya?"

"I gotta right."

"You ain't actin' like a man."

"You ain't treatin' me like one."

Bo and Enoch combed the littered hill for shed-wood and abandoned timber.

Two miles beyond, an owl watched a meadow from the branches of a dead hickory tree. Hidden in the underbrush, the fox watched the owl and the meadow. Both saw the rabbit meandering through the dying ironweed and goldenrod, and both waited for the best condition of attack. When the moment came, the owl was on wing before the fox had lifted a pad.

The wind changed, and the fox changed cover while keeping close watch on the feasting owl. The fox crept carefully, judged the distance to the nearest cover, then rushed the owl with a bark. The bird flew straight up in alarm, aimed at the thief, and dropped, only to bury its talons in ironweed and earth. Fox and prey were under cover, leaving the bird robbed and hungry in the silver dusk.

Bo built a fire while Enoch tended the dogs. Mattingly and Moore sniffed the air as they overcame their sickness. They pranced and bit the chains as Enoch checked their feet for stones or cuts. As the fire came to life, Bo felt a baseness growing within himself, felt he knew the forest better than the man with the dogs, and, for a moment, wanted to run into the darkness.

Bill began to honk his horn at the foot of the hill and continued to honk his way up the hill trail. The dogs barked from the pain in their ears. "Drunk already," Enoch shouted, laughing. Under a persimmon bush, the fox gnawed rabbit bones and rested, pausing between chews to listen.

The truck lunged into camp; Cuffy fell out, the other men stumbling behind, leaving the frothing dogs tied to the bed of the truck.

"What the hell's he doin' here?" said Cuffy, pointing at Bo.

"I invited him," Enoch said.

"Hey, Enoch," shouted Virg, looking from man to dog and back again. "You an' Matt are beginnin' to look alike."

Cuffy sauntered to the fire, took the seat opposite Bo, and they eyed each other with disgust.

"Wha's Nusty doin' here?" he taunted.

"I like it here," Bo fired back.

"Don't git too used to it."

Bo left Cuffy to join the group.

"B'god, don' tell me that dog can run," Enoch yelled at Bill.

"Bender's the best runner. Bet he sings first *and* leads 'em," Bill answered.

"I'll bet on Moore to sing out first," said Bo. "And Bender to lead."

"Least you got *half* a brain," said Bill.

"How much?" asked Bo.

"Dollar."

"Done," said Bo. Enoch bet Bill on his own, and they shook hands all around before releasing the dogs.

The men brought out their bourbon, and Enoch gave Bo a little special present—moonshine in a mason jar. Then they retired to the fire to swap tales until trail broke.

From his post in the brush the fox could hear sniffing searches being carried out. Dabbing his paws in rabbit gore for a head start, he darted over the back toward the hollow. Queen, Bill's roan hound, was first to find the trail. Instead of calling, she cut back across the ridge to where cold trail told her he was prone to cross. Moore sang out lowly as he sniffed to distinguish fox form rabbit.

"Moore," Enoch shouted, I'd know 'im anyplace."

"Dog's keen-mouthed all right," said Virg.

Bill paid each man the Dollar he owed.

"Made a mistake about that boy," Enoch bragged, embarrassing Bo. "Tell 'em 'bout yer first woman, Bo." The men leaned forward, looking at Bo.

"You tell 'em, Enoch, I ain't drunk enough."

Bo corrected Enoch's rehash from time to time as the listeners hooted their approving laughter.

"Fred said he couldn't go ahuntin'," said Cuffy, watching Bo for some reaction. "Seems somebody's been messin' whit his wife whilst he's gone." Bo stared Cuffy down, then took a full drink from his jar.

"Maybe 'twas that hippie back of Fred," Virg offered.

"Hippie just screws animals," said Cuffy.

"Or other hippies," Enoch added.

"That's what he means," Bo explained, and they all broke into a wild wind of laughter.

The last of the firewood was burning when Bill was finishing his tale. The dogs had been forgotten.

"Like I said, we's all drunk an' Cuffy an' Tom got to argyin' 'bout the weight of them two hogs . . . had 'em all clean and butchered an' packed. Them two bastards loaded 'em on the truck—guts an' all—an' took 'em to Sutton to weigh 'em. Got the guts all mixed up, an' fit ober what head went to what hog."

"Weren't much kick to that hog when I gutted 'im," Cuffy reminisced.

" 'Bout like you kicked when they brained you," Virg spouted. And the men belched laughter again.

The fox was climbing the trail to camp, the pack trailing behind. Queen waited in the brush near the men, cold-trail sure the fox would cross here. The fox circled trees, his last trick to lose the pack.

Bo was woven into the gauze-light, torn between passing out and taking another drink. He caught bits of conversation, then his mind drifted into hollow sleep, and the voices jerked him awake again.

"He's sittin' in the Holy Seat," said Bill's voice in Bo's darkness. Bo kept his eyes closed.

"That was one helluva wreck," said Enoch. "Way I figger it, she drowned."

"Whycome?" asked Virg.

"She was all wrinkly—sorta scrunged up."

"The Holy Pole is in your hold, so work yer ass to save your soul," Cuffy proclaimed.

"She was damn good, all right." Enoch's voice drifted away.

"Hell," said Virg, "I al's went last."

"First come, first served," said Bill.

"Shut up," said Cuffy. "I'm horny again."

"Hell, we all are," said Virg. "Let's dig her up."

"Maybe she's still warm," added Cuffy. The men giggled until they were coughing.

"Told her old man she had a job," Enoch laughed.

"I miss her," sighed Virg.

"I don't," shouted Cuffy. "She coulda hung us all if'n somebody didn' marry her. Nosir, I'm glad she's dead."

Bo fingered the .45 in his pocket.

But the men had whittled the time away telling lies mingled with truth until Bo could no longer distinguish between the two. He had told things, too; no truth or lie could go untold. It was fixed now; the truth and lies were all told.

The fox broke through the clearing, pausing at the sight of fire and man. Queen burst to attack just as the confused fox retreated toward her. There was a yelp, and the fox dashed for the hollow with Queen running a sight chase.

"That damn cutter," Bill shouted. Bo drunkenly swung the .45 from his coat pocket, shot at Queen, and missed. Cuffy screamed as the shot echoed form the dark western ridges. Queen paused to look at Bo, then went back to trail. Virg jumped up and kicked the gun from Bo's hand.

"Try'n save foxie," Bo slurred.

"You stupid son of a bitch," said Cuffy, and Bo looked for the pistol to kill him, but it was lost in the leaves and darkness. His head throbbed, and he looked stupidly at the men.

"Leave 'im alone," said Enoch. "Nobody never teached 'im no better."

Bo stood wavering, and said to Virg, "I's sorry, but I's tryin' to save foxie."

Cuffy spat on Bo's shoe, but he ignored it, walked to the bushes, and threw up.

"You guys piss on the fire," said Enoch. "I'll call the dogs."

Bo nearly missed the clearing in the strange, misty-gray light of Sunday afternoon. Dried oak leaves whispered in the sapless branches above him, and an autumn-blooming flower hung limply on its stem, frostbitten for its rebellion.

The remnants of the night lay strewn about the leaf-floor like a torpid ghost. The mason jar was empty, but his head felt fine—only an ache of change, like a cold coming on. He could smell cold ashes and vomit in the air, but the molten smell was gone from the wind, or perhaps the wind had carried it on.

He found his father's pistol, laced with rusty lines from the wet leaves, and shoved it into his coat pocket. As he lurched down the clay timber-trail toward the secondary, he wondered if the Impala would be ready to roll by spring.

The Mad Whore Of Peach Tree

Victor Depta

So you're here to visit your aunt Thelma. Who amongst
them told you I was mad, or did you simply think of me,
       and come?
Ah, little nephew, the years stagger by so fast.
You were the sweetest, handsomest; but you hunkered past
us like a stray dog with a puzzled look, and so obedient!
I sighed, more than once, at the way you were shunted
off and made to sleep like a boarder among your cousins.

I'm not crazy, now, but boringly sane as the new hens
in the gravel. Did you notice them? I had to pen
the cat up for a month. How could she get it in her head
that they weren't yellow mice? So not a one is dead.
You should see them fly—like chickadees with the dropsy—
to the chestnut trees and cluck like feathery hulls
when the pups quarrel. More coffee, child? What a dull
subject, for you, to have come this far to bear with.

Enough of chickens. I was all spring the mad whore
of Peach Tree. God exposed himself everywhere.
He talked from the twigs of trees with his green mouth
and uncovered his sex the first time to me in the bean sprouts.
He was showing off the tip of his first leaves
like an adolescent boy, how innocent! who unsheathes
it on his stem with unbearable tenderness.

Have they told you, yet, how I ran about the hills
like a crazy ballad? Moss or mushroom sent me reeling
from ridge to ridge; and let me tell you, more than a few
of the ladies at our church would bless me had I fallen at a pew,

rigid and dumb as a board, and not in a stinking ditch.
But God didn't call me to church. I guess I was the witch
with a rake and hoe. I certainly made beans grow.

But I learned this, child, about God:
my heart so pumps with need, that if I throbbed
with Him, we'd hurl, one being, groom and bride,
like stones, and crash amid the stirring of birds,
to join the colloquy of sunrise astir with wings.
We'd cause a flap of havoc; dawn would fling
itself into the air and reel in panic at so much joy.

Where in that happy chaos would be the soul,
and the body with its meat and bones, cupped as a watery bowl
around its being? Would I, a black snake, gulp down
the fledglings on the hill-leaf, branch and tree—devour
the sky, also, and then engorge, like that old ring of fire, the sun,
love's serpent mouth and tail, while mockingbird and thrush
cry in the wilderness without their broods?

I'm quite sane, now, and I've visited your grandmother's grave.
The irises you planted—I know you planted them, so save
yourself the protest—have done very well, both the violet
and the yellow ones with the brown speckles near the lip.
I'm keeping after Marvin. I have to pay the little brute
to mow the grass up there, and take the scythe to the brush.

And now the leaves, little nephew, humped on their points,
skitter in the road before me like grotesque crabs.
They scurry, in the chill wind, to the weeds and underbrush,
and hiss like embittered serpents to the waning sun
that paradise is finally, now, undone.

It Didn't Come From Hallmark

Victor Depta

Charlene came in and closed my book, telling me there
        was a time to think about nukes, your flesh rotting
        off your bones while you puked at one end and
        diarrheaed at the other but not right before dinner.

I love her inviting me to eat but tonight she was quiet and
        when we finished we just sat there over coffee with
        her touching the roses on the table.

I said I loved her and she told me that was natural out of a
        younger brother, especially when the older sister was
        as intelligent and alluring as she was, and she put on
        some hauteur and drank her coffee like a baroness.

I told her to quit acting stupid and I couldn't help the tears
        coming to my eyes. I want to be with you all the time,
        I said. I don't understand it and I can't stop. The
        only time everything's all right is when I'm with you.

She said she bet that was the way a little boy felt about his
        Mommy when she tucked him in bed. I told her to go
        to hell and slammed my fist on the door, crying, fumbling
        to get out when she put her arms around me and stroked
        my hair.

After a long time she said that pretty soon I'd find a love
        with more than tenderness in it and then she'd probably
        be jealous. You're my brother, she said, even if our
        mothers are different. I love you, too, but you don't
        want to be a puppy dog and neither of us would like what
        would happen and you've got to go home.

Later on she sent me a strange looking card with a note on it.
        It sure didn't come from Hallmark.

When Your Ego Bloats

Victor Depta

Damn you, uncle Walter. Unless you're hit by a semi or
    multiple sclerosis, some fate, some circumstance like
    war, which people can weep because of and curse

unless your mother creamed you half to death with a fat breast
    or a father's belt he fumbles with at his waist like a
    long, leathery, unmentionable, symbolic cock while you
    drop your pants

or just twig lashes, the unexpected ones on the path, minor
    sneers, little put-downs, frowns, *Look at your sister,*
    look at your brother, dear—or maybe a test tube frothed
    in the pituitary, or the one in the spleen got broken,
    which no hands of pity can deal with

but when your ego bloats (and, god, what a pasture of illusions
    it feeds on) and like a gassy sheep, bleats in the
    hallway, or bellows like a bull at the door, foaming
    among the picadors you call your colleagues

or when self-pity films your eyes and all your erstwhile
    friends swim by, indifferent as Jaws, well, then,
    forget it, man.

Unless you're battling the horseman in the sky, and every
    human cruelty that marches up, unless you're a doorkeeper
    in the house, like cousin Michael, or truly aware of death,
    like Grandfather, then you're merely a god damned pain
    in the neck.

Charlene's Ex

Victor Depta

Charles can't help it I guess if he's disgusted with women.
  I know he hates Charlene. She aggravates him half
  to death, only he loves her, too. He wants to think he's
  a dude laying it on the women but he's not like that.
  He'll probably marry a secretary at his lawyer's office
  six months from now, about half his age, and then he'll
  be bored and love two women.

This car radio is depressing as hell, he was saying on the way
  to work. I ought to wring its knobs off. Sounds like my

  girlfriend's twang. She's through and I'm forty-two.
  Country'n'western, very smooth, very trite, the doom
  of *good-bye* and *don't cry*.

Divorce, divorce. Kleenexes for the women, handshakes for the
  men, words I don't even listen to myself, and this
  goddamned radio where the guitar is the wail of throats
  on strings and faces pure in grief beyond any bullshit
  in the lyrics.

Jolo

Ann Pancake

Jolo.

Say it.

Say *Jolo.*

Jolo, Jolo boy (moving).

Moving through air as sticky as the blood that moves inside her, same heat as the blood, the spit inside her, that moves inside, so that there in the dark she forgets where she ends, forgets where her skin stops, her skin does not stop, she is continuous. Moving through the weed smells, all the different green smells, single, then symphonic, single, then symphonic, the river low and mucky, a fertile rotty smell, low low dog days August smell. Not a bad smell, even though it is a just short of shit smell, but the river is not unloved for it, no, actually loved by Connie more tender for it, for its spoiledness, its helplessness, for how people have done it. Moving through the frog and bug burr, the chung, chung, chung, the tiny creature roar, layers of ankles and throats and wings, a sobbing mesh, the sound, too, an extension of her, the sex noise that shirrs the rind of her head, the kernel of her chest, again, Connie not knowing where her body ends, her not knowing again, and say it. *Jolo.* The name carries the kind of wet heat, a back of the mouth under the tongue, a you-know-what-I'm-saying-heat. You do. Carried in the syllables themselves. *No*, she wants to say to the cop, *it's not like that*, she tries to say. *Fires are a dry heat*, she says, and *Jolo's wet, just say his name. Jolo.*

But Connie does not tell the cop. When he asks her the question, which triggers what it is to be with Jolo, she does not even think it in segments, in words, like that, but she thinks it all the same, in another way. Thinks it all at once, intuitive, throbbing. But all the same. Cornered in the grocery store lot after closing where she's been hauled in a Ford Fiesta by a neighbor girl who could find nobody else to ride around with that night, and in this parking lot, when the neighbor girl darts across the pavement to whisper with another carload of kids, Connie tries to follow. But the moment she shows herself in the streetlight—hulky, broad-bottomed in terry-cloth shorts—the deputy sheriff shouts her name from where he spies on them in the shadow of the store. He orders Connie over, and when she obeys, seizes her wrists in his sticky fingers without bothering to get out of the car. He pinches her wrists just inside the window where no one else in the lot can see, him cop-smug, encased in his guns and his fat, but the first time he asks her, she only stares at the puddly sundae beside him on the seat. Then he jerks her arms, and her bracelet snaps, beads tumbling into his lap, and Connie shrinks. He asks her again what she knows about Jolo's part in that summer's fires. And still all Connie can answer, and that not even out loud (not what she thinks, but what she knows) is, *Jolo*. Say his name, and you'll know it's not.

Yet Connie doesn't know. She knows no more at that point about Jolo's part in the recent fires than she knows why Jolo has chosen her, this last a daily source of stun. Although she does understand, a thick, thick knowledge, why she's drawn to him. Jolo boy. With his chest ribbed like corduroy and his melted ear, his stomach and arm skin lit like glare on the river. At first it was a prickle, then a pull. Then like how hard it is to look away when the nurse's needle enters your arm. Then, gradually, Connie learned, and yes, it was still the skin, the rosebud ear, like a brand-new animal for Connie to handle, but on top of all that, Connie learned.

Connie, on the other hand, is neither disfigured nor desirable. She was born, she knows, with a mild mistake for a face. Her hips and thighs have blossomed enormous, the way the other girls' will, it is true, shortly after high school, but instead of that inspiring sympathy for Connie, it just makes her more ignored. Connie a fleshy premonition no one wants to acknowledge, prematurely middle-aged even by the yardstick of a place where middle age can strike in one's twenties. So for sixteen years, Connie hovers along, at home, at school, a background noise, someone glimpsed only from corners of eyes, never interesting enough to hate and not even ugly enough to be noticed. And still, Jolo, that summer, chooses her.

Summers where they live. A dull pressure for three long months, a season that squats, the dirt itself on the verge of busting, everything full, until it feels like you, too (especially at fourteen, fifteen, at sixteen), are going to bust. Full. Connie grows up among plants more than people, they all do, and how they strain, strain to bust open, into berry, nut, seedpod, corn ear, like they're beings that run sap, not blood. And that summer, nearly every other night, Jolo covers eight miles on a single-speed banana-seat bike, most of the eight down off the mountain in the dark and all of the miles dark back up, Jolo moving. The bicycle lit by a single reflector and

Jolo too big for the frame, him crunched high over the metal, moving, a praying mantis on miniature wheels. He is living that summer with his grandparents, old-timey types who don't own a phone, but a booth stands near enough their house, out on that county road, that Jolo can hear it from his bedroom window. Connie lets it ring and ring and ring, while Jolo jogs out to the booth and lifts the receiver. And then they have nothing to say.

Yes, for the first two months, they communicate only by hand.

Connie waits along the river on a fraying afghan. Connie crouched there in that river odor, the odor of things dead and things going to be born, and the great organ of insect, mounting, mounting, until she hears Jolo's bike bending the brush. He reaches her, and they already know there is nothing to say, so he just drops down, and they move together. They're moving. The night fishermen across the water, mumbly drunk, to be avoided, and the single night train, baying its lonesomeness, and the corn pollen a green sensation in the back of their throats, not quite smell, not quite taste. They are moving. Jolo's stomach, his back, glow glossy even in the dark, maybe more so in the dark, and he takes Connie's hand, and he says, "Here. Put your fingers on it."

No, they say very little for the first two months, June, July, so for a long time Connie knows only the county's version of the fire eleven years ago. A scare-parable parents tell children who mess with matches. So Jolo's family wiggles through Connie's dreams long before she remembers seeing them for real, a gallery of flaming fragments, images half imagined and half heard. She sees the gooey soles of Jolo's father's melting boots, him sprawled unconscious on the couch. Jolo's mother plummeting out a window on one side of the house, his aunt Ruby Nickelson charging into the opposite side to rescue her own son, Bony (now known by his pulpit name, Little Pastor Dan). Jolo's abandoned baby brother, a black thing, curled in a burned-up bed. And once in a great while, she'll picture Jolo boy himself—this one blurry, cartoonish, hard to imagine, until that summer Jolo chooses her—yes, little Jolo, four years old, stumbling out of a wall of fire, all on his own. That-Vixboy-got-burned-up-so-bad-in-that-house-fire-up-Webb-Mountain is what the county calls Jolo, so by the time Connie is five or six, just the words "Webb Mountain" come dragging that chain: passed-out father, broken mother, saviored cousin, dead baby, charred Jolo.

But Jolo, when he starts talking, later, in August, when after their moving, Jolo will stay awhile, Jolo tells Connie that the fire was not the first time. He tells her that the first time he was even tinier, an infant in his playpen, and a stray cat got into his room. The cat snuck under his covers and started to draw breath out his mouth, nearly suffocated him dead before his father found them and beat the cat bloody with a metal trash can.

"Your mother told you?" Connie asks. "No. No," Jolo says, "I remember." And just a few years after the fire, up in New Jersey, a bunch of them were in a bad wreck that killed the one cousin who got thrown out of the car and ruined Jolo's mother's teeth, Jolo tells her, saying he can't remember that time, was knocked too hard in the head. And there have been times since, Jolo says. He won't say what.

Gradually he tells her it's not that something is trying to kill him, but that he'd just never been full-born. Says a part of him was left on some earlier other side and keeps trying to pull him back with it. Says church does nothing for him because it's the past, not the future, that gives him the tug. And each time he beats it, he comes at the spirit in another way. And although Jolo's cousin, Bony, has become a child evangelist, Jolo tells her, no. God doesn't go to revivals. Says, no. God don't go to no revivals.

God.

When Connie creeps into the barely double bed she shares with her ten-year-old sister, she does not sleep. She reaches back and cups every spent minute in her hands. The grit of the silt between her legs and the sheets, the grit in her pants, she reaches back and unbraids every minute into separate strands—touch, taste, smell, sound—and she fondles them, a second time, a third, a fourth, and even though she's alone, there is little diminishment, he, they, are that strong, that big (Connie is learning).

But her little sister starts to snore. Not loud, but enough to put a smear on things. Connie raises onto an elbow and studies her, biscuit-colored, bland and saggy, her mouth leaking onto her pillow. Then the hall floor creaks, and Connie listens to her mother shuffling to the toilet, one arm, Connie knows, braced against a wall. And the old hate wakes up inside Connie, despite that she swallows on it, hard, Connie can't help but hate her sister—her mother, her father, herself—hate her sister for her limp hair, her sinus infections, for the way she fades back and watches. Fades. Nearly every other night when Connie wedges herself out the first-story window, her parents sit stupored by some television show, suspecting nothing. Their oldest daughter, as far as they're concerned, as sexual as a potato. Now her mother shuts the bathroom door behind her as if there's somebody to watch. Connie hears water hit water.

She looks again at her sister, apologizes in her mind and tries to mean it. She touches the back of her hand to her sister's forehead, like checking for a fever, but her sister's skin feels cooler than the air. Connie rolls away. She sticks her fingers in her ears and tries again. She mouths it, tongues it, Jolo, Jolo boy, and what it calls up in her, slipperied together with the silt and the muck. The weed smells, the bed of the river. Old, old mud.

Because Connie starts to remember. All spun in on herself, curling tighter and tighter, she decides she remembers. By July, she is wondering, then she starts to remember, and, at last, in August, after Jolo tells her about the wreck and the cat and God, she believes. That Jolo found her very early on.

She remembers being four years old and riding rough in the front seat, the vents throwing odor from a mouse nest burnt up in the truck motor some time before. The pickup pulls a dirt road not much better than a jeep track, lunging at it the way an animal would. Her father, still healthy then, still of a piece, swings her out of the cab and carries her over the mud, and Connie watches him try to walk the rut sides in his good shoes. Then she can see a small half-built house in a bulldozed pit, part of this house mud-splattered vinyl siding, part naked insulation, its yard a yellow muck. Her father sets her down and tells her to stay outside. Planks have been thrown over the yard muck, and her father wobbles across them to the porch where he scraped mud off his shoes with a stick that he carries.

At the rear of the house, Connie finds a peculiar man kneeling at a window in a heap of sodden carpet rolls. And suddenly, this peculiar man, retarded somehow, or crippled up, a man's head on a child's body, slides off the carpets. He snatches her under her arms and hoists her to the sill.

At first the shock makes her squeal. But then her wonder takes her. She cups her hands around her eyes to dampen her reflection and see inside. Two coffins, both closed, one papa-sized, one baby. And, then, Connie can see (although she's not at all sure, eleven years later, in June, she becomes more sure in July, and by August, she stands convinced, even though in June, into July, she understands that he could not have been at that house, would have been at the burn center in Baltimore), Connie sees, legs dangling from his mother's lap, a little boy about her own size.

He wears nothing but a pair of shorts, despite the cold, and he is naked in other ways, strange ways, as well. Naked where his eyebrows should be, his chest naked of its nipples, his head ragged bald across its crown where hair sprouts struggle like weeds in a rock face. But what stuns Connie hardest lies between his ribs and his shorts, because this part of his body glistens a liquid glass. This part looks to her (now, as she remembers, having since seen such storms) like the aftermath of an ice storm, every limb on every ridge transfigured to a rumpled prism. The one ear has melted to a twist. A little bud unopened.

Her father doesn't remember the visit at all. Yes, Connie brings it up the summer she's fifteen, she cannot resist, even though she believes it is dangerous, thinking surely that even if they don't notice the sneaking out, her parents can't help but feel the change off her. Despite the risk, Connie brings it up to him one evening, there in the open door of the metal utility shed where her father bides his time like a dog in a pen. But he does not remember. Not the road, not the mud, not the burned-up boy. Her father only remembers the jars.

"Remember the jars?" he says. "For months after that fire, was a mayonnaise jar on every store counter in this end of the county. Had a picture of the boy taped on the front, taken before he got all fried up. They say the father started it, you know, passed out drunk smoking a cigarette. I went to school with the old boy, never was much count. Anyway, they had spaghetti dinners, rummage sales, ramp feeds, fifty-fifty raffles, I don't even know what all."

He pauses to spit in his styrofoam cup, and Connie can see the photo in her head. A K-Mart studio photo of little Jolo, pinkly skinned, and under that, a caption explaining the fire, the hospital bills, no insurance. Jolo becomes a community project, the Christian thing to do, but after about a year, her father says, Jolo's mother publishes a Notice of Appreciation in the county's weekly paper and they all disappear into New Jersey.

"So you can imagine," her father goes on, "when they show back up here five years later with the boy looking like a glazed doughnut. All that praying and fundraising for nearly nothing. Send him to Baltimore on the county nickel and end up with . . . what ? Some cut-rate job for hicks." Her father falls silent, shifts his bulk in his lawn-chair. When he heaves himself out for the evening, Connie knows it will hang all night with his print. "Yeah, some cut-rate job for hicks," he says, and he changes the subject to the heat.

But this doesn't matter. Connie can tell it herself from there. Because that first day of fifth grade, Jolo shows up on Connie's bus run, Connie recovering that day now, six years later, over and over in those nights she doesn't sleep, Connie understanding, gradually, how it all falls together. Five years after they disappear into New Jersey, Jolo's mother returns without the second husband and moves herself, Jolo, and his sister, Pelia, into a bankrupted bait shop on the hill above Connie's house—*Connie's* house. Of course, Connie doesn't know they're back as she climbs onto Bus 14 in her first-day-of-school clothes, already, at ten years old, both excruciatingly self-conscious and completely unnoticed, but five minutes later, the bus startles everyone by pulling over at the abandoned store. Jolo's mother has tried to disguise the place with curtains in the display windows and fake poinsettias on the bait coolers out front, although they never do get rid of the RC sign; they just bust out the store name with rocks and live under the RC logo alone. But all this Connie will notice later, because the first day of fifth grade, the only thing she and everyone else notice are the two new kids, and after registering that there are two, no one gives a second look to the girl.

He swings up into that bus shameless and shockful (Jolo boy). Not only does he go hatless over the skull, the curdled ear, a snail shell buttoned, but for his first day at his new school, Jolo wears one of those football jerseys made of wide loose mesh. Through the mesh they glimpse tiny teases of waxy skin. The horror and the glory in little lacquered dots. They half spy the scarlet furrows over his chest, the nipples or not? and Bus 14 falls quiet as a graveyard. Jolo drops easy into an empty seat as if he's the only person there.

From that day on, to be within eyeshot of Jolo for all the kids is a constant deliberate looking-away, a knowing better than to stare—both because of how they are raised and because of the looks Jolo gives back— but unable to resist, as though Jolo's skin has been injected with tiny magnets that suck eyes. And it's like this for Connie, too, she is no different, but only Bobby Wheazel, who is very special ed, forgets to know better and, day in and day out, gets his eyes full, until that summer Jolo chooses her. And in the meantime, the grown-ups muttering, the botched plastic surgery, confirmation of their suspicion of the overeducated and uppity, all that fundraising and praying for . . . just look at this. But it is really no big surprise. They are brought up to expect disappointment. What they can't know, Connie neither, at that time, is that it's not the doctor's fault at all. What they can't know is that Jolo's mother simply didn't keep up with the rehab. And now, this summer, Connie learns not only that his mother didn't keep up, but that Jolo sees this as a gift.

"We used to call him Bony, but now he goes by his pulpit name, Dan," Jolo says once afterwards while Connie lies on the dirty afghan, filled so rich inside for Jolo she feels her chest split open and butter spill out. Jolo does not touch her. He sits with his back against a sycamore, knees drawn to his chest, his thighs covering the places where the nipples should be. He does not touch her, but Connie can feel the current off him anyway. "Mom would keep him Saturdays while Aunt Ruby cooked at the VFW, and Ruby'd just leave him down to our place all night so she wouldn't have to wake him."

The river funk carries a memory kind of smell, the deep to it, and Jolo stirs round and round in the dirt with a branch. Aunt Ruby Nickelson and Bony moved away after the fire even faster than Jolo's family did, but even so . . . Bony still sticks to Jolo, a crusted rash. A rash that has flared up pitiless on him since that Wednesday night in early June when his grandparents came back from the Church of the Brethren where they'd heard the news that Bony, now called Dan, was expected in August on the revival circuit. Little Pastor Dan, regionally renowned for his come-to-Jesus voice, an altar call they say, like butterflies in his throat. A child evangelist delivered from a house fire at the age of three without a scar, by the grace of God delivered. Jolo gouges at the dirt with his stick. And it's coming to him now, more pressing every day, how it's time to do what he's meant to do.

"So Ruby was up the road at her place when the fire broke out, but she beat the fire trucks to it. Claims she just knew. It was Al Chance saved Pelia off the porch roof, he was Fire Chief back then. Then Mom, she jumped out the window and left little Charlie behind. She got heavy into the religion afterwards, the guilt and all. Before, we'd just been Church of the Brethern, but then she turned Assembly, and finally Holy Temple of Praise. That's another reason I moved in with Grandma and them. Too much church at Mom's."

"Like what? What kind of stuff do they do?" Connie has sat up with the listening. She's been raised tepid Methodist in a place where most churches like their spirits live. Her own religion she sees a neutered gray in the midst of all these mysteries, tangled and hot, and she has always sensed it, steaming off of Jolo, even though Jolo insists his faith is of a different kind.

Jolo just grunts.

"Oh. You know. That holy roller shit." His stick snaps off in the ground.

The insect song heartbeats out of the weeds, surge and recede, surge and recede. Jolo's ears follow it, pattern it, memory it . . . The snak-snak of the drumkit, an under-swell of bass guitar, the great "UHH"s the preacher'd insuck after every phrase, and then they'd be moving. They'd be up and moving. They preached the endtimes every Sunday, Social Security numbers, they said, the Mark of the Beast, and they held their hands over their heads when they prayed like they were asking a question, but with the palms facing down like the answer didn't matter. Jolo waits for the Holy Spirit. He grinds his teeth and tries. And pretty soon, all the others are moving, they're up and moving, leaving only Jolo and the elderly disabled behind. Jolo chill and rigid as a nickel, he sees his heart as a nickel, he does, and all the God in the place swirls Jolo right by.

It's his mother makes him continue to go. His mother, born and born and born again, and you know the state of her spirit by the clothes that she wears, those dull flappy dresses when she walks with the Lord. Then she'll backslide into her favorite black jeans, them fitting her like a snakeskin, and the pointy high-heeled boots, and her little belly, only fat part of her—

she is made long and dark and flat—paunching out over her waistband. Like a blacksnake swallowed a robin's egg, Jolo is thinking. And sometimes she stays backslid for months, once a whole year, and that is better, he knows, that is better. But in the meantime, when she's saved, she dresses him up and drags him to church. His skinny butt numbed on metal chairs, pine pews, molded plastic. In New Jersey, in West Virginia, once at a big revival in Ashland, Kentucky, the others moving and Jolo left behind. Then, one day in Sunday School, they learn about Daniel.

Those years in New Jersey, before he understood, how he kept himself covered. Long-sleeved cowboy shirts, snapped snug at the wrists, even in summer, and T-shirts under those, just to be safe, and a toboggan pulled low over his scalp, the ear. One afternoon in the New Jersey elementary school, he is cornered in the bathroom. They pin him on the floor and strip off the cowboy shirt, part of the T, Jolo's raw skull scraping the concrete as he strikes at them with his teeth. They throw the cap in a urinal. They start to rip down his pants. A teacher storms in and calls them off, but Jolo sees: Even the teacher is more curious than concerned, and this strikes Jolo. This strikes him. Jolo pulls himself up against a stainless steel stall and zips his pants. He stumbles back two steps and stares at his naked torso, warpled in the reflection there.

The Sunday they learn about Daniel, he steals the Bible comic book and studies the pictures at home in his room, the fiery furnace, the three moving, cubits and cornets, kings nibbling grass. And Jolo starts to understand. His own body, in Baltimore, all bound in white, he begins to remember, bound up in his garments, garments, he calls them, a Bible word, and Jolo starts to see. It is the past, not the future, that gives him the tug. He takes to locking himself in his bedroom, a chair jammed under the knob, and he unsnaps the shirt and reads his skin. Its brightness, how it moves on him, its light, how it gleams. He sees it lustered in perfection, a thing not of the here and now, and he starts to remember the night he walked through.

Chosen. Extraordinary. What makes him himself.

By the time he is twelve, thirteen, back in West Virginia, he knows. He bathes, pulls the plug from the drain, stands up to dry. His trunk a sea of glass, him mirroring the mirror.

"But God don't go to church," he tells Connie. "And He sure as hell don't go to no revivals."

Connie nods, and sidles a little closer to him, but Jolo doesn't notice. He swallows. "I walked through fire," he says. "Bony was carried out, and that was different.

"That was different," he says.

That summer's fires begin in late July. They are set in buildings always empty somehow: second homes, a video store closed for the night, a barn on a bankrupt farm. Connie hears about them, everybody does, but she gives them little thought—she has plenty else to think on—until the deputy sheriff in the grocery store lot. Around that time, Jolo starts coming less often, but speaks to her more. Touches her afterwards in places that aren't private, so that even Connie, who has expected all summer to be abandoned at any moment, can tell he's not leaving her yet.

But she has to make do, more and more often, with the meeting place itself. She finds herself back along the river in the days, because to place herself there, even in full light, is to conjure an imprint of the nights, and now she craves them all the time. The insect voice, collapsed thin and lacey in the sun, but the moisture, the blood temperature, amplified, oozing. The air exactly the same wetness, the same heat, inside her lungs and out, the air itself is lungy, so Connie can't track her own breathing, again, she is continuous, and she's moving. She's moving past the beer and bait trash, the stubbed-out little fires. Moving past the dirty foam boiled up in the river's elbows, and she feels for it, feels pity for the river, a river full of chicken shit and rain. She feels deep and feels for everything these days, all her feeling parts poised out on the edges of her skin, bared, and Connie, who has never before been touched by a boy, a man, now believes that it is the keloid that makes her feel, that carries with it the tight wet charge. And she's moving, wallowing in the shape of what's left over from the nights . . . but she's also dodging poison and itchweed, the small and evil plants, and always, the Jolo-conjuring diluted a little by her watching for snakes. Because that is what it is to move there in the summer. Always, a periphery of snakes.

In August, the week Little Pastor Dan arrives, there are two more fires, and Connie grows more certain. One evening on the way to the Dairy Queen, her family passes the revival. The tent is set up where you can't see it from the road—better to build the suspense—but they read the signs— "Teenage Evangelist" "Ghost-Filled Revival"—and gawk at the pasture full of parked automobiles. Connie's mother mentions she'd like to hear those butterflies, and Connie tells her fine, but Connie's not going to no revival. Yet six straight days that week, Jolo doesn't come to her.

She pauses now, there on the riverbank, late morning, the light wet and down low. She squats, and her thighs flatten out like some great underwings. Last night she listened to the sirens, less than an hour after she gave up waiting and crawled back into bed, and by ten o'clock that morning, she'd heard that it had been another weekend home, this one up on Shake Mountain. And she has called the phone booth, again and again, the ringer a mechanical locust in her ear, but nobody has answered. Still, Connie doesn't worry. It was after the second fire she'd been questioned by the cop, and at that time, the idea of Jolo as arsonist had scared her. It had. But she feels different about it since then.

She feels irradiated by it since then.

Because this is what it is to grow up between long tunnelly ridges, never considered one who'd get out, never grouped with that handful who might amount to something, absolutely nothing about you to be noticed, remembered. Not even deserving the favoritism granted the lowliest boys. To see beyond high school only pregnancy or marriage, whichever comes first, a honeymoon to Smoke Hole Caverns, the hope that your children don't hurt you too bad. But at the same time, to be susceptible, raised to obedience and easy belief. Until you piece it all together and finally know that you have been chosen by that body who walked through fire. And you feel big for the first time in your life.

Because Jolo did tell it, eventually, gradually, he told it, not as a story, not in lines, he told it in circles, concentric circles, each circle widening, filling, taking on flesh, and Connie absorbs it like that, receiving it in a sedimentation, the mesh thickening, livening, assuming texture and depth. And by the time he's told maybe eight, ten circles, Connie has it in her head like this: Jolo saying,

"It was Aunt Ruby coming in there woke me at all. Not the smoke or the heat, I would of slept dead through those. But when Bony stayed over, he slept in bed with Charlie and me, and I woke to the bounce in the springs when she snatched Bony up. Then I was coughing. Terrible coughing, jerking my head around so I couldn't hardly see, the coughing all mixed up with the stink of Bony's piss in the covers, and Charlie, he wasn't making a sound. Not a sound. Him over there on the far side of the bed where we slept, him against the wall so he wouldn't tumble out. No, I didn't even think to check on Charlie. I remember sitting up and sliding onto the floor, and I remember the heat on the flat of my feet. Then I don't remember for a while.

"Next thing I know, I'm at the top of the stairs, and I can see, even through all the smoke and flame, I can see Aunt Ruby barreling away towards the front door—she's a big woman in a big green coat, easy to see even through all that—and Bony slung over her shoulder with his mouth squawled open. They're already a good ways gone. Ruby with her back to me.

"So I stand there at the top of those stairs, coughing, smoke-tears rolling down my face, and, buddy, what a noise. Everything ripping and crashing, stuff blowing up. Then, it shuts up. Just like that. Like a hand cupping down over it, pinching it out.

"The noise shut up, and I couldn't hear nothing but my own blood rushing through me. Yeah, like I was a wee little gnat swimming my own blood, and it goes like this: WHOOM. WHOOM. WHOOM. WHOOM. Then I look over my shoulder down the hall and see flames jabbing out from under every last door. And then I know. It's coming for me.

"Yeah, then I feel it. I feel myself being pulled backwards, sucked backwards, like that. Yeah, it's put a drag on me, and I glide backwards a little, and I feel my insides start to cave like a sand washing down, and I know I'm going.

"I was scooting back across the floor, and I had my hands flung out like maybe I could stop myself, but I couldn't touch anything, the walls had drawn away, and my bare feet were picking up splinters and coals . . . when something put the brakes on me. Something reached down and handled me. And it snapped me to a stop and it stiffened my guts, and then, lo and behold, I'm moving ahead.

"Then I'm moving. I know exactly where to put my feet on those burning stairs, and once I reach the bottom, I keep knowing. Not only do I know where to find the doors in the smoke, I know where the walls are down, I'm moving. I pass through. Not only do I know where the walls are down, I know where the flames are thinnest, I can move through. I'm not scared, and I watch, and it's a beautiful thing. How it burns the different colors when it catches different things, colors you ain't never seen before, colors ain't even been thought up. I watch how it takes its time on some things, like it's loving them up, and how it hurries on the others. The paneling and curtains just zipping along, and the wallpaper running backwards to nothing the way a hornet's nest will when you torch it. And Daddy's deerheads, them smoldering, those go slow, and I pass the phone melting off the hook, and the linoleum, melting, me tracking in it like mud, and then that old trunk we had down there, come from up at Grandmommy's place, I see its lid fry open and little things flee out. I did.

"And I'm moving. I'm moving. And I don't feel or hear a single thing but blood ripping through my body and veins until I pass through the front of the house and hit the coldest air there ever was. And one of them jumped me and rolled me on the ground, and then all of it, the roaring and crashing and screams, come back over me like a thunderstorm."

Then Jolo stops. His voice drops down. It's just louder than a whisper, raspy. Prayerful. Connie leans closer, prickled in her skin.

"And you know that Bible story?"

Connie looks at him, expectant. He gazes at the dark and goes on.

"The ShadrackMeshachAbednego fire?"

Connie nods.

Jolo says, "The ones watching the furnace door, they say: 'And the fourth one, he looks like an angel.'"

Jolo turns to Connie. She's huddled on the quilt, clutching her knees, and she can feel it, currenting off him, she can. She feels her own spirit harden, lengthen, with what currents off of Jolo, now them believing together, and she starts to understand herself for the first time in her life. Jolo reaches for her hand. He lays it on his stomach. The graft tissue is a perfect surface, skin that doesn't even sweat.

"See?" Jolo says. "Purified it, He did. Breath of God."

Jolo answers the pay phone the last day of the revival. Later that afternoon, after Connie sets the table for supper, she kneels in the wind off the lint-caked box fan. Her hair streams back, and she feels the strain under her skin, so full it is, and Connie gasps a little.

She catches herself. Glances sideways, wonders if her mother heard her. But her mother keeps flouring slices of yellow squash, sliding them into hot oil. Beyond her mother, her sister, on her stomach in the living room, and Connie can tell her apart from the cement-colored carpet only by the TV glint off her glasses, her sister fading. Fading. As though she has been drained off into the television, as though that is the way the wires work. Her mother keeps rocking, back and forth, counter to stove, dripping from her arms, her throat, flesh the color of an unbaked crust. Connie turns away and coos into the fan. Her voice returns as the insect chirr. She quivers. She lifts up on her haunches in the breeze off the fan, she unfolds her arms, and the wind catches the perspiration under them and chills her, pimples her, and Connie knows how she is two of a kind.

As soon as her sister starts to snore, Connie's out the first-story window, across the yard, and over the railroad embankment. Then she's moving through the river bottom. She's moving among the plants, them pumping under their barks, their peels, and the bugs orchestrating, piles upon piles, the nearest layer always hushing as soon as she gets close, the sound always one film beyond her. She reaches the tiny clearing their bodies have rubbed in the weeds, and she drops heavy over the back to pull the afghan out of the little cave the eroded roots make there.

She knows he will be late, but by this time, she can induce it almost completely without him. She is that strong. She lies on the afghan, and she can feel in her hand the graft scars left on his thighs, his behind, the smoothness runneled. And she listens to a single nearby cricket, banjo pick, a live pick, pulled across Jolo's keloid-ripped chest. She shuts her eyes, and the sights she spells up lightning between that first fire and these recent ones. She enters Jolo and fills him behind his skin, and they move. They know where to pass, the fire shucking off their bodies, them moving, extraordinary. From inside Jolo's eyeballs she watches as they pass through the second homes, the carpet ablaze in ten thousand tiny loops, knick-knacks shattering off shelves, ammunition catching in gun cabinets and the rifles firing holes through the roof. Through the video stores, reels of tape whipping about like nests of evaporating serpents. She watches as they move through the old barn, flushed swallows and mud daubers swarming their head, silos like Roman candles, flames racing down mangers like fuses lit. And she keeps going, she moves through each fire until the one he's told her he'll set tonight. A little fire, just a practice fire. It's an old railroad shed about a mile and a half away, a place where they used to store equipment, not much bigger than a one-car garage, and it shouldn't take long. Then Connie heaves herself out of Jolo's body and slingshots eleven years into the distance, and she lights down in a hickory tree outside that burning house on Webb Mountain, and she watches Jolo boy, four years old, surface from that first fire, seething all over with flames, but not destroyed, no, spectaculared, Jolo crackled glorious all over, and Connie pops her eyes open in awe.

Connie waits a very long time. She waits so long she finally falls asleep a little, and when she wakes up, she's chilled despite the season. She clambers back over the bank to hide the afghan and head for home, but she's only a little disappointed. She stays hopeful for tomorrow.

She's almost to the tracks when she smells gasoline. It comes to her bright against the vegetation smells. She understands immediately and stops. Then Jolo steps out of the weeds and fills the smell, and although at first Connie can only see him as a blacker place against the blackish brush, when she moves right up on him, she sees the sweaty T-shirt is not scorched or singed and she believes it has worked again. She puts he body against him. He doesn't touch her back, but that's not unusual. Connie can hear his heart going in him, she listens.

Jolo grabs the fat part of her arm, and he is not gentle. He jerks her along the trail towards the tracks. They scrabble through the rockfill up the embankment, Connie slipping in the loose gravel and banging her knee, and then Jolo yanks her down so they're sitting side by side on the rail. Connie, her knee throbbing, her weight jabbed by the narrow rail, Connie still yearns at Jolo. Although it's too dark to see much, she squints down at Jolo's hands and arms to view their savioring, a sight she's never seen so fresh. And untouched they are, not a hair crisped. But then she notices the hands are trembling, and she looks him in the face. When Jolo finally speaks, he does so through clenched teeth.

"*You* know why I set them," he says.

"To make a fire big enough to walk through," she answers. She waits. They are not touching. "What's the matter?" she says.

He wipes his mouth in the bottom of the filthy shirt and turns away.

"What's the matter?" she says again. They are not touching. The railroad holds the day's heat, heavy in its ties, and now it fumes up, filling them from the bottom, a weight to it Connie feels settle in her jaws.

"I haven't yet," he answers.

"What do you mean?" Connie asks.

"I haven't walked through yet."

Connie's lungs begin to go faster, but lighter. Like little moths dissolving in her chest. After a while, she reaches her insides toward Jolo, but she gets nothing back. Her mind suddenly finds itself with no place to go. She drifts in a dark that has nothing to do with the river bottom at night, the sound of this dark like a shell to her ear, and she feels in her heart a tiny draining backwards. Then she understands, in a way without words, that she straddles a gully, the gully widening, and one side of her stays with the boy who walked through. But her other sides senses, in the middle distance, with an unfocused but gut-deep panic . . . that side backpedaling, but nonetheless sensing, Jolo's terrible ordinariness.

She braces her hands behind her on the rail and starts to struggle to her feet, not because she plans to leave, but because she might get her bearings there. Jolo snatches her back by her belt loop.

"Don't worry," he says. "I figured out what's wrong."

So Connie settles back down. On either side of her hips, she grips the rail still warm from the hours-gone sun. She repeats in her head what Jolo's said, twice. Places one warm hand on her rapid chest, coaxes her lungs to slow themselves. Connie waits. She screws up her will and tries. And, then, gradually, the roar in her ears diminishes, and she hears what she'd stopped listening to: the great organ of insect. Its surge and recede, the sobbing mesh, layers of ankles and throats and wings, it washes back, an extension of Connie, the noise shirring the rind of her head, the kernel of her chest, until her breath beats the same meter as the creatures and trees. And rushing over her comes the age in Jolo, like the age in Connie. But with Connie, the age is in the body, and with Jolo, it's deeper someplace.

Then finally she's moving. She is moving, towards that soul who walked through, and she understands, and she starts to say. Say *Jolo*, she tells herself. *Jolo.* Softly at first, she tells herself, *Jolo*, then loud as the pitch of the insect throb, say *Jolo, Jolo boy*, and finally with conviction, she is saying, *Jolo*, say *Jolo*, and you'll know, *Jolo*, she tells herself, *say it*, and Jolo says,

"With the two of us, it'll work."

Sin Boldly
from Colored People: A Memoir

Henry Louis Gates Jr.

*I*n 1968, three of the Fearsome Foursome graduated from high school. Soul Moe was called upon to serve his country in Vietnam, and Swano and I would head down to Potomac State. (Roland had been held back a couple of years.) I gave the valedictory address at graduation, defying tradition by writing my own speech—surreptitiously, because this was not allowed. All through the last six weeks of marking period I had practiced delivering the traditional prepared speech with Miss Twigg, our senior English teacher, then had gone home to rehearse my real speech with Mama. Mama had a refined sense of vocal presentation and a wonderful sense of irony and timing. My speech was about Vietnam, abortion, and civil rights, about the sense of community our class shared, since so many of us had been together for twelve years, about the individual's rights and responsibilities in his or her community, and about the necessity to defy norms out of love. I searched the audience for Miss Twigg's face, just to see her expression when I read the speech! She turned as red as a beet, but she liked the speech, and as good as told me so with a big wink at the end of the ceremony.

My one year at Potomac State College of West Virginia University, in Keyser, all of five miles away, was memorable for two reasons: because of my English classes with Duke Anthony Whitmore and my first real love affair, with Maura Gibson.

I came to Potomac State to begin that long, arduous trek toward medical school. I enrolled in August 1968, a week before Labor Day, and I was scared to death. While I had been a good student at Piedmont High, I had no idea how well I would fare in the big-time competition of a college class that included several of the best students from Keyser High, as well as bright kids from throughout the state. I had never questioned my decision to attend Potomac State; it was inevitable: you went there after Piedmont High, as sure as the night follows the day. My uncles Raymond and David had attended it in the fifties, my brother in the early sixties, and my cousin Greg had begun the year before. I would attend too, then go off to "the university"—in Morgantown—to become a doctor.

Greg had told me about life on campus, about the freedom of choice, about card parties in the Union, and, of course, about the women. But he had also told me one thing early in his freshman year that had stayed with me throughout my senior year in Piedmont. "There's an English teacher down there," he had said, "who's going to blow your mind."

"What's his name?" I responded.

"Duke Anthony Whitmore," he replied.

"*Duke?*" I said. "What kind of name is Duke? Is he an Englishman?"

"No, dummy," Greg replied. "He's a white guy from Baltimore."

So as I nervously slouched my way through registration a year later, I found myself standing before the ferocious Mr. Gallagher, who enjoyed the reputation of being tough. He gave me the name of my adviser.

I looked at the name; it was not Whitmore. "Can I be assigned to Mr. Whitmore?" I ventured. "Because I've heard quite a lot about him from my cousin."

"You'll have to ask him," Mr. Gallagher said. "He's over there."

I made my way to Mr. Whitmore's table, introduced myself tentatively, stated my case, telling him my cousin Greg had said that he was a great teacher, a wonderful inspiration, etc., etc. What Greg had really said was: "This guy Whitmore is *crazy*, just like you!" It was love at first sight, at least for me. And that, in retrospect, was the beginning of the end of my twelve-year-old dream to becoming a doctor.

Learning English and American literature from the Duke was a game to which I looked forward every day. I had always loved English and had been blessed with some dedicated and able teachers. But reading books was something I had always thought of as a pastime, certainly not as a vocation. The Duke made the study of literature an alluring prospect.

Duke Whitmore did not suffer fools gladly. He did not suffer fools at all. Our classes—I enrolled in everything he taught, despite his protests, which I have to say weren't very strenuous—soon came to be dominated by three or four voices. We would argue and debate just about everything from Emerson and Thoreau to the war in Vietnam and racial discrimination. He would recite a passage from a poem or play, then demand that we tell him, rapid-fire, its source.

"*King Lear*," I responded one day.

"What act, what scene, Mr. Gates?" he demanded.

"Act Three, Scene Four," I shouted out blindly, not having the faintest clue as to whether the passage that he had recited was from *Hamlet* or the Book of Job.

"Exactly," he responded with a certain twinkle in his eye.

"Sin boldly," he would tell me later, citing Martin Luther. My reckless citation was wrong, of course, but he wished to reward me for my audacity.

It was a glorious experience. Words and thoughts, ideas and visions, came alive for me in his classroom. It was he who showed me, by his example, that ideas had a life of their own and that there were other professions as stimulating and as rewarding as being a doctor.

After an academically successful year, Professor Whitmore encouraged me to transfer to the Ivy League. I wrote to Harvard, Yale, and Princeton. Since I had cousins who had gone to Harvard and Princeton, I decided to try for Yale. I sent off the application and took a summer job in the personnel office of the paper mill. I'd been hired for the express purpose of encouraging a few black people to transfer into the craft unions; I recruited them and administered the necessary test. In three months, each union had been integrated, with barely an audible murmur from its members. Things were changing in Piedmont—a little.

Though we didn't become an item until our freshman year at Potomac State, Maura Gibson and I had known each other from a distance in high school. I used to run into her at the bowling alley and at Jimmy's Pizza next door. She was sharp on her feet and loved to argue. Once, she took me to task for talking about race so much. You can't talk about the weather without bringing up race, she charged. I was embarrassed about that at first, then pleased.

Once we were at college, Maura and I started having long talks on the phone, first about nothing at all and then about everything. The next thing I remember happening between us was parking in her green Dodge up in the colored cemetery on Radical Hill, near where just about all the Keyser colored, and much of the white trash, lived. "Radical" is a synonym in the valley for tacky or ramshackle. I'm not sure which came first, the name or what it came to mean. That's where we were when Horse Lowe (the coach of the college's football team and the owner of the property that abuts the colored cemetery) put his big red face into Maura's window, beat on the windshield with his fist, then told me to get the hell off his property.

Horse Lowe would wait until a couple had begun to pet heavily, then he'd sneak up on the car. He liked to catch you exposed. Even so, we used to park up there all the time. I figured that he'd get tired of throwing us out before I got tired of parking.

On weekends during the summer of 1969, I'd drive over to Rehoboth Beach, in Delaware, to see Maura, who was working as a waitress at a place called the Crab Pot. I'd leave work on Friday at about four o'clock, then drive all the way to Delaware, through Washington and the Beltway, past Baltimore and Annapolis, over the Chesapeake Bridge, past the Ocean City, arriving at Rehoboth before midnight, with as much energy as if I had just awakened. We'd get a motel room after her shift ended, and she'd bring a bushel of crabs, steamed in the hot spice called Old Bay. We'd get lots of ice-cold Budweiser and we'd have a feast, listening to Junior Walker play his saxophone, play "What Does It Take" over and over and over again. "What does it take to win your love for me? . . ."

Since Maura was white, I felt that I was making some sort of vague political statement, especially in the wake of Sammy Davis, Jr., and *Guess Who's Coming to Dinner*. Others concurred. We were hassled at the beach. Somehow, for reasons having to do with nudity and sensuality, blacks were not allowed to walk along most beachfronts or attend resorts. I personally integrated many places at Rehoboth Beach that summer.

I was used to being stared at and somewhat used to being the only black person on the beach, or in a restaurant, or at a motel. But I hadn't quite realized how upset people could be until the day that some white guy sicced his Saint Bernard on me as Maura and I walked by. Certainly Maura and I had been no strangers to controversy, but we usually took pains not to invite it. Back home, we had sneaked around at first, hiding in cemeteries and in a crowd of friends, almost never being seen together in public alone. Until we were found out—by her father, of all people. A man called " 'Bama," of all things.

It was the evening we had agreed to meet at the big oak tree on Spring Street in Keyser, near one of her friends' houses. I picked her up in my '57 Chevrolet, and we went up to harass the Horse. Afterward, I dropped her off, then drove the five miles back to Piedmont. By the time I got home, Maura had called a dozen times. It turned out that her father had followed her down the street and hidden behind a tree while she waited, had watched her climb into my car. He knew the whole thing.

And he, no progressive on race matters, was sickened and outraged.

Soon, it seemed, all of the Valley knew the whole thing, and everybody had an opinion about it. We were apparently the first interracial couple in Mineral County, and there was hell to pay. People began making oblique threats, in the sort of whispers peculiar to small towns. When friends started warning my parents about them, they bought me a '69 Mustang so I could travel to and from school—and the colored graveyard—safely. (The Chevy had taken to conking out unpredictably.) Some kids at Potomac State started calling us names, anonymously, out of dormitory windows. And in the middle of all this chaos, 'Bama Gibson, Maura's father, decided he was going to run for mayor.

Lawd, Lawd, Lawd.

In his own redneck way, 'Bama Gibson was a perfectly nice man, but he was not exactly mayoral material. He had been a postman and became some sort of supervisor at the post office. He was very personable, everybody liked him, and he knew everybody's business, the way a postman in any small town does. With the whole town talking about how terrible it was that his daughter was dating a colored boy, and the men giving him their sympathy and declaring what they'd do to that nigger if that nigger ever touched their daughter, old 'Bama up and announced his candidacy.

Dr. Church, former president of the college, was the obvious front-runner. People were saying he'd already started to measure the mayor's office for new curtains. Certainly no one would have given 'Bama any hope of beating Dr. Church, even before my nappy head came on the horizon. With you on these crackers' minds, Daddy told me, he's got two chances: slim and none. Boy, how do you *get* into all this trouble?

Meantime, at the height of the campaign, Roland, Jerry, Swano, and I decided to integrate the Swordfish, a weekend hangout where all the college kids went to listen to a live band—usually E. G. Taylor and the Sounds of Soul, a white band with a black, Eugene Taylor, as lead singer. Eugene could *sing*. He wasn't so great with learning the words, but that Negro could warble. He'd make up words as he went along, using sounds similar to those he could not remember but making no sense.

Still, we wanted the right to hear Eugene mess up James Brown's words, same as anybody else, so we started to plot our move. Late one Friday night, when the Swordfish was rocking and packed, we headed up New Creek in our Soul Mobile, which we had washed for the occasion, even replacing the old masking tape over the holes in the roof. The Fearsome Foursome made their date with destiny. We were silent as we drove into the parking lot. There was nothing left to say. We were scared to death but just had to get on with it.

We parked the car and strolled up the stairs to the Swordfish. Since there was no cover charge, we walked straight into the middle of the dance floor. That's when the slo-mo started, an effect exacerbated by the strobe lights. Everybody froze: the kids from Piedmont and Keyser who had grown up with us; the students from Potomac State; the rednecks and crackers from up the hollers, the ones who came to town once a week all dressed up in their Sears, Roebuck perma-pressed drawers, their Thom McAn semi-leather shoes, their ultimately white sox, and their hair slicked back and wet-looking. The kids of rednecks, who liked to drink gallons of 3.2 beer, threaten everybody within earshot, and puke all over themselves— they froze too, their worst nightmare staring thin in the face.

After what seemed like hours but was probably less than a minute, a homely white boy with extra-greasy blond hair recovered and began to shout "Niggers" as his face assumed the ugly mask of hillbilly racism. I stared at this white boy's face, which turned redder and redder as *he* turned into the Devil, calling on his boys to kick our asses: calling us niggers and niggers and niggers to help them summon up their courage. White boys started moving around us, forming a circle around ours. Our good friends from Keyser and Potomac State were still frozen, embarrassed that we were *in* there, that we had violated their space, dared to cross the line. No help from them. (I lost lots of friends that night.) Then, breaking through the circle of rednecks, came the owner, who started screaming: Get out of here! Get out of here! and picked up Fisher and slammed his head against the wall. It wasn't easy to see because of all the smoke and because of the strobe effect of the flashing blue lights, but I remember being surprised at how Roland's Afro had kept it's shape when his head sprang back off the wall, the way a basketball keeps its shape no matter how much or how hard you dribble it.

Moe and I hauled Fisher off the ground, with Swano's broad shoulders driving through the 'necks the way Bubba Smith used to do for the Baltimore Colts. I wondered if Roland's head would stop bleeding. Fuck you, motherfucker, I heard myself say. We're gonna shut your racist ass down. We're gonna shut your ass down, repeated Moe and Swano in chorus. Take a good look around you, you crackers, cuz this is your last time here.

We dragged Fisher to the car, ducking the bottles and cans as we sped away. Roland's head had stopped its bleeding by the time we passed Potomac Valley Hospital, which we called the meat factory because one of the doctors was reputed to be such a butcher, so we drove on past it and headed for my house. What'll y'all do now? Daddy asked as Mama bandaged Roland Fisher's head.

And yes, the place was shut down. We called the State Human Rights Commission on Monday, and the commissioner, Carl Glass, came up to Piedmont a few days later. He interviewed the four of us separately, and then he went out to the Swordfish and interviewed the proprietor, who by this time had told everybody white and colored in Keyser that he was going to get that troublemaker Gates. He swore to the commissioner that he would close down before he let niggers in. The commissioner took him at his word and sent an official edict telling him to integrate or shut down. As the man promised, he shut it down. And that is why the Swordfish nightclub is now Samson's Family Restaurant, run by a very nice Filipino family.

Well, all of this broke out in the middle of 'Bama Gibson's campaign to be the first postman elected as Mayor of Keyser, West Virginia, The Friendliest City in the U. S. A., as the road sign boasted—to which we chorused "bullshit" whenever we passed it.

The whole town talked about this campaign, from sunup to sundown. And there were some curious developments. Our family doctor, Dr. Staggers (our high school principal, Mr. Staggers's son), went out of his way to tell me that lots of his friends, well-educated and liberal, had decided to suspend disbelief and vote for 'Bama, just to prove (as he put it) that Keyser is not Birmingham. Then the colored people, who never voted, decided to register and turn out for good ole 'Bama. The college kids at Potomac State, the ones not busy calling Maura "nigger-lover" from their dormitory windows, turned out in droves. And all the romantics who lived in Keyser, those who truly respected the idea of love and passion, voted for 'Bama. All both of them. Bizarrely enough, the election was turning into a plebiscite on interracial relationships.

I stayed out of Keyser on the day of the election, terrified that I'd already caused Maura's father to lose. If it's close, there's no sense aggravating the ones sitting on the fence, rubbing their nose in it, Daddy had said. And so I waited for Maura's phone call, which came around eleven-thirty and informed me that we had nothing more to worry about, her father had trampled Dr. Church. No longer would the police follow us, daring us to go even one mile over the speed limit. That's what she told me, and I could scarcely believe it. I started parking my car on red lines and in from of fire hydrants, just to test her assertion. She was right.

It was also because of 'Bama's new office that I learned that the West Virginia State Police had opened a file on me in Mineral County, which identified me for possible custodial detention if and when race riots started. Maura gave me the news late one night, whispering it over the phone. Old 'Bama, whom victory had made magnanimous, had wanted me to know and to be warned.

I remember the feeling sick and scared . . . and then, when that passed, a little flattered. I was eighteen, had scarcely been outside Mineral County, and someone in authority decided I was dangerous? I mean, *I* liked to think so. But that an official establishment should collude with my fantasies of importance was quite another matter.

I took it as a sign that it was time for me to leave the Valley and go Elsewhere. I did leave it, that very fall, packing my bags for New Haven. But leaving it *behind* was never a possibility. It did not take me long to realize that.

The "Personal Statement" for my Yale application began: "My grandfather was colored, my father was Negro, and I am black." And it concluded: "As always, whitey now sits in judgment of me, preparing to cast my fate. It is your decision either to let me blow with the wind as a non-entity or to encourage the development of self. Allow me to prove myself."

I wince at the rhetoric today, but they let me in.

Twilight In West Virginia:
Six O'clock Mine Report

Irene McKinney

*Bergoo Mine No. 3 will work: Bergoo Mine
No. 3 will work tomorrow. Consol. No. 2
will not work: Consol. No. 2 will not
work tomorrow.*

Green soaks into the dark trees.
The hills go clumped and heavy
over the foxfire veins
at Clinchfield, One-Go, Greenbrier.

At Hardtack and Amity the grit
abrades the skin. The air is thick
above the black leaves, the open mouth
of the shaft. A man with a burning

carbide lamp on his forehead
swings a pick in a narrow corridor
beneath the earth. His eyes flare
white like a horse's, his teeth glint.

From his sleeves of coal, fingers
with black half-moons: he leans
into the tipple, over the coke oven
staining the air red, over the glow

from the rows of fiery eyes at Swago.
Above Slipjohn a six-ton lumbers down
the grade, its windows curtained with soot.
No one is driving.

The roads get lost in the clotted hills,
in the Blue Spruce maze, the red cough,
the Allegheny marl, the sulphur ooze.

The hill-cuts drain; the roads get lost
and drop at the edge of the strip job.
The fires in the mines do not stop burning.

Deep Mining

Irene McKinney

Think of this: that under the earth
there are black rooms your very body

can move through. Just as you always
dreamed, you enter the open mouth

and slide between the glistening walls,
the arteries of coal in the larger body.

I knock it loose with the heavy hammer.
I load it up and send it out

while you walk up there on the crust,
in the daylight, and listen to the coal-cars

bearing down with their burden.
You're going to burn this fuel

and when you come in from your chores,
rub your hands in the soft red glow

and stand in your steaming clothes
with your back to it, while it soaks

into frozen buttocks and thighs.
You're going to do that for me

while I slog in the icy water
behind the straining cars.

Until the swing-shift comes around.
Now, I am the one in front of the fire.

Someone has stoked the cooking stove
and set brown loaves on the warming pan.

Someone has laid out my softer clothes,
and turned back the quilt.

Listen: there is a vein that runs
through the earth from top to bottom

and both of us are in it.
One of us is always burning.

Visiting My Gravesite:
Talbott Churchyard, West Virginia

Irene McKinney

Maybe because I was married and felt secure and dead
at once, I listened to my father's urgings about "the future"

and bought this double plot on the hillside with a view
of the bare white church, the old elms, and the creek below.

I plan now to use both plots, luxuriantly spreading out
in the middle of a big double bed. —But no,

finally, my burial has nothing to do with my marriage, this lying
      here
in these same bones will be as real as anything I can imagine

for who I'll be then, as real as anything undergone, going back
and forth to "the world" out there, and here to this one spot

on earth I really know. Once I came in fast and low
in a little plane and when I looked down at the church,

the trees I've felt with my hands, the neighbors' houses
and the family farm, and I saw how tiny what I loved or knew
            was,

it was like my children going on with their plans and griefs
at a distance and nothing I could do about it. But I wanted

to reach down and pat it, while letting it know
I wouldn't interfere for the world, the world being

everything this isn't, this unknown buried in the known.

Fodder

Irene McKinney

So I was the Scavenger-Child, whuffling
in filthy attics, scrounging for
broken-backed edition of Edgar Allen Poe
covered with pigeon-droppings, accumulating
old yellowed books from abandoned schoolhouses

buried in the woods, smelling of piss
and mire and all abuzz with giant wasps
building a nest in a pump organ.
These were my fabulous loves, my secret
foods. There were my handholds

into shaky light, my emergence from
the pit, and loving the furniture of
the pit, my dedication to the darkness
and the shadows of fireflies' bodies
found between the smelly pages, the vile

effluvium of bookworms' paths trekking
with intention through one after the other,
out one cover into the next, eating
their way through shelf after shelf,
Byron, *Sheep Shearing in America*,

Kiss me Deadly to Paradise Lost, and
Lo! The Bird. Why should a hungry worm
care what it ate? It was all paper
and words, all black magic marks
in an unmarked world, all height and

depth and beautiful fodder, a method
of moving the eyes until they brimmed
with startlement, the swollen pupils
reading themselves to death, and up
beside it, and into it.

For Women Who Have Been Patient All Their Lives

Irene McKinney

1.

There is anger in the stiff bedsprings
and under the house in the black powdered dirt,
ground into the blunt cracked hands of my father.

Something is coming, my mother says
There will be something for all of us

The strip-miners come, the loggers;
anger gathers at the lip of the cracked well,
in the bins of wheat in the shambled granary.

Someone will pay, it won't be us
We have learned to wait

in the cold morning with snow on the beds,
at night in the stale quilts
and worn grunts of our men.

2.

Mother, from the roots of your hair
from your heavy white body

from your great splayed feet
from the blue bowls of your breasts.

from the steamy washtub
from the wet rags, sour milk

from the belly of the stove
from the lobs of dough, the biscuits

from the whine of the babies
I was one, dragging at you

from the dark barrow of your bed
where you wait in your sleep

What you have given cannot say its name

From blind love for your sisters
and the ease of women

from these, who you are
reach out to me

and I, your bony daughter
schooled in your kitchen

will reach back to give you
what I have, these words

the spilling of anger and love
saved like money for years.

Viridian Days

Irene McKinney

I was an ordinary woman, and so
I appeared eccentric, collecting gee-gaws
of porcelain and cobalt blue, mincing
deer-meat for the cat. I was unhooked

from matrimony, and so I rose up
like a hot-air balloon, and drifted
down eventually into the countryside,
not shevelled New England nor the

grandeur of the West, but disheveled
West Virginia, where the hills are flung
around like old green handkerchiefs
and the Chessie rumbles along, shaking

the smooth clean skin of the river.
If I wanted to glue magazine pictures
to an entire wall, or walk around nude,
I did so, having no standard to maintain

and no small children to be humiliated
by my defection. I spent years puttering
around in a green bathrobe, smelling of
coffee, perfume, sweat, incense, and

female effluvia. Why not. That was
my motto. I collected books like some
women collect green stamps, but I read
them all, down to the finest print,

the solid cubes of the footnotes. Since no one
was there, nobody stopped me. Raspberry vines
slash at the Toyota's sides as I come in.
Flocks of starlings, grosbeaks, mourning doves

lift the air around the house. Fragments
of turkey bones the dog chewed on, a swarm
of ladybugs made into a red enameled necklace,
hulls of black sunflower seeds piled

on the porchboards. Locust, hickory, sweet gum
trees. Absolute silence stricken by crow calls.
Copper pans, eight strands of seed beads,
dolphin earrings. I climb over the fence

at the edge of the woods, back and forth
over it several times a day, gathering ferns,
then digging in the parsley, -shaggy, pungent, green.

Cheers

Jayne Anne Phillips

*T*he sewing woman lived across the tracks, down past Arey's Feed Store. Row of skinny houses on a mud alley. Her rooms smelled of salted grease and old newspaper. Behind the ironing board she was thin, scooping up papers that shuffled open in her hands. Her eyebrows were arched sharp and painted on.

She made cheerleading suits for ten-year-olds. Threading the machine, she clicked her red nails on the needle and pulled my shirt over my head. In the other room the kids watched *Queen for a Day*. She bent over me. I saw each eyelash painted black and hard and separate. Honey, she said. Turn around this way. And on the wall there was a postcard of orange trees in Florida. A man in a straw hat reached up with his hands all curled. Beautiful Bounty said the card in wavy red letters.

I got part of it made up, she said, fitting the red vest. You girls are bout the same size as mine All you girls are bout the same. She pursed her red lips and pinched the cloth together. Tell me somethin Honey. How'd I manage all these kids an no man. On television there was loud applause for the queen, whose roses were sharp and real. Her machine buzzed like an animal beside the round clock. She frowned as she pressed the button with her foot, then furled the red cloth out and pulled me to her. Her pointed white face was smudged around the eyes. I watched the pale strand of scalp in her hair. There, she said.

When I left she tucked the money in her sweater. She has pins between her teeth and lipstick gone grainy in the cracks of her mouth. I had a red swing skirt and a bumpy *A* on my chest. Lord, she said. You do look pretty.

Bess

Jayne Anne Phillips

*Y*ou have to imagine: this was sixty, seventy, eighty years ago, more than
the lifetimes allotted most persons. *Lord save us*, is what we used to say—
we younger ones—as an expression, sometimes in jest. Later I said it in
earnest, in the long winters, light in the rooms so dim and the rooms
themselves like shadowy caves. Some months we children took lessons at
home, as Coalton was thirty minutes wagon ride and snow too deep for the
wheels; drifts on the road were waist-high. Pa did have a sledge but
traveled any distance only in emergency. A few times, in a snap freeze, the
snow grew shiny and hard, gleaming as though a mirror were shattered
across its whole surface. Pa marked a track with sticks and bundled us in
furs. We rode round, runners of the sledge tracing a circle past the house
and the naked oaks. The belled harness jingled and beyond the oaks were
fields on all sides, sloping flat to the woods. We were warned not to go out
of track. Further out the snow was soft in spots and would swallow us right
up, Pa said. This was probably only a story, though we lost an animal
nearly every winter, in just that way—goats or hogs lost in a drift, frozen
perfectly until a thaw revealed them.

From the age of eight or nine, my brother Warwick drove the sledge.
We sisters sat wrapped together in blankets and the bear rug, our faces
covered except for our eyes. Warwick sat forward with the whip and reins,
making the horse step quickly to stay warm. Pa followed on snowshoes;
behind us he looked like a bulky troll against the white, which fairly
glinted like a glassy sea with slopes. The circle, round the big house and
the empty guesthouse, was perhaps a half-mile. Warwick whistled and
shouted to the horse, his voice high-pitched, a child's voice floating out
and freezing. It was like flying, slicing through the wind with the air so
cold we couldn't see into it.

Finally Warwick let us off by the big porch that was heaped with
snow, then drove the sledge to the barn where Pa met him. We sisters went

in to the fire, all of us shining with cold, and the fire warmed us, turned us one by one to our winter selves, dim in the dim house, the windows all shuttered against the cold, the lamps throwing off small glows.

Our parents joked about their two families, first the six sons, one after the other; then a few years later the four daughters, Warwick, and me. Another daughter after the boy was a bad sign, Pa said; there were enough children. I was the last, youngest of twelve Hampsons, and just thirteen months younger then Warwick. Since we were born on each other's heels, Mam said, we would have to raise each other.

Warwick, Ava, and I shared one room, the three other sisters another. In winter only the big kitchen was kept truly warm. It was considered dangerous to have wood stoves or coal burners in children's bedrooms; we slept under feather comforters, close to each other. Ava was four years older and often appointed to watch Warwick and me. She longed for the company of the older sisters and yet took a kind of pride in her responsibility. I remember her teaching us, with chalks on a slate, gravely, the letter *S*. I was not even talking yet; she taught me to hiss, then drew one line and changed the *S* to an *8*. *S*, *8*. Something was flickering all around us. Doubtless it was the fire, lit on a winter evening when the dark came so early. I remember no one's face, but I see her hand on the slate beside the magic form. Those long winters inside were not bad times at first, but in later weeks a strange loneliness came—late in the cold, the last few weeks before it broke, we seldom talked or read aloud or argued anymore, or played games. We lived instead in silence, only doing what we were told to do, and waiting.

We could see no other farms from our house, not a habitation or the smoke of someone's chimney; we could not see the borders of the road anymore but only the cover of snow, the white fields, and mountains beyond. The mountains were an awesome height; you could not see where the sky began. The house in this whiteness seemed small, alien, as though we might be covered up and vanish; no one would know. Sounds were so muffled; except for the wind, one could have fantasies of deafness. The power of the Scriptures in such a setting was great and we heard the Bible aloud nearly every evening. Twilight, because the valley was deep, came as early as three or four in the afternoon; the world, the snow, seemed to fly in the face of the Word. *Remove not the old landmarks, venture not into the fields of the fatherless*; yet the snow still fell.

Winter frightened me, but it was summers I should have feared. Summers, when the house was large and full, the work out-of-doors so it seemed no work at all, everything done in company. Summers all the men were home, the farm was crowded, lively; it seemed nothing could go wrong then.

The six elder brothers had all left home at sixteen to homestead somewhere on the land, each going first to live with the brother established before him. They worked mines or cut timber for money to start farms and had an eye for women who were not delicate. Once each spring they were all back to plant garden with Pa, and the sisters talked amongst themselves about each one. All older than the girls and distant enough to be mysterious, they were comely men and this week alone appeared all together without their wives, filling the house after the long silent winter and taking hours to eat big suppers the sisters served after nightfall.

Noons we took turns carrying water to them on horseback, corked bottles we'd filled in the cold creek. We sat astride and they drank at our knees. Each had a favorite sister; they were a bit shy when alone with the one they liked most. Sometimes there was an awkward silence while they drank. They were strong men; they were all alive then. To think of them, drinking cold water and sweating, squinting against the sun at a face.

By late June the brothers had brought their families, each a wife and several children. All the rooms in the big house were used, the guesthouse as well, swept and cleaned. There was always enough space because each family lived in two big rooms, one given to parents and youngest baby and the other left for older children to sleep together, all fallen uncovered across a wide cob-stuffed mattress. Within those houses were many children, fifteen, twenty, more. I am speaking now of the summer I was twelve, the summer Warwick got sick and everything changed.

He was nearly fourteen. We slept in the big house in the same room but chose favorite cousins to share the space, as the four elder sisters in summer had their own two rooms over the sun porch, open to river breeze; they were all young ladies now and I had little to do with them. Ava told me I was more a boy than a girl. I didn't care; the young cousin all wanted to be chosen, as our room was bay-windowed, very large, and directly above the parlor, the huge oak tree lifting so close our window it was possible to climb out at night and sit hidden on the branches. Adults on the porch were different from high up, the porch lit in the dark and chairs creaking as the men leaned and rocked, murmuring, drinking homemade beer kept cool in cellar crocks.

Late one night that summer, Warwick woke me, pinched my arms inside my cotton shift and held his hand across my mouth. He walked like a shadow in his white nightclothes, motioning I should follow him outside; I could see his clothes and not his body in the dark. Warwick was quickly through and I was slower, my weight still on the sill as he settled himself, then lifted me over when I grabbed a higher branch, my feet on his chest and shoulders. We climbed into the top branches that grew next the third floor of the house and sat cradled where three branches sloped; Warwick whispered not to move, stay behind the leaves in case they look. We were outside Claude's window, seeing into the dim room.

Claude was youngest of the older brothers and his wife was hugely with child, standing like a white column in the middle of the floor. Her white chemise hung wide round her like a tent and her sleeves were long and belled; she stood, both hands pressed to the small of her back, leaning as though to help the weight at her front. Then I saw Claude kneeling, darker than she because he wasn't wearing clothes. He touched her feet and I thought at first he was helping her take off her shoes, as I helped the young children in the evenings. But he had nothing in his hands and was lifting the thin chemise above her knees, higher to her thighs, then above her hips as she was twisting away but stopped and moved more toward him, only holding the cloth bunched to conceal her belly. She pressed his head away from her, the chemise pulled to her waist in back and his one hand there trying to hold her. Then he backed her three steps to the foot of the bed and she half leaned, knees just bent; he knelt down again, his face almost at her feet and his mouth moving like he was biting her along her legs. She held him just away with her hands and he touched over and over the big globed belly, stroking it long and deeply like you would stroke a scared animal. Suddenly he held her at her knees and tipped her whole body back, moved her thighs apart, and was right up against her with his face, eating: it looked backwards and terrible, like a big crouched cat suckling its smaller mother—she leaning back totally now with both hands over her mouth. The he stood quickly and turned her so her belly was against the heaped sheets. She grasped the bed frame with both hands so when he pulled her hips close she was bent prone forward from the waist; now her hands were occupied and he uncovered all of her, pushing the chemise to her shoulders and past her breasts in front; the filmy cloth hid her head and face, falling even off her shoulders so it hung halfway down her arms. She was all naked globes and curves, headless and wide-hipped with the swollen belly big and pale beneath her like a moon; standing that way she looked all dumb and animal like our white mare before she foaled. All this time she was whimpering, Claude looking at her. We saw him, he started to prod himself inside her very slow, tilting his head and listening.

. . . I put my cool hands over my eyes then, hearing their sounds until Warwick pulled my arms down and made me look. Claude was tight behind her, pushing in and flinching like he couldn't get out of her; she bawled once. He let her go, stumbling; they staggered onto the bed, she lying on her back away from him with the bunched chemise in her mouth. He pulled her to him and took the cloth from her lips and wiped her face.

This was perhaps twenty minutes of a night in July, 1900. I looked at Warwick as though for the first time. When he talked he was so close I could feel the words on my skin distinct from night breeze. "Are you glad you saw?" he whispered, his face frightened.

He had been watching them from the tree for several weeks.

"Warwick. Warwick, are you here?"

Thick wide door of the barn shuts behind me; inside it is darker than morning in the field, where the light seems nearly ivory, indirect and still diffuse, early. Inside, the barn is a color nearly olive, furred with warmth and the smells of animals close all night. Coolness come finally just at dawn is only barely felt. Morning, early morning, as the Independence Day parade begins at noon in Coalton and we have both horses to curry and brush.

"Warwick, you have the ribbon? I brought the satin but the rest was gone from the sewing box."

He says, "I have the grosgrain, there, in the basket."

Now I hear Mags and Race, snorting in the far stalls at the end and Warwick is there. I don't see the combs, the silver shine in his hands, but hear their teeth on the horses' long necks and see Warwick. Both arms moving smooth and repetitive as in some purposeful dance except all his body is still, just standing, while his arms stay lifted, stroking. He watches his hands, the combs, and the horses whinny because I'm closer and they smell apples.

"Ava is making the carriage streamers," I tell him.

The apples are in my apron and I reach for them, not looking; they're hard and small and sweet; the horses jostle and lower their long heads to mouth my palm with their velvety lips that leave no wetness. There is the sound of the apples cracking and the big breathing of horses. Warwick steps back. There are the combs in his palms, their leather straps across the back of his hands.

"Are the rest of them awake?" he asks.

"Yes, up cooking food for the picnic. Where did you sleep?"

"Out here."

He touches my shoulder with the side of his wrist and his face is still in half-shadow. While he talks my eyes get used to the dimness and I see his mouth, the line of his jaw. He has a thin, narrow face that is sensitive and changing; already he is a head taller than me.

"You didn't mean to watch them," he says. "I led you into it. You won't tell anyone?"

"No. But if you watch them again I don't want to know."

"I won't watch them. Here, take the grosgrain first. You do Mags."

He puts the combs down where they glint in straw and we prop the basket of ribbons between us, against the stall. The horses stand very still, almost somnolent, while we touch them. Our fingers in their long manes are plaiting the rough hair, the hair coarse and cool and dead against the warmth of their broad necks. In the quiet the horses feel big and human, their hard heads pressed close our shoulders.

"You remember when Claude got married?" Warwick says.

His hands are faster; he knots the red grosgrain into each plait and crosses thin ribbons, red, blue, down each length to keep the braids tight. Mags and Race stay still, only shifting their weight and moving hindquarters to stand where the straw was thicker.

"I remember, we all went down to Bluefield on the train. Was it two years ago?"

"She was in a family way. Then, at the wedding."

"How would you know?'

"Claude told me. He said she was, and he had made it right to her and did not regret it. She lost that baby early on and felt badly, like he had married her now for no reason—but Claude said he would have anyway, got married, because he was her first."

"Her first?"

"Yes, he knew he was. He was her first and a woman belongs to that man, whether she is with him later or not."

"I don't believe you, Warwick. What about the Jones girl, the one hurt last spring by that tramp?"

He touches Race under her mane, pulls a lock of the coarse hair straight.

"Well?" I ask him.

"The tramp was lynched, wasn't he? If the girl had been a tramp herself, the man would have been let go or jailed. But she was young and her father dead and her brothers not grown, so the townsmen met in Coalton and found the man."

"But the tramp can't own her when he's dead. Who owns her then?"

Warwick is still a moment in the shady light, his hands moving, and between us the basket is nearly empty. The straw bottom looks white in this dimness.

"I don't know," he says. "I guess then she's a kind of orphan."

The satin ribbon is knotted in a coil beneath grosgrain, slick and silky by the nubby darker red—unrolling it I feel the basket shift and almost fall. Warwick catches it, kneeling down beside me to hold it with one hand.

"But a woman does belong to her first man and that is the truth," he says.

"I think it's a lie."

"How do you mean?"

"I know, I know it is."

"How can you know?"

"I feel it, I'm certain."

"You feel it because you don't know."

In old photographs of Coalton that July 4th, the town looks scruffy and blurred. The blue of the sky is not shown in those black-and-white studies, nor the colors of the streamered buildings and the flags, the finery worn by the crowd. Wooden sidewalks on the two main streets were broad and raised; that day people sat along them as on low benches, their feet in the dusty road, waiting for the parade. We were all asked to stay still as a photographer took pictures of the whole scene from a near hillside. People did sit quite still, or stand in place, some of them in windows of the old hotel; then there was a prayer blessing the new century and the cornet band assembled. The parade was forming out of sight, by the river, and most townspeople driving decorated carriages had already driven out—Warwick had gone, with Claude and Pa, and some of the young cousins. It would be a big parade; we had word that local merchants had hired part of a circus traveling through Bellington. I ran up the hill to see if I could get a glimpse of them; Mam was calling me to come back and my shoes were blond to the ankles with dust. Below me the crowd began to cheer. The ribboned horses danced with fright and kicked, jerking reins looped over low branches of trees and shivering the leaves. From up the hill I saw dust raised in the woods and heard the crackling of what was crushed. There were five elephants; they came out from the trees along the road and the trainer sat on the massive harnessed head of the first. He sat in a sort of purple chair, swaying side to side with the lumbering swivel of the head. The trainer wore a red cap and jacket; he was dark and smooth on his face and held a boy close his waist. The boy was moving his arms at me and it was Warwick; I was running closer and the trainer beat with his staff on the shoulders of the elephant while the animal's snaky trunk, all alive, ripped small bushes. Warwick waved; I could see him and ran, dodging the men until I was alongside. The earth was pounding and the animal was big like a breathing wall, its rough side crusted with dirt and straw. The skin hung loose, draped on the limbs like sacking crossed with many creases. Far, far up, I saw Warwick's face; I was yelling, yelling for them to stop, stop and take me up, but they kept on going. As the elephants passed, dust lifted, and ribbons and hats, the white of the summer skirts swung and billowed. The cheering was a great noise under the trees and birds flew up wild. Coalton was a sea of yellow dust, the flags snapping in that wind and banners strung between the buildings broken, flying.

Warwick got it in his head to walk a wire and none could dissuade him. Our Pa would not hear of such foolishness so Warwick took out secretly to the creek every morning and practiced on the sly. He constructed a thickness of barn boards lengthwise on the ground, propped with nailed supports so he could walk along an edge. First three boards, then two, then one. He walked barefoot tensing his long toes and cradled a bamboo fishing pole in his arms for balance. I followed along silently when I saw him light out for the woods. Standing back a hundred feet from the creek bed, I saw through dense summer leaves my brother totter magically just above the groundline; thick ivy concealed the edges of the boards and made him appear a jerky magician. He often walked naked since the heat was fierce and his trousers too-large hand-me-downs that obstructed careful movement. He walked parallel to the creek and slipped often. Periodically he grew frustrated and jumped cursing into the muddy water. Creek bottom at that spot was soft mud and the water perhaps five feet deep; he floated belly-up like a seal and then crawled up the bank mud-streaked to start again. I stood in the leaves. He was tall and still coltish then, dark from the sun on most of his body, long-muscled; his legs looked firm and strong and a bit too long for him, his buttocks were tight and white. It was not his nakedness that moved me to stay hidden, barely breathing lest he hear the snap of a twig and discover me—it was the way he touched the long yellow pole, first holding it close, then opening his arms gently as the pole rolled across his flat still wrists to his hands; another movement, higher, and the pole balanced like a visible thin line on the tips of his fingers. It vibrated as though quivering with a sound. Then he clasped it lightly and the pole turned horizontally with a half-rotation; six, seven, eight quick flashes, turning hard and quick, whistle of air, snap of the light wood against his palms. Now the pole lifted, airborne a split second and suddenly standing, earthward end walking Warwick's palm. He moved, watching the sky and a wavering six feet of yellow needle. The earth stopped in just that moment, the trees still, Warwick moving, and then as the pole toppled in a smooth arc to water he followed in a sideways dive. While he was under, out of earshot and rapturous in the olive water, I ran quick and silent back to the house, through forest and vines to the clearing, the meadow, the fenced boundaries of the high-grown yard and the house, the barn, where it was shady and cool and I could sit in the mow to remember his face and the yellow pole come to life. You had to look straight into the sun to see its airborne end and the sun was a blind white burn the pole could touch. Like Warwick was prodding the sun in secret, his whole body a prayer partly evil.

That night I saw our mother hold his feet in her lap. She ran the cold edge of her steel darning needle up and down, up and down his flesh, taking painlessly the splinters from his skin. I stood with a lamp, hidden from sight at the porch door; beyond the filtered light of the globe close my face I saw my brother, my mother, two lumps in pale garments, moving, and past them the foreshortened planks of porch floor shaded a graduated dark. The round porch pillars were lost at one fat end in eaves. Low grass of the yard rumpled like carpet to the fence, pickets waist-high and blurred at field's edge. Out there the dogs bayed long-drawn howls, scouting near the creek for coons while dusk held. The dogs moved in a pack, eyes squinted near shut in the high sharp grass.

The sky those summer nights was like the pale inside of an over-turned blue bowl, blue and light longer than the earth or the fields were light. Fireflies blinked in the tall black grass while it was still nearly daytime. Close by, crickets made a shrill weeping under the house; cats slid, hunting; Warwick called our mother "Mam" and she touched his feet, silent, Warwick looking away across the yard. Meadows had lost defini-tion. Breeze wavered the whole slow mass like deep water and made a sound, a sighing pitched low and perfect: I was standing with the lamp in my hand and thought the house moved beneath my feet, slipped and slid with a creaking like a ship, like we were all afloat. The wick in the lamp flared up then, the fire leaped in the globe. As though in reply the wind murmured loud beyond the wheat and the grasses, far out in the woods. Mam and Warwick sat still, their heads lifted, listening.

Suddenly I was ashamed and blew out the light lest they know I watched them. I lowered my eyes and gazed at my own feet until I saw clearly their white shapes on the floor. When I looked again, Mam had turned her back to him. He sat leaning against the broad porch column, long legs extended so he braced her back with his feet, and then he moved, slowly, one foot flat to the base of her spine and the other higher, nearly to the blades of her shoulders; and so he bent his knees and rocked her, both of them quiet; he took all her weight and rocked her with his legs as though she were in those long full skirts some voluminous silent object. All this in silence but for a creaking of boards as her weight shifted.

Stubborn as the devil's agent, she called him, but she was partial to her male children and Warwick was the youngest of the boys. She allowed disobedience from none but him; he was always wild and taken with strange notions. Born that way and encouraged too by his position in the family: next-to-last of twelve, largely overlooked by the older brothers and easy victor over sisters closer his age. He was good at shenanigans and saved himself many a cuff or belting by a witticism at the right moment. Regardless, he didn't care if he was hit and never altered his behavior due to any punishment. *Deliver my soul from the sword*, we read for summer lessons, Warwick halting and angry at being inside the warm kitchen, *and my darling from the power of the dog.* His eyes were long-lashed and narrow, yellow-brown, lightened with bright slashes the color of copper; he squinted sideways at me and touched big Malantha, the fat hound, with his feet, shoving her secretly toward me under the table so she woke and yawned with my whole foot wet in her big jowled mouth.

One day, of course, he saw me watching him practice, and knew in an instant I had watched him all along; by then he was actually walking a thick rope strung about six feet off the ground between two trees. For a week he'd walked only to a midpoint, as he could not rig the rope so it didn't sag and walking all the way across required balance on the upward slant. That day he did it; I believe he did it only that once, straight across. I made no sound but as he stood there poised above me his eyes fell upon my face; I had knelt in the forest cover and was watching as he himself had taught me to watch. Perhaps this explains his anger—I see still, again and again, Warwick jumping down from the rope, bending his knees to an impact as dust clouds his feet but losing no balance, no stride, leaping toward me at a run. His arms are still spread, hands palm-down as though for support in the air, and then I hear rather than see him because I'm running, terrified—shouting his name in supplication through the woods as he follows, still coming after me wild with rage as I'd never seen anyone. Then I was nearly out of breath and just screaming, stumbling—

It's true I led him to the thicket, but I had no idea where I was going. We never went there as it was near a rocky outcropping where copperheads bred, and not really a thicket at all but a small apple orchard gone diseased and long dead. The trees were oddly dwarfed and broken, and the ground cover thick with vines. Just as Warwick caught me I looked to see those rows of small dead trees; then we were fighting on the ground, rolling. I fought with him in earnest and scratched his eyes; already he was covered all over with small cuts from running through briers. This partially explains how quickly he was poisoned, but the acute nature of the infection was in his blood itself. Now he would be diagnosed severely allergic and given antibiotics; then we knew nothing of such medicines. The sick were still bled. In the week he was most ill, Warwick was bled twice daily, into a bowl. The doctor theorized, correctly, that the poison had worsened so as to render the patient's blood toxic.

Later Warwick told me, if only I'd stopped yelling—Now that chase seems a comical as well as nightmarish picture; he was only a naked enraged boy. But the change I saw in his face, that moment he realized my presence, foretold everything. Whatever we did from then on was attempted escape from the fact of the future.

"Warwick? Warwick?"

The narrow sun porch is all windows but for the house wall. He sleeps here like a pupa, larva wrapped in a woven spit of gauze and never turning. His legs weeping in the loose bandages, he smells of clear fluid seeped from wounds. The seepage clear as tears, clear as sweat but sticky on my hands when my own sweat never sticks but drips from my forehead onto his flat stomach, where he says it stings like salt.

"Warwick. Mam says to turn you now."

Touching the wide gauze strips in the dark. His ankles propped on rolls of cloth so his legs air and the blisters scab after they break and weep. The loose gauze strips are damp when I unwrap them, just faintly damp; now we don't think he is going to die.

He says, "Are they all asleep inside?"

"Yes. Except Mam woke me."

"Can't you open the windows? Don't flies stop when there's dew?"

"Yes, but the mosquitoes. I can put the netting down but you'll have that dream again."

"Put it down but come inside, then I'll stay awake."

"You shouldn't, you should sleep."

Above him the net is a canopy strung on line, rolled up all the way round and tied with cord like a bedroll. It floats above him in the dark like a cloud the shape of the bed. We keep it rolled up all the time now since the bandages are off his eyes; he says looking through it makes everyone a ghost and fools him into thinking he's still blind. Before, he didn't know the difference and so the netting was down and the room cooler, breeze through all the open windows helped him heal. That was night. Days the doctor told us to keep the windows shut so sun poured through the glass panes, dried the blisters and new rash. So hot Ava stood and fanned him with Mam's big palm fan, while I was the only one allowed to touch him because I don't catch poison.

Now I stand on a chair to reach the knotted cords, find them by feel, then the netting falls all around him like a skirt.

"All right, Warwick, see me? I just have to unlatch the windows."

Throw the hooks and windows swing outward all along the sunporch walls. The cool comes in, the lilac scent, and now I have to move everywhere in the dark because Mam says I can't use the lamp, have kerosene near the netting.

"I can see you better now," he says from the bed.

I can tell the shadows, shapes of the bed, the medicine table, the chair beside him where I slept the first nights we moved him to the sun porch. Doctor said he'd never seen such a poison, Warwick's eyes swollen shut, his legs too big for pants, soles of his feet oozing in one straight seam like someone cut them with scissors. Mam with him day and night until her hands broke out and swelled; then it was only me, wrapping him in bandages she cut and rolled wearing gloves.

"Let me get the rosewater," I whisper.

Inside the tent he sits up to make room. Hold the bowl and the cloth, crawl in and it's like sitting low in high fields hidden away, except there isn't even sky, no opening at all.

"It's like a coffin, that's what," he'd said when he could talk.

"A coffin is long and thin," I told him, "with a lid."

"Mine has a ceiling," Warwick said.

Inside everything is clean and white and dry; every day we change the white bottom sheet and he isn't allowed any covers. He's sitting up—I still can't see him in the dark; even the netting looks black, so I find him, hand forehead nose throat.

"Can't you see me? There's a moon, I see you fine."

"Then you've turned into a bat. I'll see in a moment, it was light in the kitchen."

"Mam?"

"Mam and three lamps. She's rolling bandages this hour of the night. She doesn't sleep when you don't."

"I can't sleep."

"I know."

He only sleeps in daytime when he can hear people making noise. At night he wakes up in silence, in the narrow black room, in bandages in the tent. For a while when the doctor bled him he was too weak to yell for someone.

"I won't need bandages much longer," he says.

"A little longer," I tell him.

"I should be up walking. I wonder if I can walk; like before I wondered if I could see."

"Of course you can walk, you've only been in bed two weeks, and a few days before upstairs—"

"I don't remember when they moved me here, so don't it seem like always I been here?"

Pa and Dennis and Claude and Mam moved him, all wearing gloves and their forearms wrapped in gauze I took off them later and burned in the woodstove.

"Isn't always. You had deep sleeps in the fever, you remember wrong."

I start at his feet which are nearly healed, with the sponge and the cool water. Water we took from the rain barrel and scented with torn roses, the petals pounded with a pestle and strained, since the doctor said not to use soap.

The worst week I bathed him at night so he wouldn't get terrified alone. He was delirious and didn't know when he slept or woke. When I touched him with the cloth he made such whispers, such inside sounds; they weren't even words but had a cadence like sentences. When he whispered them to me it was all right; I wasn't scared, but that one noon his fever was highest and the room itself like an oven—he shouted, on and on—Mam made everyone pray, even the men called in from work in the fields. Satan was inside Warwick. That is not God's language, she said, Satan is trying to take him. She yelled louder than Warwick as though he might hear if she shouted the devil down: *He delighteth not in the strength, He taketh not pleasure in the legs of a man, the Lord taketh pleasure in them that fear Him. . . .Fear Him! hope in His Mercy, He casteth forth His ice like morsels—*

I was rubbing Warwick with alcohol to take the sweat, he was wet and smelled of poison, his legs arms eyes all bandaged and hands and legs tied down so he wouldn't thrash and make his raw skin bleed—I was terrified there in the hot narrow room, sun in the windows horribly bright. Voices in the kitchen, the other side of the wall. *Thou hast made him lower than angels . . . he did fly up*, Mam shouted, and Warwick in the darkness in his secret place, all round about him like black water boiling in the dark. I could see him vanishing like something sucked down a hole, like fire ducked into a slit. If he could hear them praying, if he could feel this heat and the heat of his fever, blind as he was then in bandages, and tied, if he could still think, he's think he was in hell. I poured the alcohol over him, and the water from the basin, I was bent close his face just when he stopped raving and I thought he had died. He said a word.

"Bessie," he said.

Bless me, I heard. I knelt with my mouth at his ear, in the sweat, in the horrible smell of the poison. "Warwick," I said. He was there, tentative and weak, a boy waking up after sleeping in the blackness three days. "Stay here, Warwick. Warwick."

I heard him say the word again, and it was my name, clearly.

"Bessie," he said.

So I answered him. "Yes, I'm here. Stay here."

Later he told me he slept a hundred years, swallowed in a vast black belly like Jonah, no time anymore, no sense but strange dreams without pictures. He thought he was dead, he said, and the moment he came back he spoke the only word he'd remembered in the dark.

Sixteen years later, when he did die, in the mine—did he say a word again, did he say that word? Trying to come back. The second time, I think he went like a streak. I had the color silver in my mind. A man from Coalton told us about the cave-in. The man rode out on a horse, a bay mare, and he galloped the mare straight across the fields to the porch instead of taking the road. I was sitting on the porch and saw him coming from a ways off. I stood up as he came closer. I knew the news was Warwick, and that whatever had happened was over. I had no words in my mind, just the color silver, everywhere. The fields looked silver too just then, the way the sun slanted. The grass was tall and the mare moved through it up to her chest, like a powerful swimmer. I did not call anyone else until the man arrived and told me, breathless, that Warwick and two others were trapped, probably suffocated, given up for dead. The man, a Mr. Forbes, was surprised at my composure. I simply nodded; the news came to me like an echo. I had not thought of that moment in years—the moment Warwick's fever broke and I heard him speak—but it returned in an instant. Having once felt that disappearance, even so long before, I was prepared. Memory does not work according to time. I was twelve years old, perceptive, impressionable, in love with Warwick as a brother and sister can be in love. I loved him then as one might love one's twin, without a thought. After that summer I understood too much. I don't mean I was ashamed; I was not. But no love is innocent once it has recognized its own existence.

At eighteen, I went away to a finishing school in Lynchburg. The summer I came back, foolishly, I ran away west. I eloped partially because Warwick found fault with anyone who courted me, and made a case against him to Mam. The name of the man I left with is unimportant. I do not really remember his face. He was blond but otherwise he did resemble Warwick—in his movements, his walk, his way of speaking. All told, I was in his company eight weeks. We were traveling, staying in hotels. He'd told me he was in textiles but it seemed actually he gambled at cards and roulette. He had a sickness for the roulette wheel, and other sicknesses. I could not bear to stand beside him in the gambling parlors; I hated the noise and the smoke, the perfumes mingling, the clackings of the wheels like speeded-up clocks and everyone's eyes following numbers. Often I sat in a hotel room with a blur of noise coming through the floor, and imagined the vast space of the barn around me: dark air filling a gold oval, the tall beams, the bird sounds ghostly, like echoes. The hay, ragged heaps that spilled from the mow in pieces and fell apart.

The man who was briefly my husband left me in St. Louis. Warwick came for me; he made a long journey in order to take me home. A baby boy was born the following September. It was decided to keep my elopement and divorce, and the pregnancy itself, secret. Our doctor, a country man and friend of the family, helped us forge a birth certificate stating that Warwick was the baby's father. We invented a name for his mother, a name unknown in those parts, and told that she'd abandoned the baby to us. People lived so far from one another, in isolation, that such deceit was possible. My boy grew up believing I was his aunt and Warwick his father, but Warwick could not abide him. To him, the child was living reminder of my abasement, my betrayal in ever leaving the farm.

Lately I have a dream. As is true in fact, I am the last one left. The farmhouse is deserted but still standing; I walk away from it. There is mist from the creek and the moist smell of day lilies, mustard bitters of their furred sepals broken in the black ivy. Thick beds of the dark-veined leaves are a tangle in the undergrowth. There, in the thicket where I fought with Warwick, I find the yellow rope, bleached pale as rain in those leaves. The frayed fibers are a white fuzz along the ground. I kneel down to touch the leaves, and the dirt beneath is cool as cellar air, pliable as sand. I dig a hole, as though a grave is there, a grave I will discover. Cards I find, and a knife. And the voice of a preacher, wet and charred: *One man among a thousand I found, but a woman among all these I have not found.*

The funeral was held at the house. Men from the mine saw to it Warwick was laid out in Coalton, then they brought the box to the farm on a lumber wagon. The lid was kept shut. That was the practice then; if a man died in the mines his coffin was closed for services, nailed shut, even if the man was unmarked.

The day after Warwick's funeral, all the family was leaving back to their homesteads, having seen each other in a confused picnic of food and talk and sorrowful conjecture. Half the sorrow was Warwick alive and half was Warwick dead. His dying would make an end of the farm. I would leave now for Bellington, where, in a year, I would meet another man. Mam and Pa would go to live with Claude and his wife. But it was more than losing the farm that puzzled and saddened everyone; no one knew who Warwick was, really. They said it was hard to believe he was inside the coffin, with the lid nailed shut that way. Touch the box, anywhere, with the flat of your hand, I told them. They did, and stopped that talk.

The box was thick pine boards, pale white wood; I felt I could fairly look through it like water into his face, like he was lying in a piece of water on top of the parlor table. Touching the nailed lid you felt first the cool slide of new wood on your palm, and a second later, the depth—a heaviness, the box was so deep it went clear to the center of the earth, his body contained there like a big caged wind. Something inside, palpable as the different air before flash rains, with clouds blown and air clicking before the crack of downpour.

I treated the box as though it were living; it had to accustom itself to the strange air of the house, of the parlor, a room kept for weddings and death. The box was simply there on the table, long and pure like some deeply asleep, dangerous animal. The stiff damask draperies at the parlor windows looked as though they were about to move, gold tassels at the hems suspended and still.

The morning before the service most of the family had been in Coalton, seeing to what is done at a death. I had been alone in the house with the coffin churning what air there was to breathe. I had dressed in best clothes as though for a serious, bleak suitor. The room was just lighted with sunrise, window shades pulled halfway, their cracked sepia lit from behind. One locust began to shrill as I took a first step across the floor; somehow one had gotten into the room. The piercing, fast vibration was very loud in the still morning: suddenly I felt myself smaller, cramped as I bent over Warwick inside his white tent of netting, his whole body afloat below me on the narrow bed, his white shape in the loose bandages seeming to glow in dust light while beyond the row of open windows hundreds of locusts sang a ferocious pattering. I could scarcely see the parlor anymore. My vision went black for a moment, not black but dark green, like the color of the dusk those July weeks years before.

A Patch Of Earth
from The Milkweed Ladies

Louise McNeill

*T*he farm, a wide plateau of rocky, loam-dark fields, lies above Swago Crick, along the Greenbrier River of West Virginia and some twenty-five to thirty miles north of the Virginia line. This patch of earth is held within a half stadium of limestone cliffs and mountain pastures. On the surface, the Swago Farm is quiet and solid, green in summer and in winter deep with snow. It has its level fields, its fence rows and hilly pastures. There are some two hundred acres of trees and bluegrass, running water, and the winding, dusty paths that cattle and humans have kept open through the years. There are three small woodlands, two of them still virgin and mostly of oak.

On one of the knolls is the weedy myrtle-grown graveyard where we have buried our people for 150 years. Before then, we buried them where we now forget. We call the knoll the Graveyard Hill, and the cattle graze there outside its wire fence and crooked gate. Higher up on the ridge-top and canting over toward Captain Jim's orchard is a rusty pole set like a crucifix—a television antenna that stands as though it were put there to mark our soldiers' graves. One grave is for Captain Jim, my father's father, who went with the Virginia Rebels; another is for the boy, Elbert Messer, who was fatally wounded in World War I.

Some of the gravestones are too old to read, their names eaten away by time and water; the faint rock-etchings are filled now with gray moss. It is one of these stones that marks the grave of our great, great, great cousin Jacob, who died back in the 1800s when he was just nineteen. Cousin Jacob was sick of the "bloody flux" a long time before he died and used to come up here on the hill to sit under an oak tree and read his Bible. So they buried him under the oak, and for a hundred years it stood there, heavy with age and old funeral keenings, and was called the Jacob Tree. But that tree is gone now, and Little Manfred's tree too, and the willow tree Granny Fanny planted over the grave of her dead baby back in 1875.

But even older than the old graves were the primordial oceans that once covered our fields and cast their seashells into our rock. When the ancient waters receded, strands of pink and broken coral were left scattered—as they are still scattered—across the meadows. This is not coal country. No rotting swamps lay over these slopes and upland valleys, only the oceans weaving and receiving as they laid the pink coral down: coral rock and white limestone rock, and the underground steams sucking in the dark. Through all our generations, we have picked and hauled corals and piled them in roseate heaps along the fence rows and in the swamp.

So it was with us, and is with us still, over two hundred years and nine generations of the farm keeping us, and we believing that we keep the farm. But that is not the way it is in the real truth of it, for the earth holds us and not the other way. The whole great rolling earth holds us, or a rocky old farm down on Swago Crick.

Until I was sixteen years old, until the roads came, the farm was about all I knew: our green meadows and hilly pastures, our storied old men, the great rolling seasons of moon and sunlight, our limestone cliffs and trickling springs. It was about all I knew, and, except for my father and before him, the old Rebel Captain, all that any of us had even known: just the farm and our little village down at the crossroads, and the worn cowpaths winding the slopes; or we kids driving the cows home in the summer evenings; or the winter whiteness and stillness, Aunt Malindy's "old woman in the sky" picking her geese, the "old blue misties" sweeping out of the north.

Some of our tales were old and old, going back into time itself, American time. Living so long there in the same field under the same gap in the mountain, we had seen, from our own ragged little edge of history, the tall shadows passing by. "Old Hickory" in his coach passed along our dug road one morning; General Lee one evening on his way to the Gauley rebel camps. Then, in 1863, as we watched from our cliff walls and scrub oak bushes, the great Yankee army passed on its way to the Battle of Droop: all day long the clank and spur and roll of their passage, 2,000 3,000 4,000, hard, blue Yankees, their bayonet tips made bloody in the sunset.

Grandpa Tom, our "old one," had gone with George Rogers Clark to Kaskaskia and had run the Falls of the Ohio under an eclipse of the sun. Uncle Bill went to Point Pleasant against old Cornstalk and his Ohio Shawnee; then Little Uncle John to the War of 1812; Captain Jim to the Virginia Rebels, his brother Al to the Yankees. My father, in 1906, sailed with Teddy Roosevelt's Great White Fleet; then Cousin Paul and Cousin Coe "to make the world safe for Democracy."

But before I grew up and went out into the world—and a bloody thing I found it—we were all at home there in our faded cottage in the meadow, all of us safe and warm. Sometimes now, a quiet sense comes to me, the cool mist blowing in my face as though I am walking through islands of fog and drifting downhill slowly southward until I feel the mountains behind my shoulder. Walking on, I can see the light in the "big room" window as I come to our cottage standing in the meadow under "Bridger's" Mountain, as it was always stands on the fore-edges of my memory, and the old farm where I ran the April fields and pastures to my great rock up in the woodland where the lavender hepaticas grew. Then I knew just the earth itself: the quiet measure of the seasons; the stars in the sky; the wheat field in August, golden: darkness and day; rain and sunlight; the primal certainty of spring. Then we were all there together, the years not yet come on us, these seventy-five years of war and money and roaring turnpikes and torrents of blood.

I know, deep down, that our one old farm is only a ragged symbol, a signet mark for all the others, the old and far older hard-scrabble mountain farms of Kentucky, Tennessee, North Carolina, and Virginia, all the briery fields scattered across the mountains south. And how the earth holds us is still a dark question. It is not the sucking deepness that draws us, for the earth is mother, protector, the home; but the oppressor too. It requires, sometimes, the very lifeblood of its own, and imprisons the fly-away dreams and bends the backs of men and women. Yet to love a familiar patch of earth is to know something beyond death, "westward from death," as my father used to speak it.

We could sense, just beyond our broken-down line fences, the great reach of the American continent flowing outward. Because we stood so long in one place, our rocky old farm and the abundant earth of the continent were linked together in the long tides of the past. Because the land kept us, never budging from its rock-hold, we held to our pioneer ways the longest, the strongest; and we saw the passing of time from a place called solid, from our own slow, archean, and peculiar stance.

Night At The Commodore
from The Milkweed Ladies

Louise McNeill

After I left the farm, I often felt as I had when I used to plumb the depth of water as a child. In summer, after every big rainstorm, a flood would come, and our tiny cow-spring trickle would become a roaring stream that flowed foamy and green over the leaning grasses. I would go out barefoot in the early morning with a long straight pole; and with my dress tied up above my knees I would wade along the shallows to measure the deep holes. I felt my way out into the current and walked slowly upstream, my feet and legs stinging with the cold. As I walked on and on up through the wild morning, I would become John Ridd of *Lorna Doone* with his trident, walking up the spate of Doone Valley. Then the mountains would come dark and close around me. I walked until I could feel the black danger and death in it. As I am walking still. For you walk to death, don't you? Because you cannot ride.

Aunt Malindy told me that old women in the night can see; and now that I am old and often cannot sleep at night, I see pictures in the dark. I close my eyes and long-ago pictures float before me, all in color and shadow, framed in the soft fog of the years. Most often, I seem to be standing in our yard at home and looking in through the "big room" window, and we are all there together in the firelight. G.D., my brother Ward, Uncle Dock, and Cousin Rush are by the fireplace spitting and smoking and talking about Over the Mountain; and I am there myself, listening. Farther back from the fire, Mama is peeling apples; Granny Fanny is winding her hanks of wool, and her old gargoyle clock is ticking. Elizabeth is holding Little Jim on her lap, and Aunt Malindy sits in the rocker in her fat black sateen dress, her hands folded in perfect content. Up above us, the picture of Captain Jim hangs on the wall.

I can see all this before me in the night, and then it fades away and I see my brother Young Jim, now sixty-nine years old, still farming our land, sowing lime by helicopter over Bridger's Gap. Or I see Blix, Jim's and

Annabelle's son; and then Blix's only son, Little Jamie, nine years old, who sometimes helps his grandfather turn out the coral rocks or wrestle big bales of hay up into the barn that was once our faded cottage. Sometimes I see my hepatica rock, with the walking fern and maidenhair; or my white calf named Lily. Sometimes I can see Clarence Smith, our funeral director, looking down at G.D.'s grave and saying, "Many a lame dog did this man help over the stile." Then, and quite suddenly, I may see a dying soldier in my picture; and there is blood and mud and death.

These days I see the war pictures more and more: the mixed up pictures from the Second World War, which was *my* war more than any of the others I have lived through. Often I see Howard Wilfong from my 1930 one-room school. Howard is in the control tower of his ship, the *U.S.S. Borie*, when suddenly a Jap kamikaze plane screams down and takes the tower. Old women in the night can see. Some nights I cannot sleep at all.

When I left the farm, it seemed that suddenly, or *almost* suddenly, I was out in the world. Roger and I were married and traveling the old trains hooting through the pass: the C. and O.'s Sportsman and Fast Flying Virginian; the Silver Rocket hurtling through the prairie night; the Southern through the piney woods of Georgia; the old sit-up-all-night Pacemaker roaring west to Chicago. All at once I was buying my suits at Lord and Taylor's; and I, still in my Sears Roebuck shoes! On one of these wandering train rides, Roger and I and our baby, Doug, came one early September to visit with G.D. and Mama on the farm.

We were all sitting on the front porch that night: G.D. and Mama, Rog and I, my brother Jim, and our old collie herd dog lying at Jim's feet. We were sitting and talking, or not talking; and it was a still, crisp, fragrant night. The clover meadow was in new stubble, the wisteria shadows falling over the porch swing; and down under the wisteria, the crickets were crying their "six weeks till frost." Then the collie got up, whining a little. He turned around backward and looked down at his bed. A strange pale light began moving in over the porch railing. Suddenly we all saw a faint glow quivering in the sky over Bridger's Gap: the Northern Lights!

We ran out into the yard and looked up over us. The whole round of the heavens was beginning to quiver with a wild, flickering crown. At first from the north; then the east and south and west joined; and the green-red-blue-gold-purple spear tent was streaming up to the point of the heavens and riving as it came: the great crown borealis of September 1941.

As I stood there, a kind of awe and fear came to me, as though God had not yet unloosed His might. But He had it, held back somewhere in the banked fire of the Worlds. The borealis began to fade and die down, and we went back to the porch. The blue September fog spread across the meadows. We sat there in the quiet darkness, September 8, 1941, just three months before Pearl Harbor.

Roger and I spent the years of the war teaching at the rich boys' prep school in Aiken, South Carolina. I planted my iris roots from the farm again, this time in front of a faculty cottage. Doug was a year old in October 1941 and just beginning to talk. One of his first words was "airplane," for the bombers flew everyday over the school playing field in black formation. The war leaped and swirled around us in a kind of controlled madness; or it dragged on and on in an eternity of waiting, like water dripping from a roof edge.

Now the time is only a cry and a shuffle of mixed-up names: Bataan Death March, Burma Road, Java Sea; and the *Lexington*, FDR, Adolph Hitler, cattle cars, Guadalcanal, gas station, Savo Island, Iwo Jima, ration cards, Gabriel Heater, Betty Grable, Casablanca, Anzio Beach. The news came from home that Cousin Bill had gone with Patton, and Cousin Buck went down over the English Channel. Double cousin J.B. was in the 82ND Airborne—Salerno, Normandy, wounded in the Battle of the Bulge. Then, after the war, "Red" Jeffries, from up the Crick, came home from Bataan and sat in J.B.'s filling station drinking pop. Finally we learned the date on which Howard Wilfong died: August 12, 1945—three days after peace was declared.

It's been more than forty years now since the night at the Commodore Hotel, but it still comes back to me out of the shadows and will not stop. It is still as clear as it was on its own stabbing hour. I forget where we had been or where we were going that hot August night, but Rog and Doug and I were getting off a train in Grand Central Station. Long, long before, there had been Old Tom's bison coming down to the salt lick in the twilight; and now I was taking a yellow taxi to the Commodore Hotel.

As soon as we were registered, Rog went off on some errand. I took Doug and an evening paper and went to our room. I gave Doug a quick bath and stuffed him into bed. Then, relaxing over a cigarette and a glass of water, I sat down to read the evening news. When I looked at the headlines, I saw a word, a phrase, that I had never seen before. It was big and black, leaping out at me from the front page, and it was spelled
A-T-O-M-I-C B-O-M-B.

August 6 and 7, 1945: the news story about a place called Hiroshima, a mushroom cloud uprisen, a triumph, burning flesh. I sat there staring down at the black newsprint, and something tore loose in my soul. Then, as from some far leafy distance, I saw Old Tom and George Rogers Clark wading the frozen swamps of the Wabash. So it was all for this? The blood on the snow at Valley Forge, on the sands of Guadalcanal? All for this that old Tim McCarty, because he knew "the hard price of Freedom," gave his sons? "Daniel, Preston, Justin, James, Thomas."

I got up and walked slowly over to the window where the lights of the neon towers were piercing across the north. Then it came to me, there above the roaring traffic and strange light of this strange city. It came to me, in the old superstitions of us mountain people, like a fireball in the night, a Death Omen. Aunt Malindy had seen hers in the sky over Buckley Mountain the night her brother Potts had been killed at Gettysburg; now mine over Hiroshima and over the Commodore Hotel. Only mine wasn't about Brother Potts. It was more about the human race, and more than that, about Earth itself.

That was the night the world changed. It wasn't joy that died, or faith, or resolution; for all these come back. It was something else, something deep and earth-given that died that night in the Commodore. Never again would I be able to say with such infinite certainty that the earth would always green in the springtime, and the purple hepaticas come to bloom on my woodland rock. For there, the earth and its seasons, had always been my certainty—going beyond death, beyond the death of all my people, even beyond the death of the farm; the sun in the morning, the darkness at night, the certain roll of the seasons, the "old blue misties" sweeping out of the north.

About the Contributors

Maggie Anderson

Maggie Anderson was born in New York City and moved to West Virginia at the age of thirteen. She received an M.A. in English and an M.S.W. from West Virginia University. Anderson has won several literary honors, including the Pushcart Prize. She has also been listed in *Contemporary Writers* and *Who's Who in U.S. Writers, Editors, and Poets*. Her works include *A Space Filled with Moving, Cold Comfort, Years that Answer, The Great Horned Owl,* and *Windfall: New and Selected Poems*. Anderson teaches at Kent State University, where she directs the Wick Poetry Program and edits the Wick Poetry Series.

Tom Andrews

Tom Andrews (1961-2001) grew up in Charleston, West Virginia. In 1984, he won the Academy of American Poets prize at Oberlin College. He graduated from Hope College, and in 1985 was awarded the Hoyns Fellowship at the University of Virginia, where he received his M.F.A. His second collection of poems, *The Hemophiliac's Motorcycle*, inspired by his own battle with the disease, won the 1993 Iowa Poetry Prize. He also wrote *Codeine Diary: A Memoir* and a chapbook, *Hymning the Kanawha*. Andrews taught at the University of Virginia, University of Michigan, Ohio University, and Purdue University.

Pinckney Benedict

Pinckney Benedict was raised in Greenbrier County, West Virginia. He received his bachelor's degree from Princeton University and an M.F.A. from the University of Iowa. Benedict has won several awards, including the Chicago Tribune's Nelson Algren Award, the James Michener Fellowship, and the Pushcart Prize. He was the first recipient of the Steinbeck Award for best novel of the year "in the tradition of John Steinbeck." Benedict's works include two collections of short fiction, *Town Smokes* and *The Wrecking Yard*, and a novel, *Dogs of God*. He is an associate professor of English at Hollins University.

Richard Currey

Richard Currey was raised in Wood County, West Virginia. After service in the U.S. Navy, he graduated from the MEDEX/Physician Assistant Program at Howard University. His first prose work was *Crossing Over*, a collection of stories based upon his experiences in Vietnam. Other works include *Fatal Light*, *The Wars of Heaven*, and *Lost Highway*. Currey has received two National Endowment for the Arts Fellowships, and the O. Henry and Pushcart Awards. Besides fiction, Currey has written numerous essays on healthcare and medical ethics. He currently lives in Maryland.

Mark DeFoe

Mark DeFoe was born in Oklahoma, and has lived in West Virginia for more than twenty-five years. He received his B.A. and M.A. degrees from Oklahoma University and a Ph.D. from the University of Denver. Past editor of the *Laurel Review*, Defoe has also published works including *Aviary, Air,* and *Palmate*. Among the several awards that his poetry has won are first place awards from the *Tulane Review* and *Black Warrior Review*. DeFoe is Chair of the English Department at West Virginia Wesleyan College.

Victor Depta

Victor Depta was born and raised in Accoville, West Virginia. He received his B.A. from Marshall University and a Ph.D. in American Literature from Ohio University. His works include *A Doorkeeper in the House, The Helen Poems, Azrael on the Mountain, The Silence of Blackberries, The Gates of Paradise*, and *Plays from Blair Mountain: Four Comedies*. Depta has also published a novel, *Idol and Sanctuary*. He is managing editor of the Blair Mountain Press and teaches English at the University of Tennessee at Martin.

Henry Louis Gates Jr.

Henry Louis Gates Jr. was born and raised in Piedmont, West Virginia. He received his bachelor's degree in English from Yale University, and his M.A. and Ph.D. from Clare College at the University of Cambridge. He is author of *Colored People: A Memoir*, *Thirteen Ways of Looking at a Black Man*, and *The Future of the Race*, among many others. Gates's awards include the MacArthur Foundation "Genius Grant", the George Polk Award for Social Commentary, and the Golden Plate Achievement award. He was also named one of the 25 most influential people in America by Time Magazine. Professor of Humanities at Harvard University, he chairs the Afro-American Studies Program and directs the W.E.B. DuBois Institute for Afro-American Research.

Denise Giardina

Denise Giardina was born in Black Wolf, West Virginia, and moved to Charleston at the age of thirteen. She earned her bachelor's degree from West Virginia Wesleyan College. Giardina pursued postgraduate work at Marshall University and later received her Master of Divinity degree from the Virginia Theological Seminary. She is the author of several novels, including *Good King Harry*, *Storming Heaven*, and *Unquiet Earth*. Her latest novel is *Saints and Villians*. She lives in Charleston and teaches at West Virginia State College.

Davis Grubb:

Davis Grubb (1919-1980) was born in Moundsville, West Virginia. He attended the Carnegie Institute of Technology (Now Carnegie-Mellon University) from 1938-39. He is the author of *The Watchmen, A Dream of Kings, Twelve Tales of Suspense and the Supernatural, Fool's Parade*, and many other works. He is most famous for his novel is *Night of the Hunter*, which was adapted into a now-classic movie. His many short stories appeared in journals including *Collier's, Cosmopolitan,* and *Holiday.*

Lisa Koger:

Lisa Koger was born and raised in Gilmer County, West Virginia. She received her B.A. from West Virginia University, and also holds degrees from the University of Tennessee and the University of Iowa. She is the author of *Farlanburg Stories*, and her work has appeared in several periodicals. She is the recipient of several awards, including the James Michener Award, a National Writer's Voice Project Residency, and a Kentucky Arts Council Fellowship. Koger lives in Somerset, Kentucky.

Lee Maynard:

Lee Maynard was born and raised in Wayne County. He earned his B.A. from West Virginia University. He has been published more than 100 times in several periodicals such as *The Saturday Review, Reader's Digest*, and *Columbia Review of Literature*. Maynard has also worked as a screenwriter, novelist, and editor. In 1995, he received a Literary Fellowship in Fiction from the National Endowment from the Arts for his unpublished novel *Screaming with the Cannibals*. Maynard lives in New Mexico.

John McKernan:

John McKernan received his M.F.A. from Columbia University and his Ph.D. from Boston University. His books of poetry include *Walking along the River* and *Erasing the Blackboard*. His *Postcard from Dublin* won the 1997 Dead Metaphor Press Chapbook Contest, and his work has appeared in journals and magazines including *Atlantic Monthly, The New Yorker, The Paris Review,* and *Virginia Quarterly*. McKernan currently lives in Barboursville, West Virginia, and teaches at Marshall University.

Llewellyn McKernan:

Llewellyn McKernan grew up in rural southern Arkansas, but has lived in West Virginia for over twenty years. She received her B.A. from Hendrix College in Arkansas, an M.A. in creative writing from Brown University, and an M.A. in English from the University of Arkansas. Besides writing poetry, McKernan is an author of children's books and editor of the journal *Dickinsonian*. She has also published two books of poetry, *Short and Simple Annals* and *Many Waters*. She currently lives in Barboursville, West Virginia.

Irene McKinney:

Irene McKinney received her B.A. from West Virginia Wesleyan College, an M.A. from West Virginia University, and a Ph.D. from the University of Utah. She is the author of four collections of poetry, including *Six O'Clock Mine Report* and *Quick Fire and Slow Fire*. McKinney is West Virginia's poet laureate, and has received fellowships from the National Endowment for the Arts and the West Virginia Commission on the Arts. Her many honors include the Utah Arts Council Prize in Fiction, the *Cincinnati Review* Annual Poetry Prize, and an award from the Bread Loaf Writers' Conference. She is co-founder and editor of *Trellis*, a West Virginia poetry magazine. She lives in Belington, West Virginia, and teaches literature at West Virginia Wesleyan College.

Louise McNeill:

Louis McNeill (1911-1993) grew up in Pocahontas County, West Virginia. She received her B.A. from Concord College, her M.A. from Miami University of Ohio, and her Ph.D. from West Virginia University. She is the author of the memoir *The Milkweed Ladies*, and five books of poetry, including *Gauley Mountain*, *Paradox Hill*, and *Hill Daughter*. Her works have been published in journals including *The Atlantic Monthly*, *Harper's Poetry*, and *The Saturday Review*. Her literary awards include the *Atlantic Monthly* Poetry Prize, the annual book award of the West Virginia Library Association, and the 1988 Appalachian Gold Medallion from the University of Charleston. She was poet laureate of West Virginia from 1977 until her death.

Ann Pancake:

Ann Pancake grew up in Romney, West Virginia. She received a B.A. from West Virginia University, an M.A. in English from the University of North Carolina, and a Ph.D. from the University of Washington. Her works have appeared in several journals, including *Virginia Quarterly Review* and *Shenandoah*. *Given Ground*, a collection of short stories, won the Bakeless Literary Publication Prize for Fiction. She has also won the Tennessee Williams Scholarship in Fiction, the Thomas Wolfe Fiction Prize, and the National Endowment for the Arts Creative Writers' Fellowship Grant. Pancake has taught extensively in Japan, American Samoa, and Thailand. She currently teaches at Penn State-Erie.

Breece Pancake:

Breece Pancake (1952-1979) was born in Milton, West Virginia. He graduated from Marshall University in 1974. In 1977, he received the prestigious Hoyns Fellowship and became a teaching assistant at the University of Virginia. Several of Pancake's stories were published during his life, but his only book, *The Stories of Breece D'J Pancake*, was published posthumously.

Jayne Anne Phillips:

Jayne Anne Phillips was raised in Buckhannon, West Virginia. She received her B.A. from West Virginia University and her M.F.A. from the University of Iowa. Phillips is the author of two collections of short stories, *Fast Lanes* and *Black Tickets*, and three novels, *Motherkind*, *Shelter*, and *Machine Dreams*. Her literary honors include a Guggenheim Fellowship, two National Endowment for the Arts Fellowships, the Sue Kaufmann Prize, and an Academy Award in Literature from the American Academy and Institute of Arts and Letters. Phillips is currently writer in residence at Brandeis University.

Timothy Russell:

Timothy Russell grew up in Follansbee, West Virginia. He received his B.A. from West Liberty College and his M.A. from the University of Pittsburgh. He has written several chapbooks of haiku, and has won awards including the fourth Shiki Internet Haiku Contest and the 1993 Terrence Des Pres prize in poetry from *Triquarterly*  *Magazine* for *Adversaria*, his first full-length book. Russell is a retired steel-mill worker now residing in Ohio.

Mary Lee Settle:

Mary Lee Settle was born in Charleston, West Virginia, and spent the majority of her childhood in southern Appalachia. Settle has received two Guggenheim Fellowships, and the 1978 National Book Award for *Blood Tie*. Other novels include the "Beulah Quintet" of *Prisons, O Beulah Land, Know Nothing, The Scapegoat,* and *The Killing Ground*. Her latest work was *Addie: A Memoir*, in 1998. She currently lives and writes in Charlottesville, Virginia.

A.E. Stringer:

A.E. Stringer earned his B.A. in English from Ohio University, his M.A. in English from Colorado State University, and his M.F.A. in creative writing from the University of Massachusetts. *Channel Markers* is his first collection of poems. His work has appeared in journals including *The Nation*, *Ohio Review*, *Iron-wood*, and the *New Virginia Review*. Stringer is a professor of English at Marshall University.

Meredith Sue Willis:

Meredith Sue Willis was raised in Shinnston, West Virginia. She received her B.A. from Barnard College, and her M.F.A. from Columbia University. She has written twelve books of fiction and non-fiction, including *Higher Ground, Only Great Changes*, *Trespassers*, *A Space Apart*, and *In the Mountains of America*. Her newest novel is *Oradell at Sea* in 2002. She is the recipient of several awards and fellowships from the National Endowment for the Arts, the New Jersey State Council on the Arts, and the West Virginia Library Association. She currently works as a writer in the schools in New York and New Jersey and teaches novel writing at New York University.